WIDGEY Q BUTTERFLUFF

WIDGEY Q. BUTTERFLUFF
BY STEPH CHERRYWELL

SLG PUBLISHING

DAN VADO — PRESIDENT AND PUBLISHER
JENNIFER DE GUZMAN — EDITOR-IN-CHIEF

P.O. BOX 26427
SAN JOSE, CA 95159
WWW.SLGCOMIC.COM

FIRST PRINTING: JANUARY 2010
ISBN-13: 978-1-59362-184-1

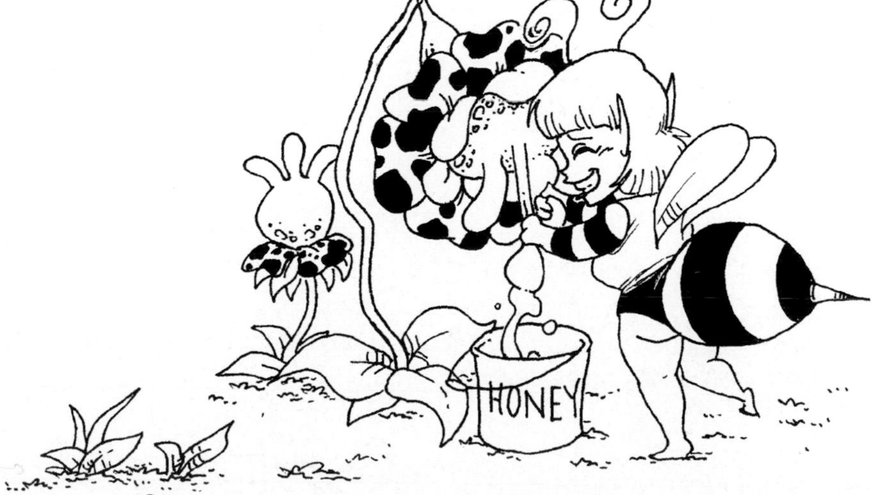
HONEY

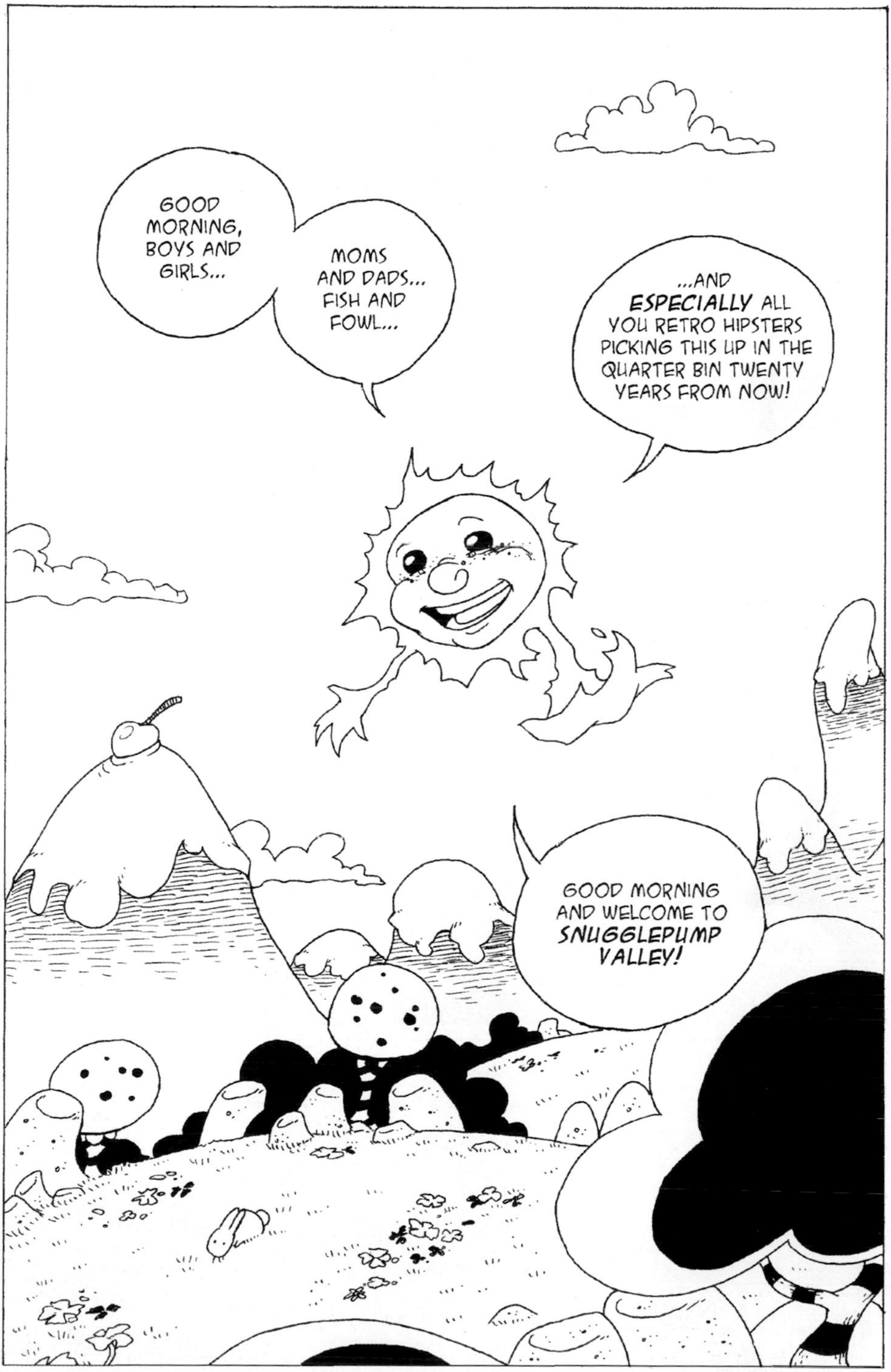
GOOD MORNING, BOYS AND GIRLS...
MOMS AND DADS... FISH AND FOWL...
...AND **ESPECIALLY** ALL YOU RETRO HIPSTERS PICKING THIS UP IN THE QUARTER BIN TWENTY YEARS FROM NOW!
GOOD MORNING AND WELCOME TO **SNUGGLEPUMP VALLEY!**

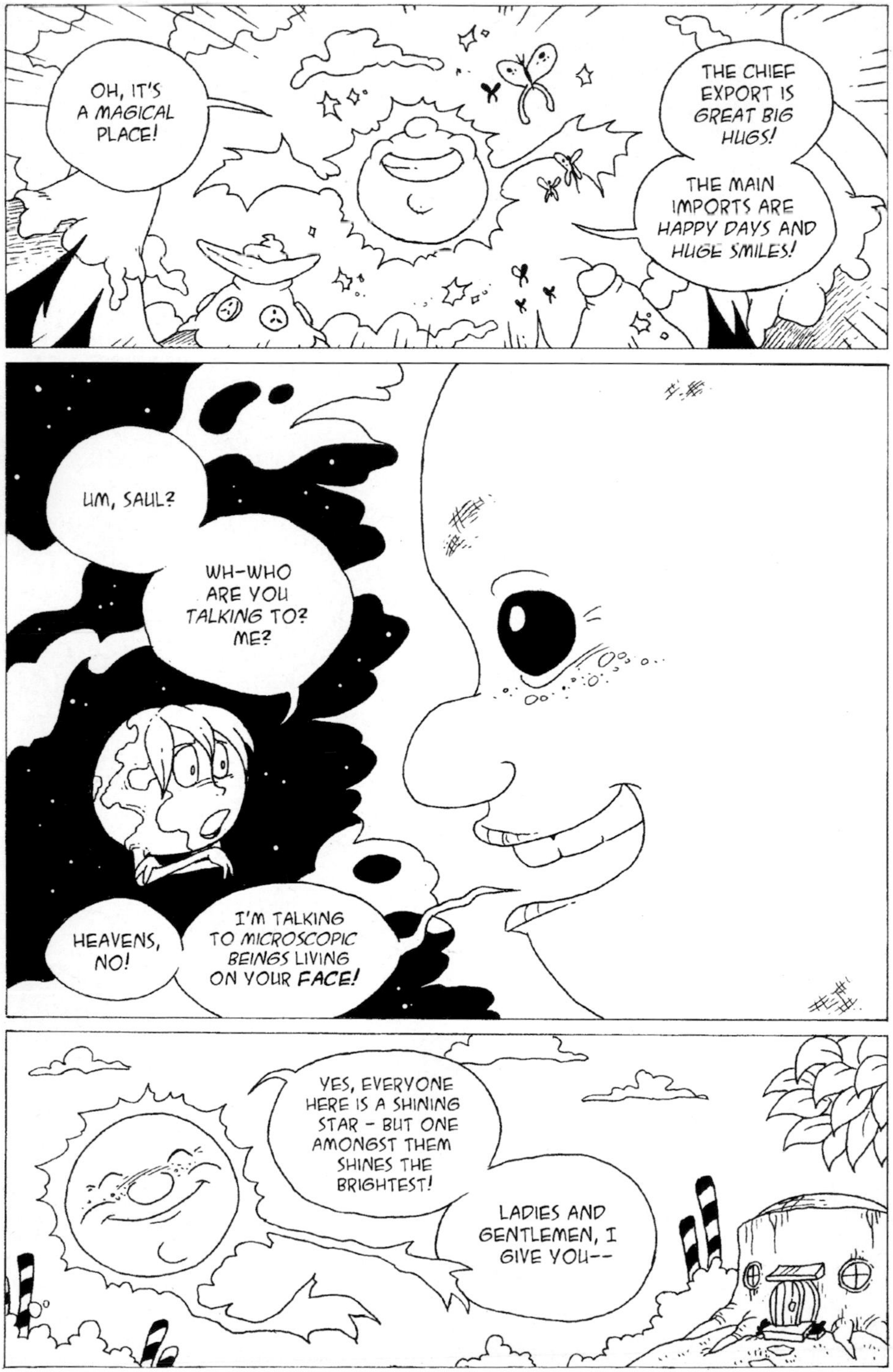
OH, IT'S A MAGICAL PLACE!
THE CHIEF EXPORT IS GREAT BIG HUGS!
THE MAIN IMPORTS ARE HAPPY DAYS AND HUGE SMILES!
UM, SAUL?
WH-WHO ARE YOU TALKING TO? ME?
HEAVENS, NO!
I'M TALKING TO MICROSCOPIC BEINGS LIVING ON YOUR FACE!
YES, EVERYONE HERE IS A SHINING STAR - BUT ONE AMONGST THEM SHINES THE BRIGHTEST!
LADIES AND GENTLEMEN, I GIVE YOU--

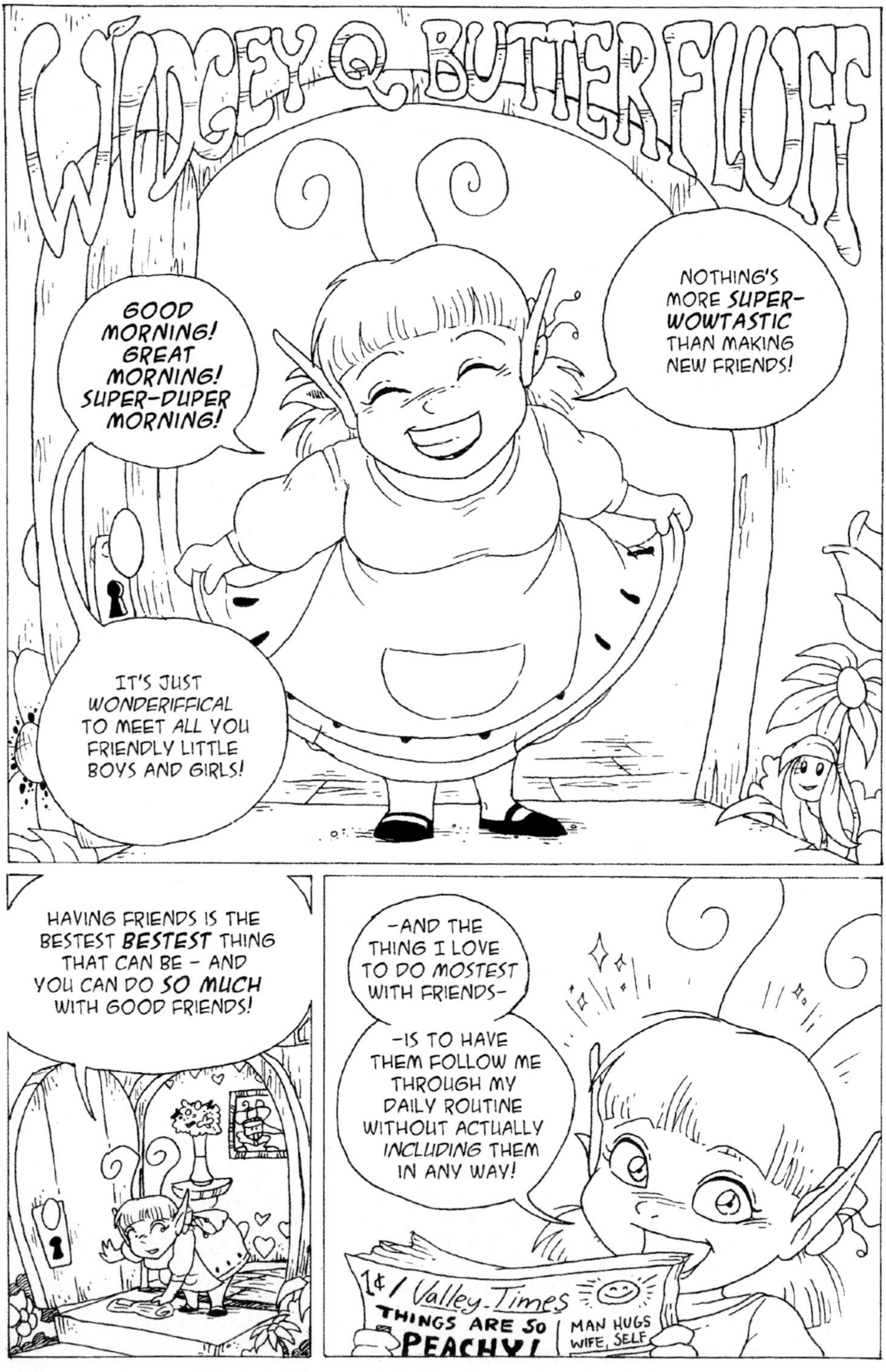
WIDGEY Q. BUTTERFLUFF
GOOD MORNING! GREAT MORNING! SUPER-DUPER MORNING!
NOTHING'S MORE SUPER-WOWTASTIC THAN MAKING NEW FRIENDS!
IT'S JUST WONDERIFFICAL TO MEET ALL YOU FRIENDLY LITTLE BOYS AND GIRLS!
HAVING FRIENDS IS THE BESTEST BESTEST THING THAT CAN BE - AND YOU CAN DO SO MUCH WITH GOOD FRIENDS!
-AND THE THING I LOVE TO DO MOSTEST WITH FRIENDS-
-IS TO HAVE THEM FOLLOW ME THROUGH MY DAILY ROUTINE WITHOUT ACTUALLY INCLUDING THEM IN ANY WAY!
1¢ / Valley Times
THINGS ARE SO PEACHY!
MAN HUGS WIFE, SELF

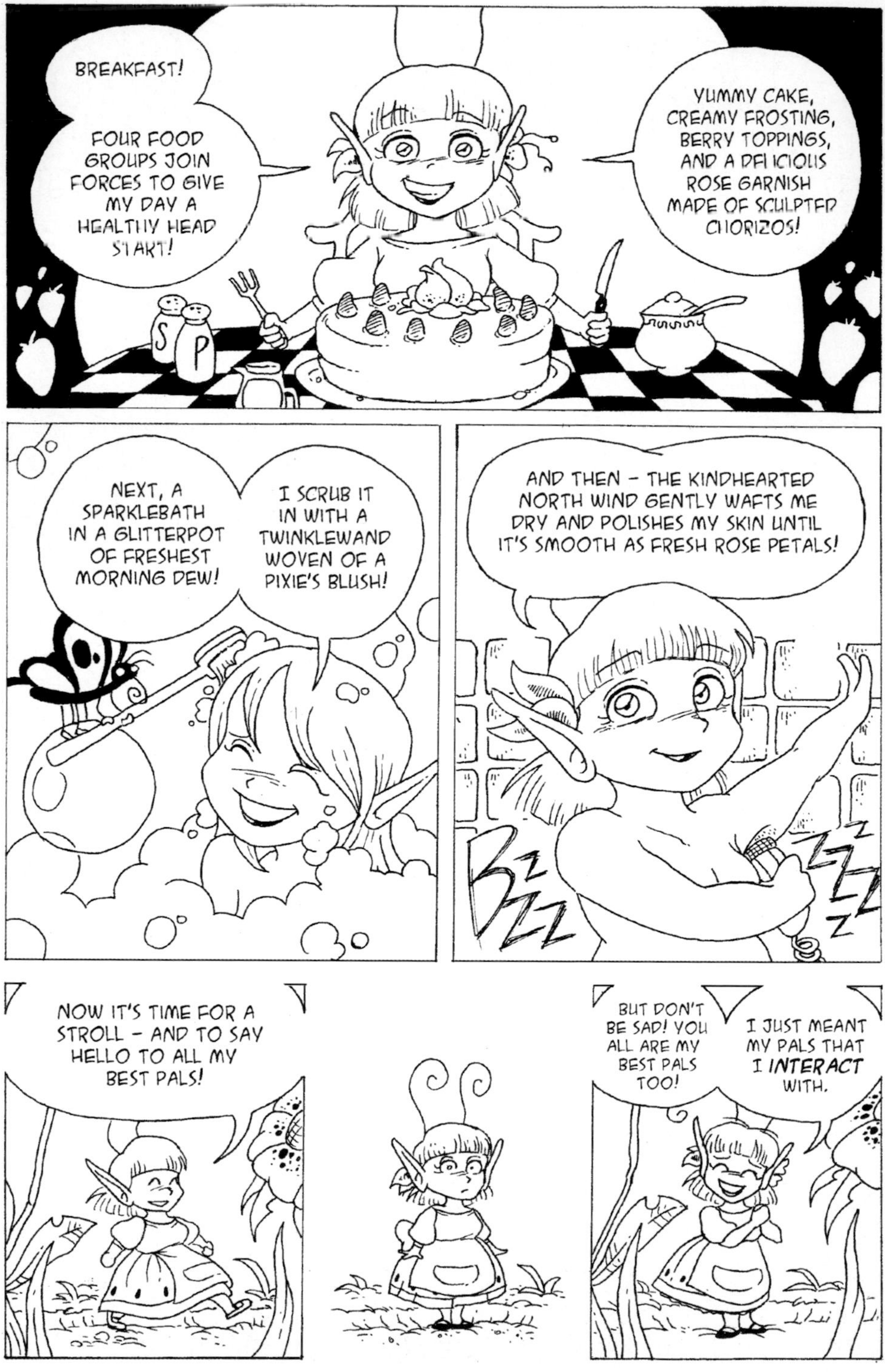
BREAKFAST!
FOUR FOOD GROUPS JOIN FORCES TO GIVE MY DAY A HEALTHY HEAD START!
YUMMY CAKE, CREAMY FROSTING, BERRY TOPPINGS, AND A DELICIOUS ROSE GARNISH MADE OF SCULPTED CHORIZOS!
S
P
NEXT, A SPARKLEBATH IN A GLITTERPOT OF FRESHEST MORNING DEW!
I SCRUB IT IN WITH A TWINKLEWAND WOVEN OF A PIXIE'S BLUSH!
AND THEN - THE KINDHEARTED NORTH WIND GENTLY WAFTS ME DRY AND POLISHES MY SKIN UNTIL IT'S SMOOTH AS FRESH ROSE PETALS!
BZZZ
ZZZZZ
NOW IT'S TIME FOR A STROLL - AND TO SAY HELLO TO ALL MY BEST PALS!
BUT DON'T BE SAD! YOU ALL ARE MY BEST PALS TOO!
I JUST MEANT MY PALS THAT I *INTERACT* WITH.

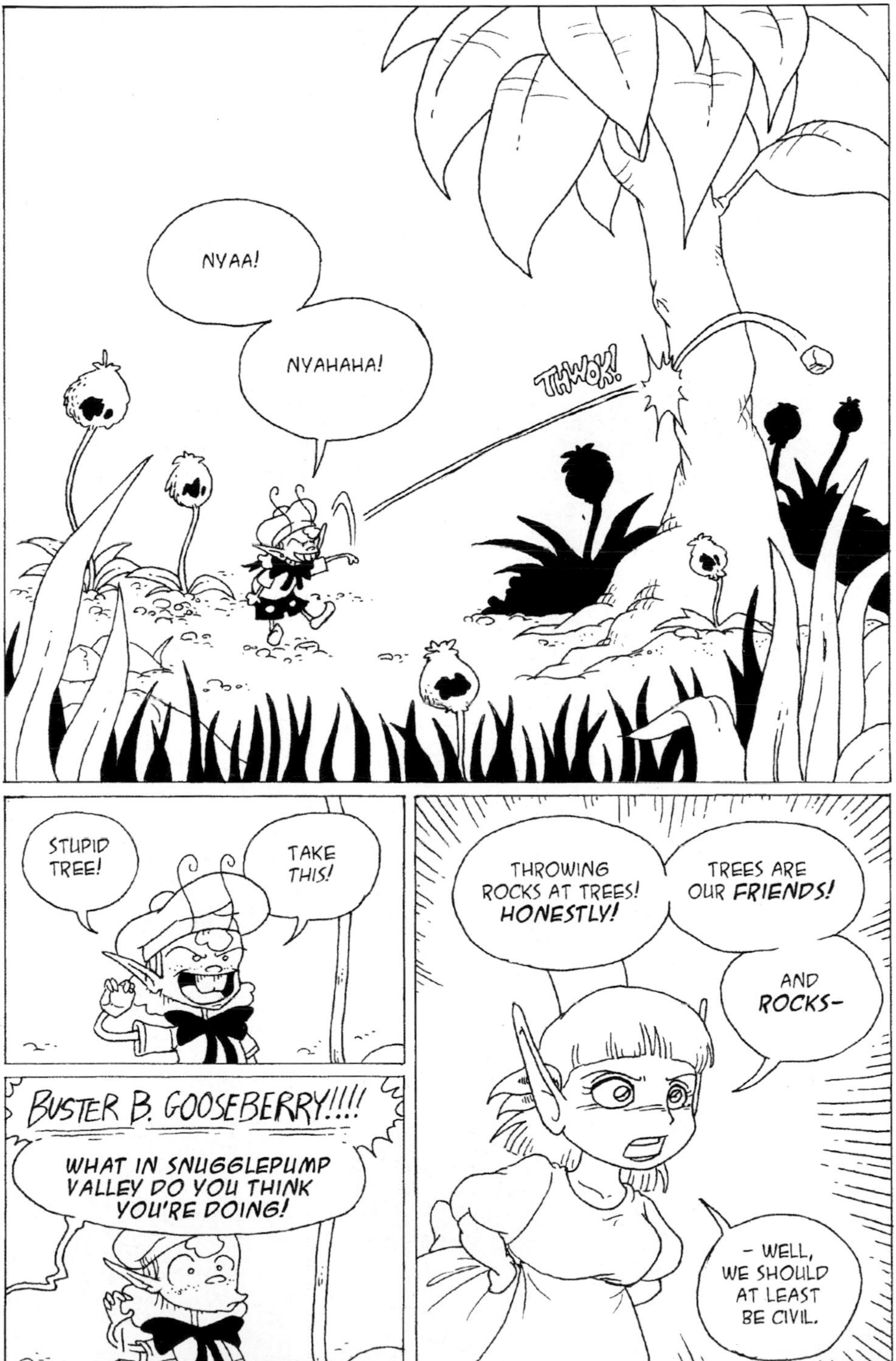
NYAA!
NYAHAHA!
THWOK!
STUPID TREE!
TAKE THIS!
BUSTER B. GOOSEBERRY!!!!
WHAT IN SNUGGLEPUMP VALLEY DO YOU THINK YOU'RE DOING!
THROWING ROCKS AT TREES! HONESTLY!
TREES ARE OUR FRIENDS!
AND ROCKS-
- WELL, WE SHOULD AT LEAST BE CIVIL.

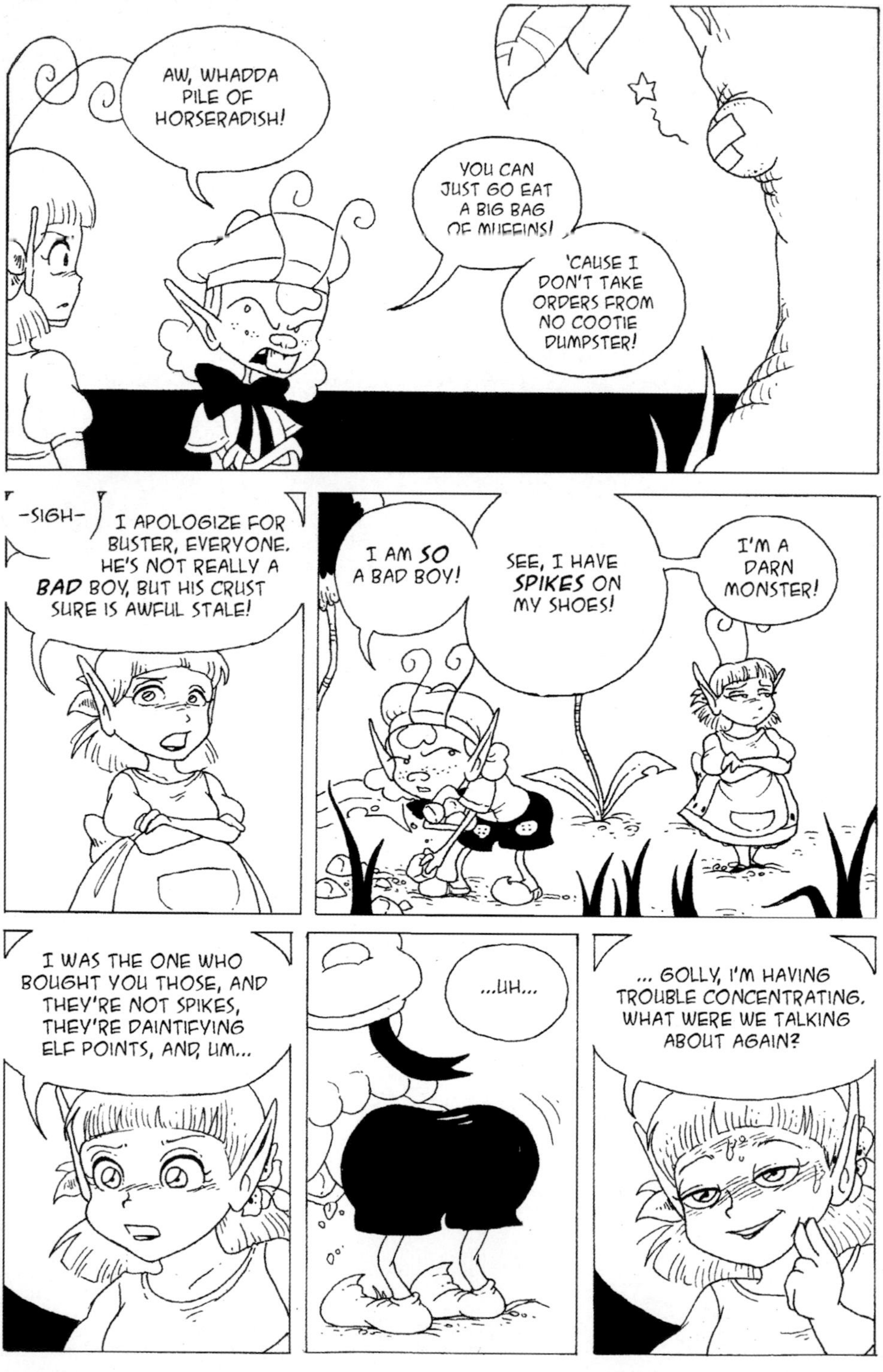
AW, WHADDA PILE OF HORSERADISH!
YOU CAN JUST GO EAT A BIG BAG OF MUFFINS!
'CAUSE I DON'T TAKE ORDERS FROM NO COOTIE DUMPSTER!
-SIGH-
I APOLOGIZE FOR BUSTER, EVERYONE. HE'S NOT REALLY A BAD BOY, BUT HIS CRUST SURE IS AWFUL STALE!
I AM SO A BAD BOY!
SEE, I HAVE SPIKES ON MY SHOES!
I'M A DARN MONSTER!
I WAS THE ONE WHO BOUGHT YOU THOSE, AND THEY'RE NOT SPIKES, THEY'RE DAINTIFYING ELF POINTS, AND, UM...
...UH...
... GOLLY, I'M HAVING TROUBLE CONCENTRATING. WHAT WERE WE TALKING ABOUT AGAIN?

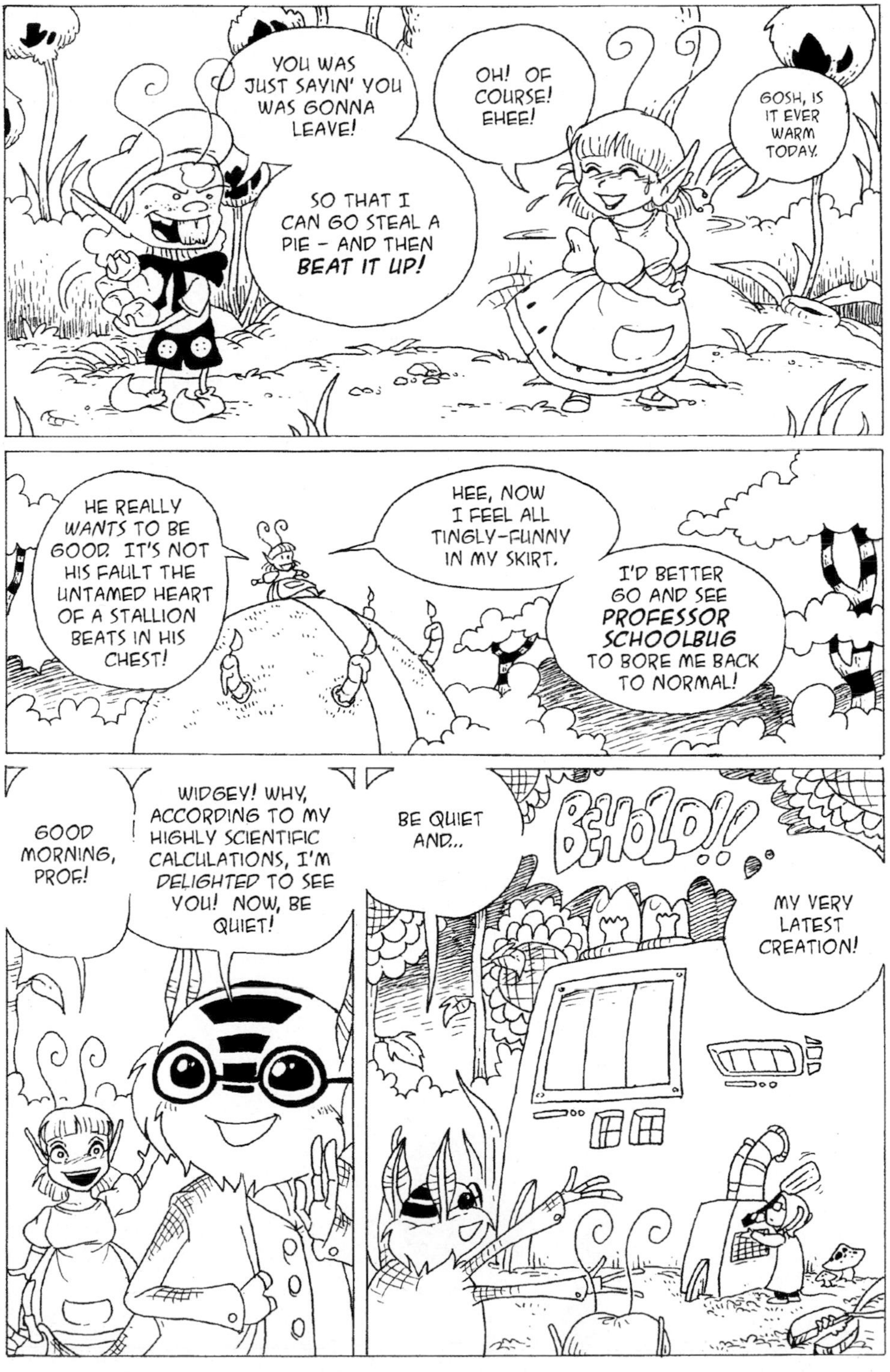
YOU WAS JUST SAYIN' YOU WAS GONNA LEAVE!
SO THAT I CAN GO STEAL A PIE - AND THEN BEAT IT UP!
OH! OF COURSE! EHEE!
GOSH, IS IT EVER WARM TODAY.
HE REALLY WANTS TO BE GOOD. IT'S NOT HIS FAULT THE UNTAMED HEART OF A STALLION BEATS IN HIS CHEST!
HEE, NOW I FEEL ALL TINGLY-FUNNY IN MY SKIRT.
I'D BETTER GO AND SEE PROFESSOR SCHOOLBUG TO BORE ME BACK TO NORMAL!
GOOD MORNING, PROF!
WIDGEY! WHY, ACCORDING TO MY HIGHLY SCIENTIFIC CALCULATIONS, I'M DELIGHTED TO SEE YOU! NOW, BE QUIET!
BE QUIET AND...
BEHOLD!!
MY VERY LATEST CREATION!

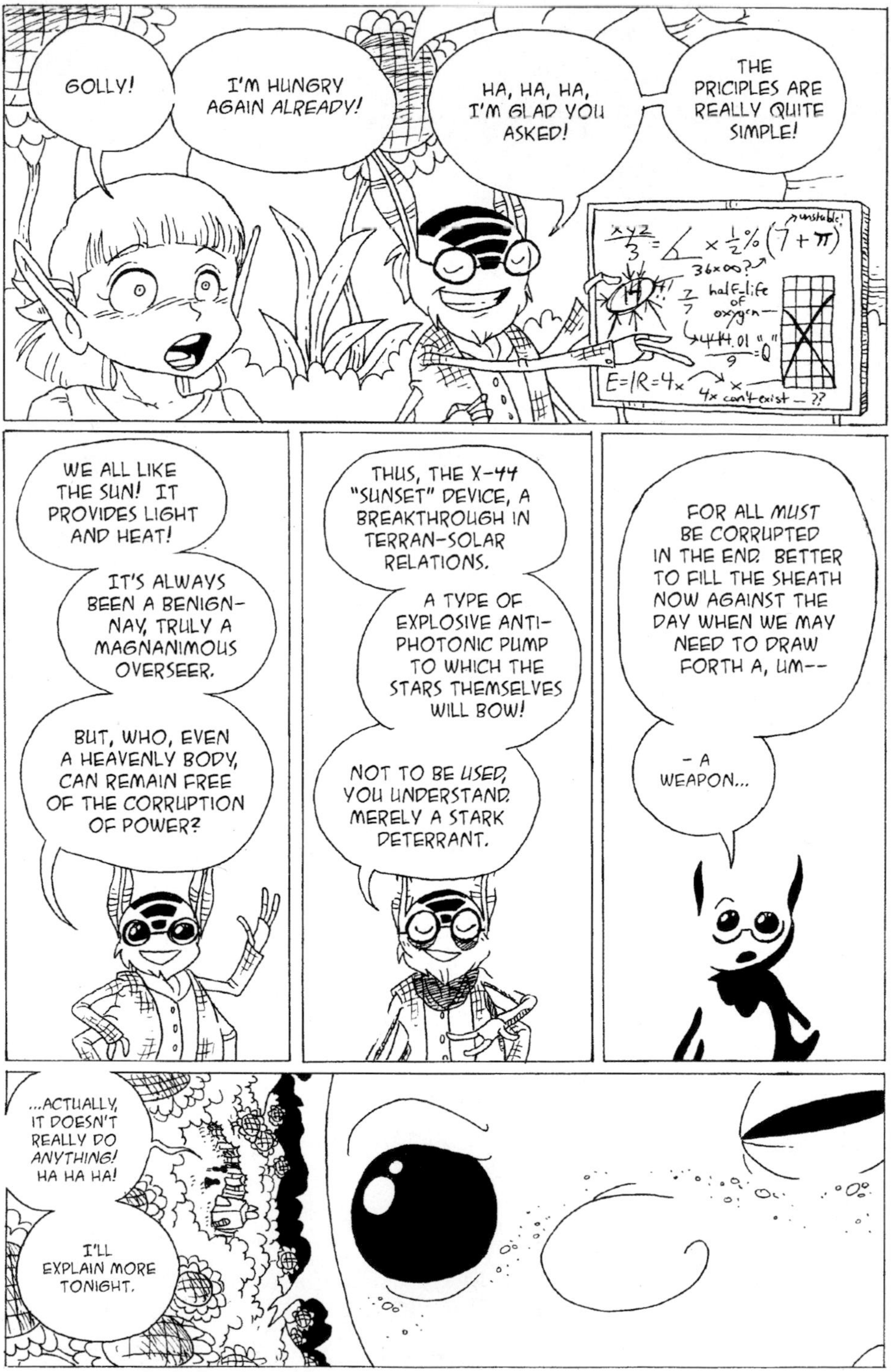
GOLLY!
I'M HUNGRY AGAIN ALREADY!
HA, HA, HA, I'M GLAD YOU ASKED!
THE PRICIPLES ARE REALLY QUITE SIMPLE!
WE ALL LIKE THE SUN! IT PROVIDES LIGHT AND HEAT!
IT'S ALWAYS BEEN A BENIGN- NAY, TRULY A MAGNANIMOUS OVERSEER.
BUT, WHO, EVEN A HEAVENLY BODY, CAN REMAIN FREE OF THE CORRUPTION OF POWER?
THUS, THE X-44 "SUNSET" DEVICE, A BREAKTHROUGH IN TERRAN-SOLAR RELATIONS.
A TYPE OF EXPLOSIVE ANTI-PHOTONIC PUMP TO WHICH THE STARS THEMSELVES WILL BOW!
NOT TO BE USED, YOU UNDERSTAND. MERELY A STARK DETERRANT.
FOR ALL MUST BE CORRUPTED IN THE END. BETTER TO FILL THE SHEATH NOW AGAINST THE DAY WHEN WE MAY NEED TO DRAW FORTH A, UM--
- A WEAPON...
...ACTUALLY, IT DOESN'T REALLY DO ANYTHING! HA HA HA!
I'LL EXPLAIN MORE TONIGHT.

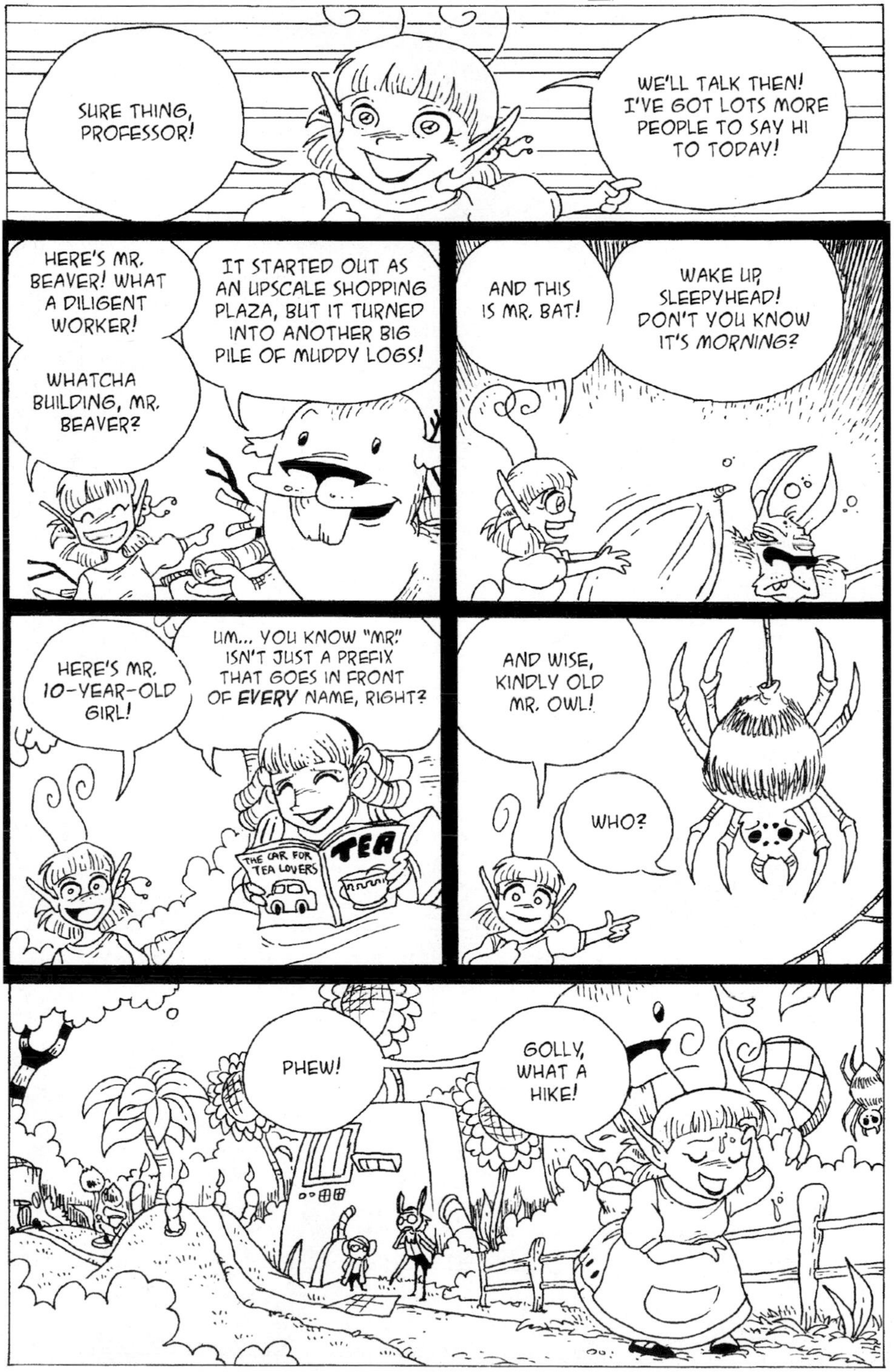
SURE THING, PROFESSOR!
WE'LL TALK THEN! I'VE GOT LOTS MORE PEOPLE TO SAY HI TO TODAY!
HERE'S MR. BEAVER! WHAT A DILIGENT WORKER!
WHATCHA BUILDING, MR. BEAVER?
IT STARTED OUT AS AN UPSCALE SHOPPING PLAZA, BUT IT TURNED INTO ANOTHER BIG PILE OF MUDDY LOGS!
AND THIS IS MR. BAT!
WAKE UP, SLEEPYHEAD! DON'T YOU KNOW IT'S *MORNING*?
HERE'S MR. 10-YEAR-OLD GIRL!
UM... YOU KNOW "MR." ISN'T JUST A PREFIX THAT GOES IN FRONT OF **EVERY** NAME, RIGHT?
THE CAR FOR TEA LOVERS
TEA
AND WISE, KINDLY OLD MR. OWL!
WHO?
PHEW!
GOLLY, WHAT A HIKE!

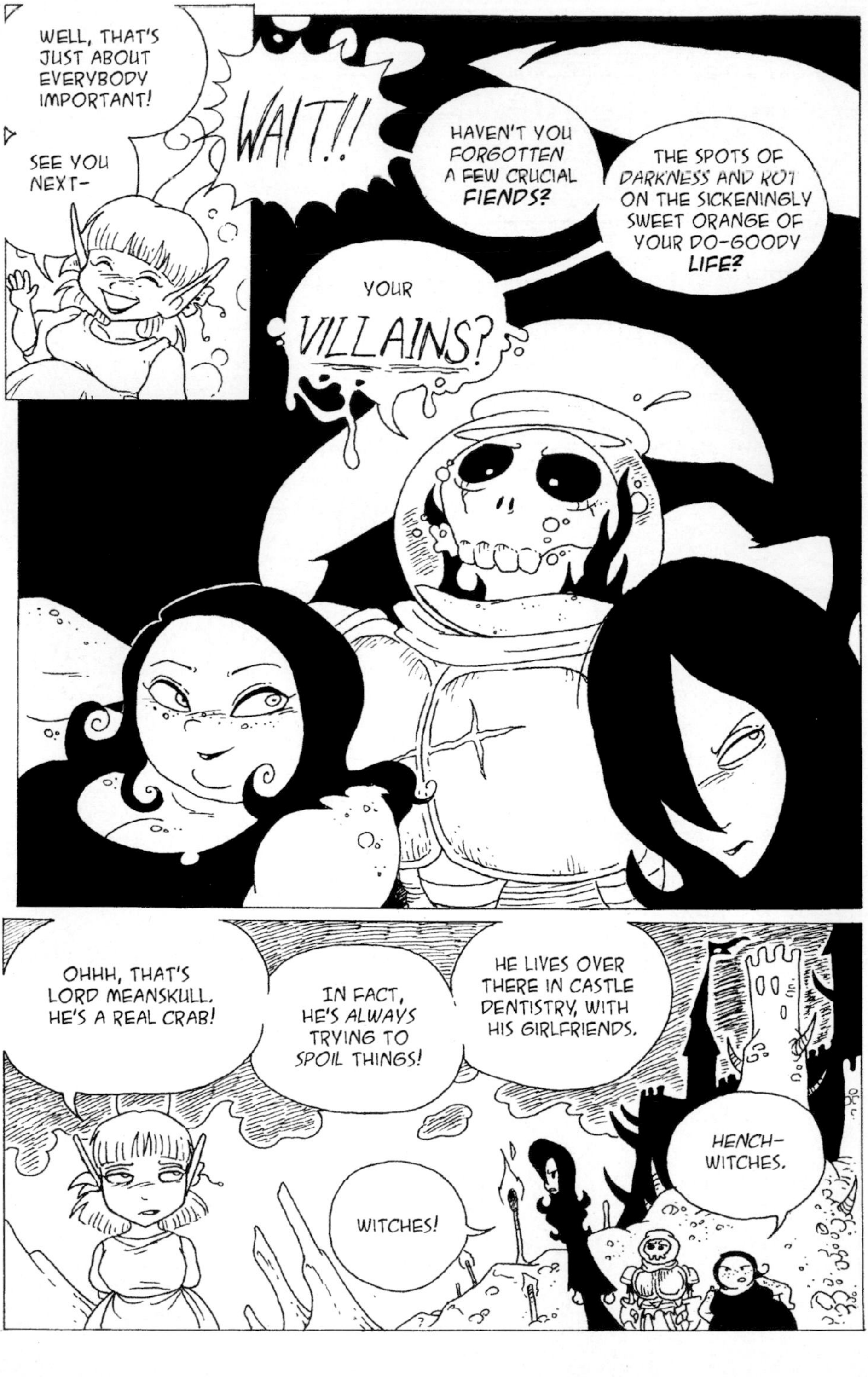
WELL, THAT'S JUST ABOUT EVERYBODY IMPORTANT!
SEE YOU NEXT-
WAIT!!
HAVEN'T YOU FORGOTTEN A FEW CRUCIAL FIENDS?
THE SPOTS OF DARKNESS AND ROT ON THE SICKENINGLY SWEET ORANGE OF YOUR DO-GOODY LIFE?
YOUR VILLAINS?
OHHH, THAT'S LORD MEANSKULL. HE'S A REAL CRAB!
IN FACT, HE'S ALWAYS TRYING TO SPOIL THINGS!
HE LIVES OVER THERE IN CASTLE DENTISTRY, WITH HIS GIRLFRIENDS.
WITCHES!
HENCH-WITCHES.

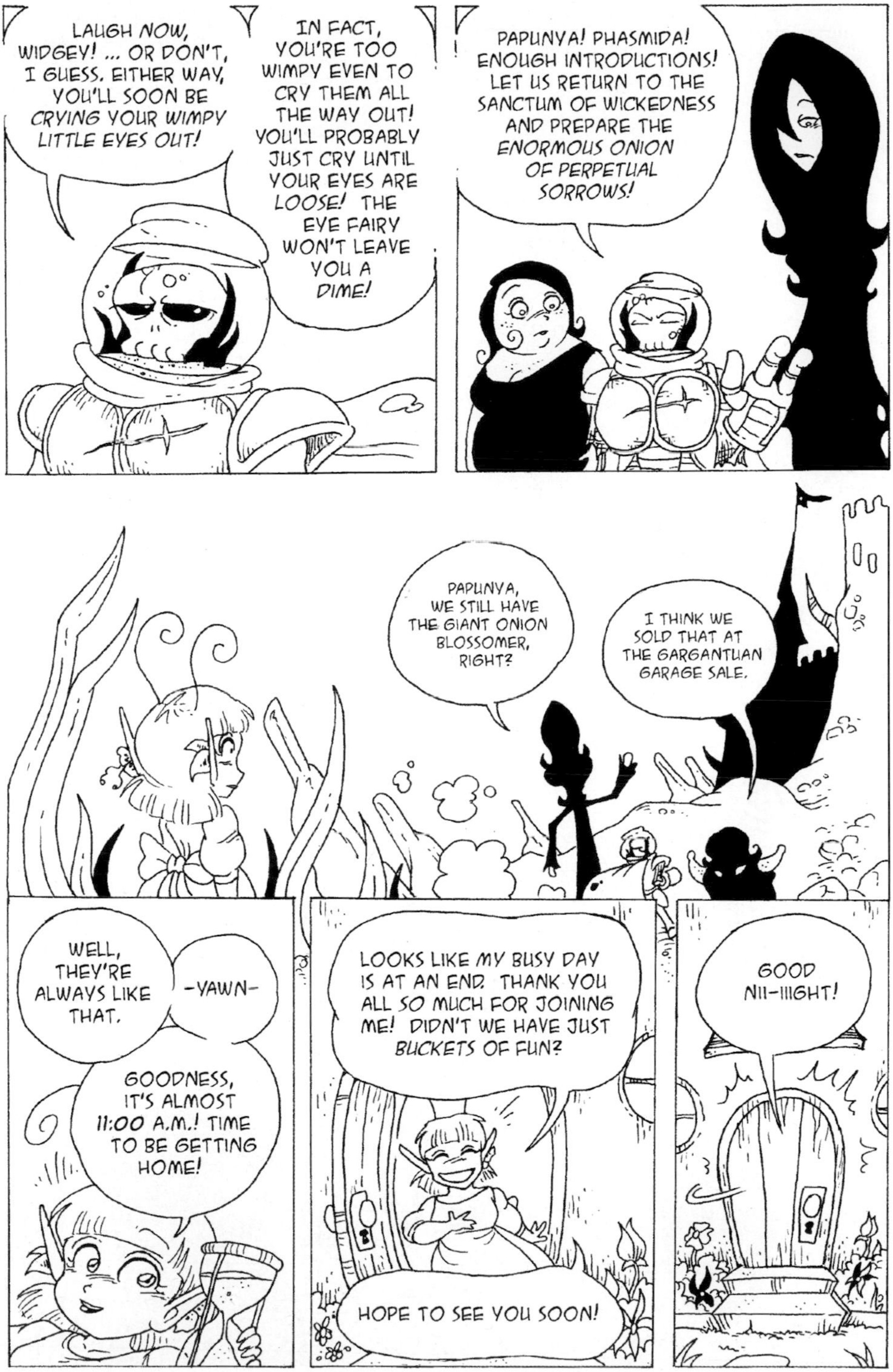
LAUGH NOW, WIDGEY! ... OR DON'T, I GUESS. EITHER WAY, YOU'LL SOON BE CRYING YOUR WIMPY LITTLE EYES OUT!
IN FACT, YOU'RE TOO WIMPY EVEN TO CRY THEM ALL THE WAY OUT! YOU'LL PROBABLY JUST CRY UNTIL YOUR EYES ARE LOOSE! THE EYE FAIRY WON'T LEAVE YOU A DIME!
PAPUNYA! PHASMIDA! ENOUGH INTRODUCTIONS! LET US RETURN TO THE SANCTUM OF WICKEDNESS AND PREPARE THE ENORMOUS ONION OF PERPETUAL SORROWS!
PAPUNYA, WE STILL HAVE THE GIANT ONION BLOSSOMER, RIGHT?
I THINK WE SOLD THAT AT THE GARGANTUAN GARAGE SALE.
WELL, THEY'RE ALWAYS LIKE THAT.
-YAWN-
GOODNESS, IT'S ALMOST 11:00 A.M.! TIME TO BE GETTING HOME!
LOOKS LIKE MY BUSY DAY IS AT AN END. THANK YOU ALL SO MUCH FOR JOINING ME! DIDN'T WE HAVE JUST BUCKETS OF FUN?
HOPE TO SEE YOU SOON!
GOOD NII-IIIGHT!

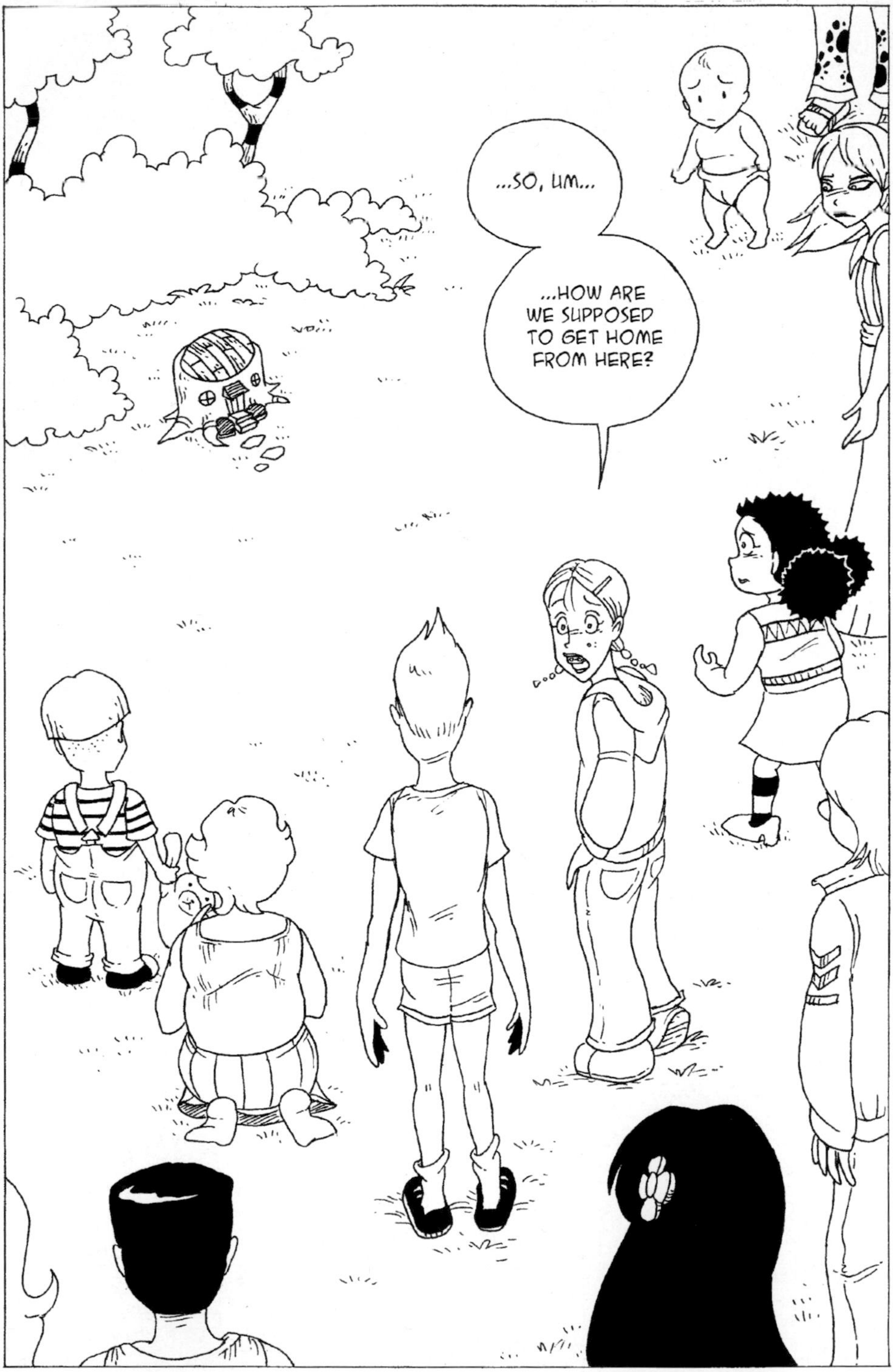
...SO, UM...
...HOW ARE WE SUPPOSED TO GET HOME FROM HERE?

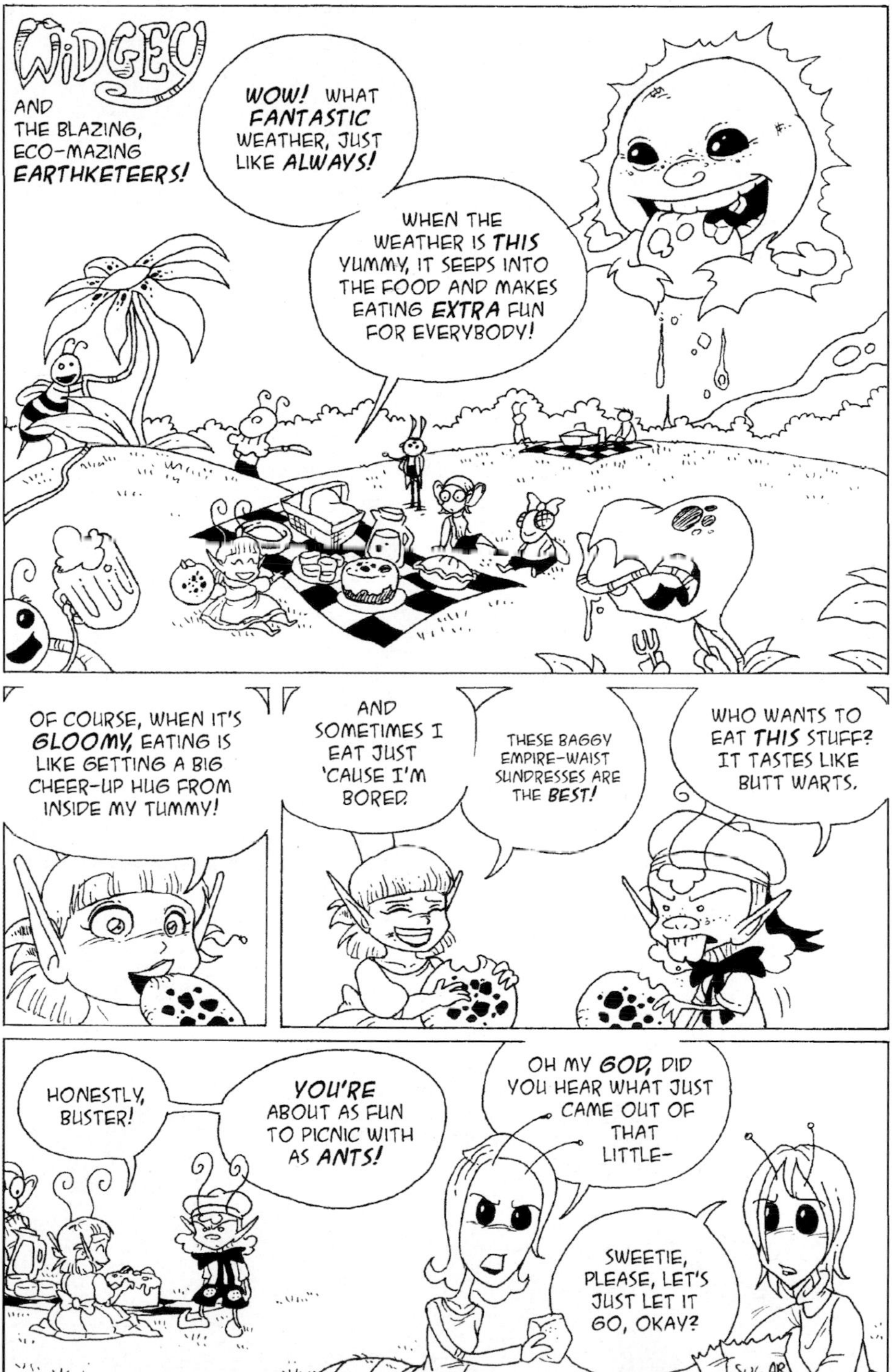
WIDGEY
AND THE BLAZING, ECO-MAZING EARTHKETEERS!
WOW! WHAT FANTASTIC WEATHER, JUST LIKE ALWAYS!
WHEN THE WEATHER IS THIS YUMMY, IT SEEPS INTO THE FOOD AND MAKES EATING EXTRA FUN FOR EVERYBODY!
OF COURSE, WHEN IT'S GLOOMY, EATING IS LIKE GETTING A BIG CHEER-UP HUG FROM INSIDE MY TUMMY!
AND SOMETIMES I EAT JUST 'CAUSE I'M BORED.
THESE BAGGY EMPIRE-WAIST SUNDRESSES ARE THE BEST!
WHO WANTS TO EAT THIS STUFF? IT TASTES LIKE BUTT WARTS.
HONESTLY, BUSTER!
YOU'RE ABOUT AS FUN TO PICNIC WITH AS ANTS!
OH MY GOD, DID YOU HEAR WHAT JUST CAME OUT OF THAT LITTLE-
SWEETIE, PLEASE, LET'S JUST LET IT GO, OKAY?
SUGAR

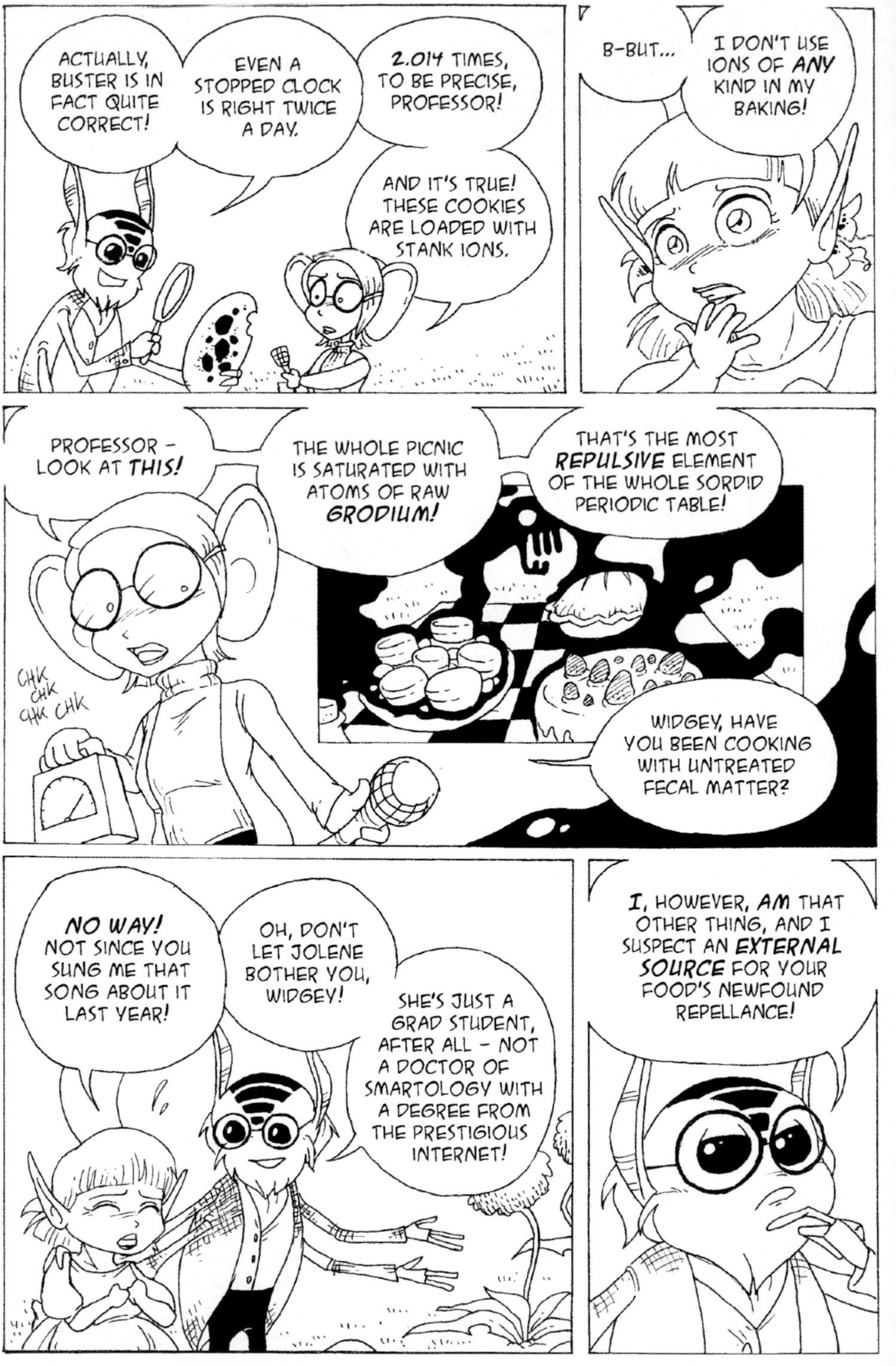
ACTUALLY, BUSTER IS IN FACT QUITE CORRECT!
EVEN A STOPPED CLOCK IS RIGHT TWICE A DAY.
2.014 TIMES, TO BE PRECISE, PROFESSOR!
AND IT'S TRUE! THESE COOKIES ARE LOADED WITH STANK IONS.
B-BUT...
I DON'T USE IONS OF ANY KIND IN MY BAKING!
PROFESSOR - LOOK AT THIS!
THE WHOLE PICNIC IS SATURATED WITH ATOMS OF RAW GRODIUM!
THAT'S THE MOST REPULSIVE ELEMENT OF THE WHOLE SORDID PERIODIC TABLE!
CHK CHK CHK CHK
WIDGEY, HAVE YOU BEEN COOKING WITH UNTREATED FECAL MATTER?
NO WAY! NOT SINCE YOU SUNG ME THAT SONG ABOUT IT LAST YEAR!
OH, DON'T LET JOLENE BOTHER YOU, WIDGEY!
SHE'S JUST A GRAD STUDENT, AFTER ALL - NOT A DOCTOR OF SMARTOLOGY WITH A DEGREE FROM THE PRESTIGIOUS INTERNET!
I, HOWEVER, AM THAT OTHER THING, AND I SUSPECT AN EXTERNAL SOURCE FOR YOUR FOOD'S NEWFOUND REPELLANCE!

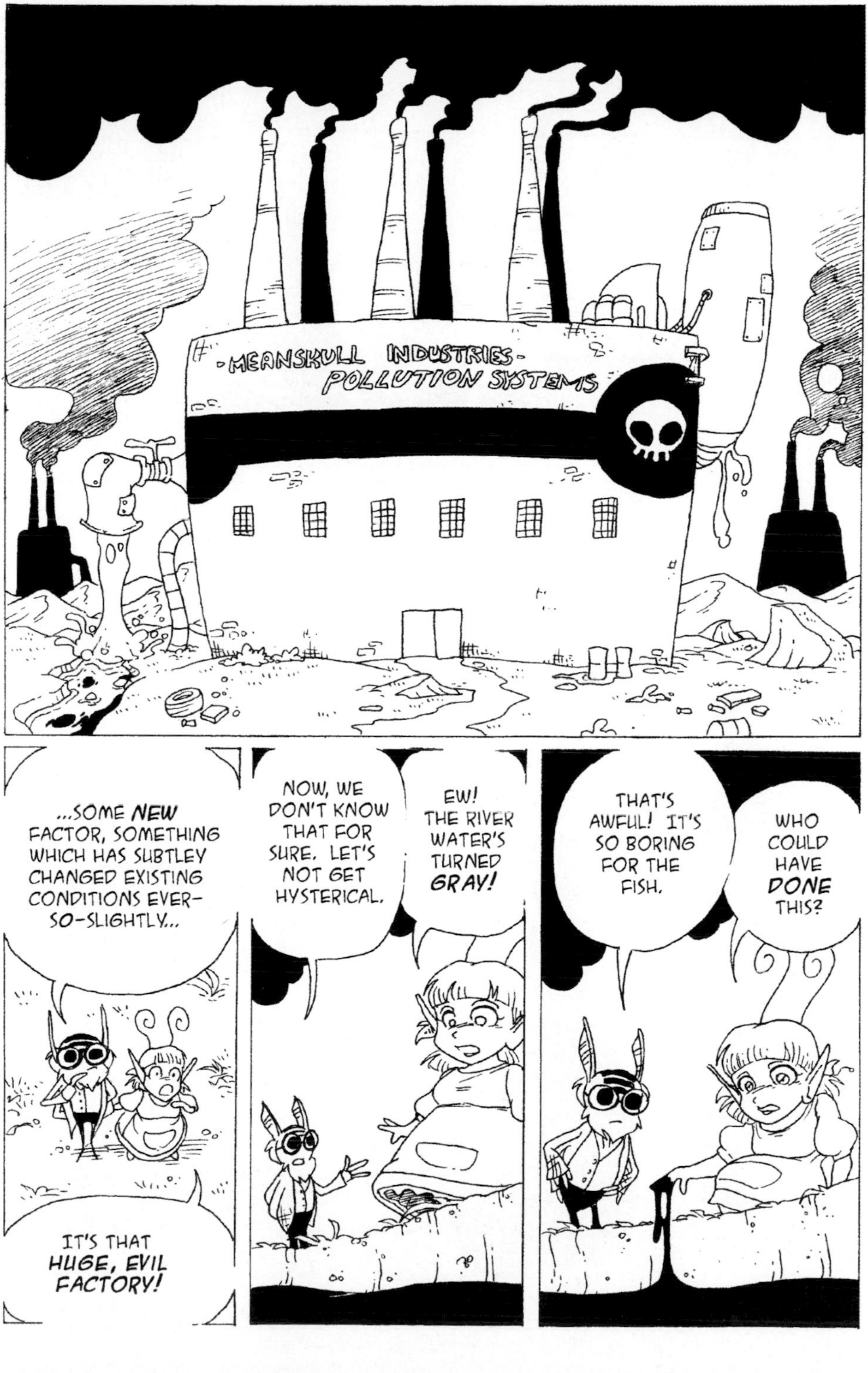
-MEANSKULL INDUSTRIES-
POLLUTION SYSTEMS
...SOME NEW FACTOR, SOMETHING WHICH HAS SUBTLEY CHANGED EXISTING CONDITIONS EVER-SO-SLIGHTLY...
IT'S THAT HUGE, EVIL FACTORY!
NOW, WE DON'T KNOW THAT FOR SURE. LET'S NOT GET HYSTERICAL.
EW! THE RIVER WATER'S TURNED GRAY!
THAT'S AWFUL! IT'S SO BORING FOR THE FISH.
WHO COULD HAVE DONE THIS?

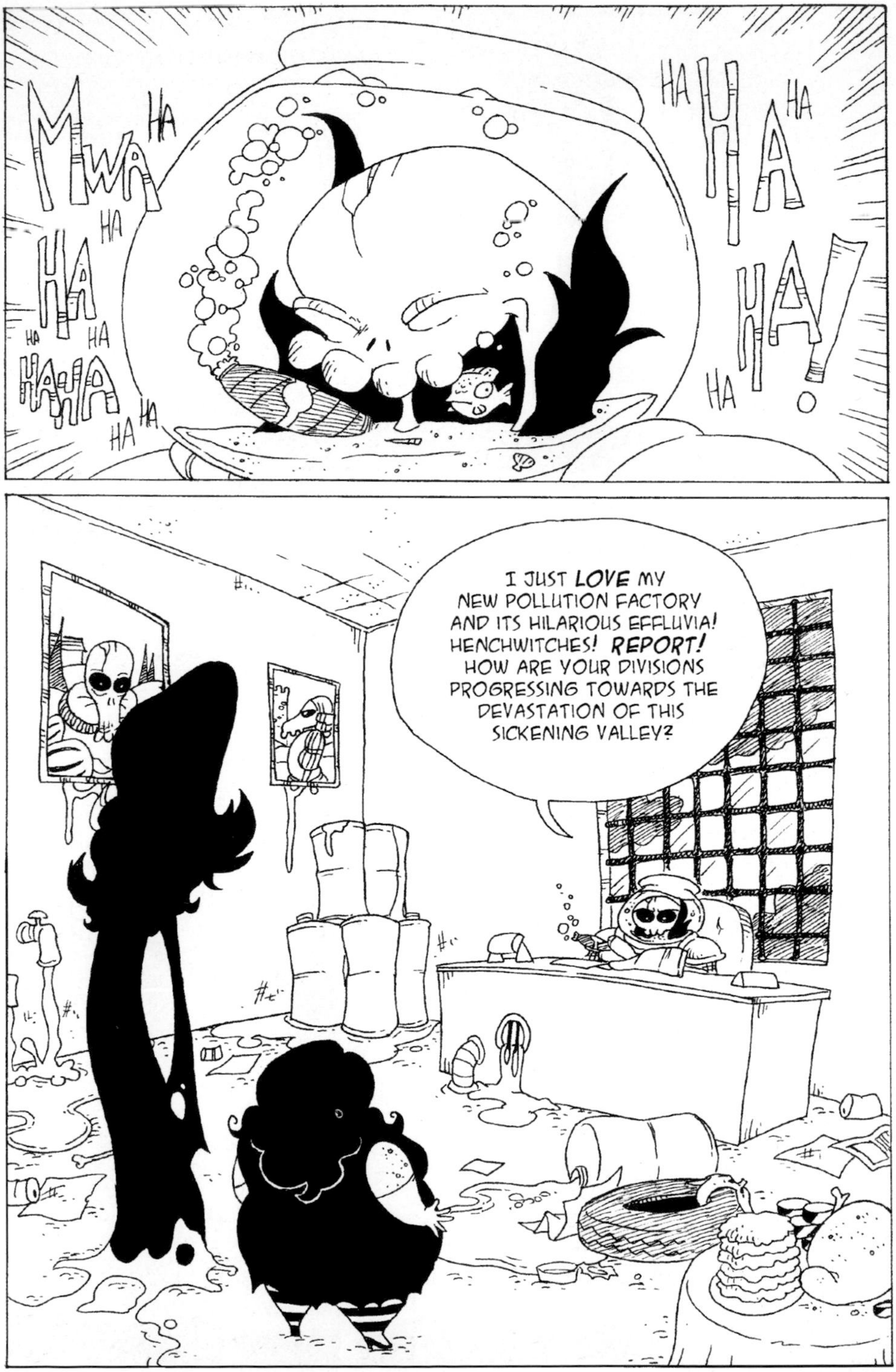
MWA HA
HA HA
HA HA
HAHA
HA HA
HA HA HA HA HA HA! HA
I JUST LOVE MY NEW POLLUTION FACTORY AND ITS HILARIOUS EFFLUVIA! HENCHWITCHES! REPORT! HOW ARE YOUR DIVISIONS PROGRESSING TOWARDS THE DEVASTATION OF THIS SICKENING VALLEY?

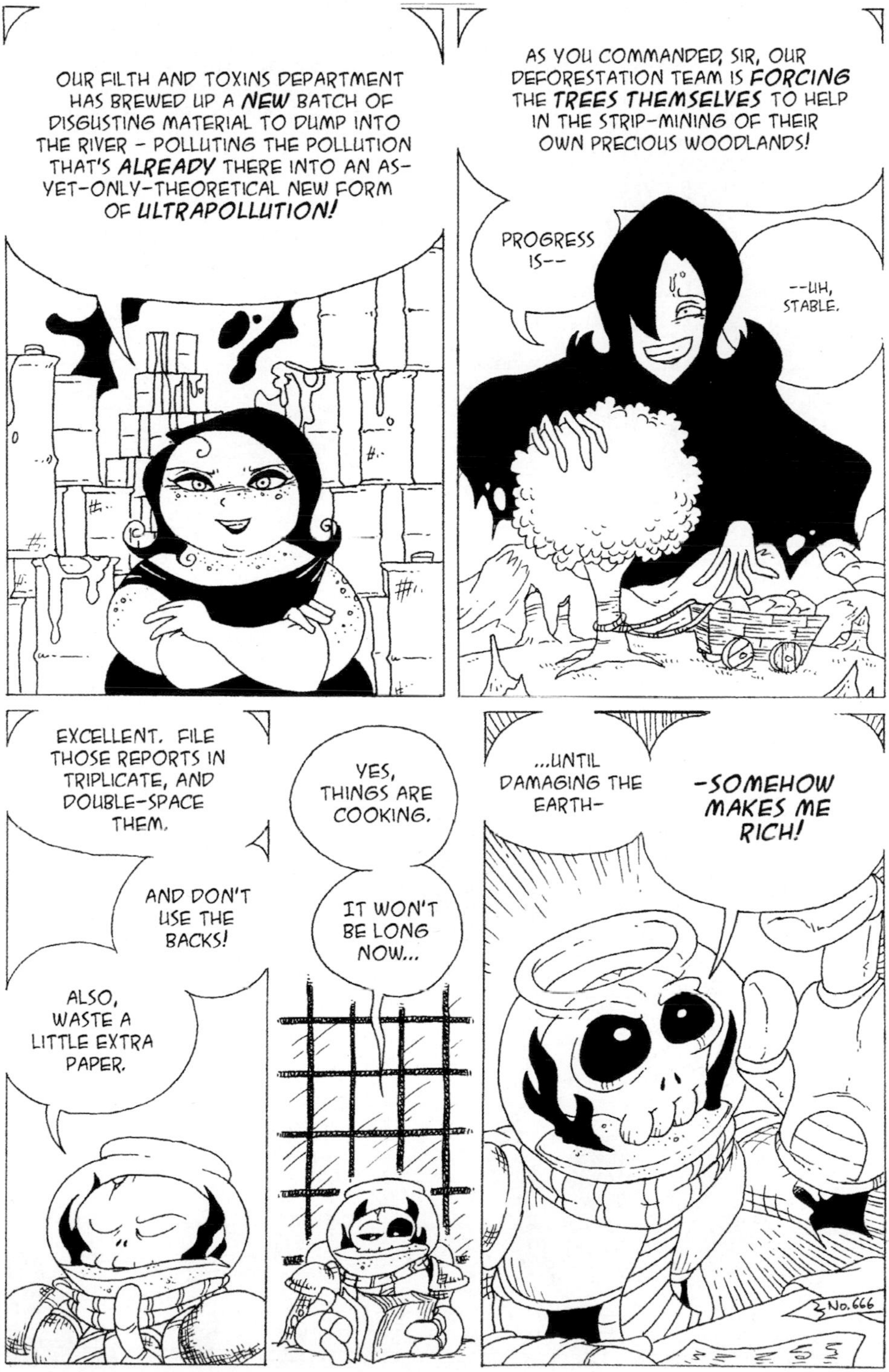
OUR FILTH AND TOXINS DEPARTMENT HAS BREWED UP A NEW BATCH OF DISGUSTING MATERIAL TO DUMP INTO THE RIVER - POLLUTING THE POLLUTION THAT'S ALREADY THERE INTO AN AS-YET-ONLY-THEORETICAL NEW FORM OF ULTRAPOLLUTION!
AS YOU COMMANDED, SIR, OUR DEFORESTATION TEAM IS FORCING THE TREES THEMSELVES TO HELP IN THE STRIP-MINING OF THEIR OWN PRECIOUS WOODLANDS!
PROGRESS IS--
--UH, STABLE.
EXCELLENT. FILE THOSE REPORTS IN TRIPLICATE, AND DOUBLE-SPACE THEM.
AND DON'T USE THE BACKS!
ALSO, WASTE A LITTLE EXTRA PAPER.
YES, THINGS ARE COOKING.
IT WON'T BE LONG NOW...
...UNTIL DAMAGING THE EARTH-
-SOMEHOW MAKES ME RICH!
No. 666

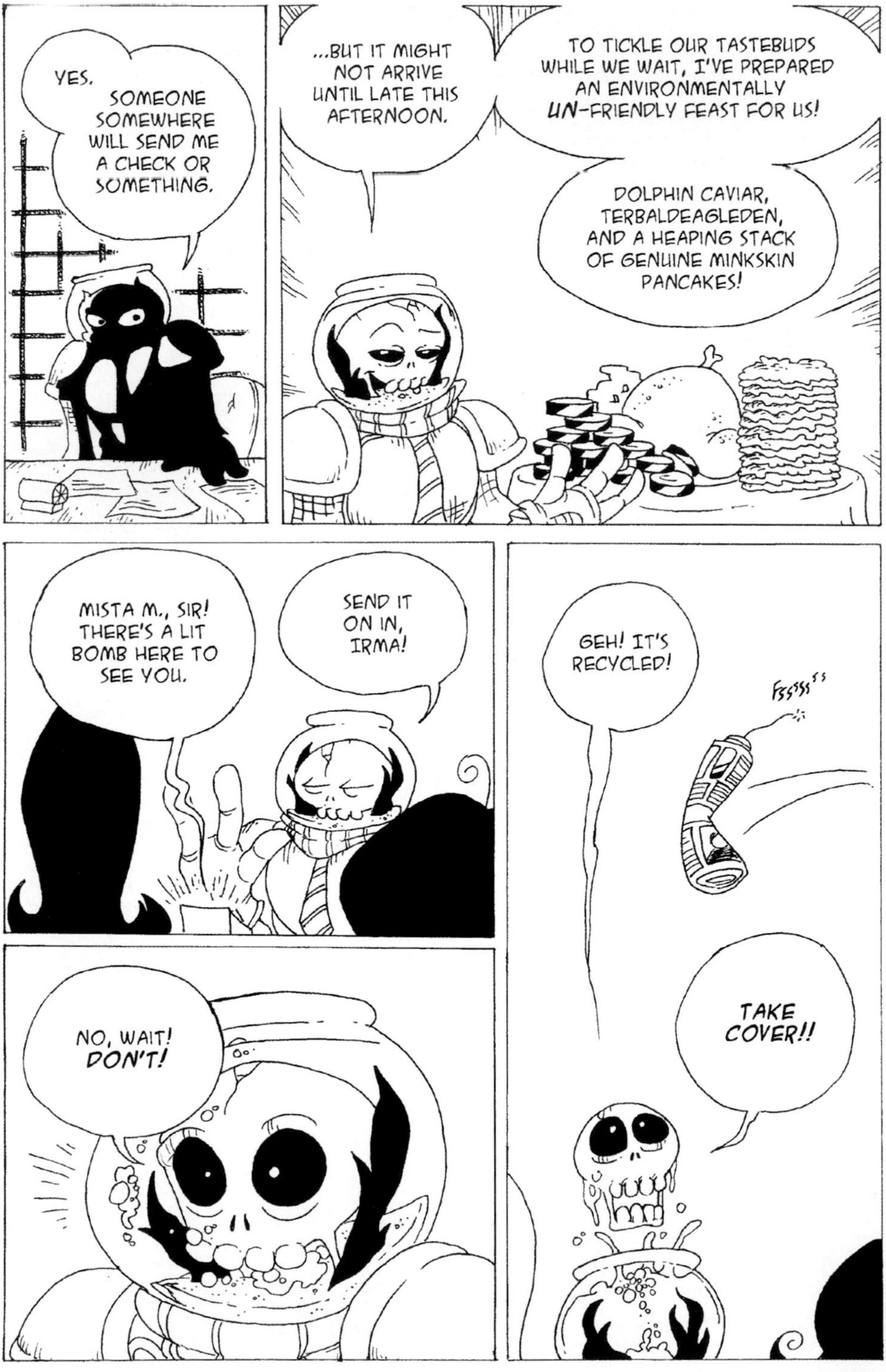
YES. SOMEONE SOMEWHERE WILL SEND ME A CHECK OR SOMETHING.
...BUT IT MIGHT NOT ARRIVE UNTIL LATE THIS AFTERNOON.
TO TICKLE OUR TASTEBUDS WHILE WE WAIT, I'VE PREPARED AN ENVIRONMENTALLY *UN*-FRIENDLY FEAST FOR US!
DOLPHIN CAVIAR, TERBALDEAGLEDEN, AND A HEAPING STACK OF GENUINE MINKSKIN PANCAKES!
MISTA M., SIR! THERE'S A LIT BOMB HERE TO SEE YOU.
SEND IT ON IN, IRMA!
NO, WAIT! *DON'T!*
GEH! IT'S RECYCLED!
Fssssss
TAKE COVER!!

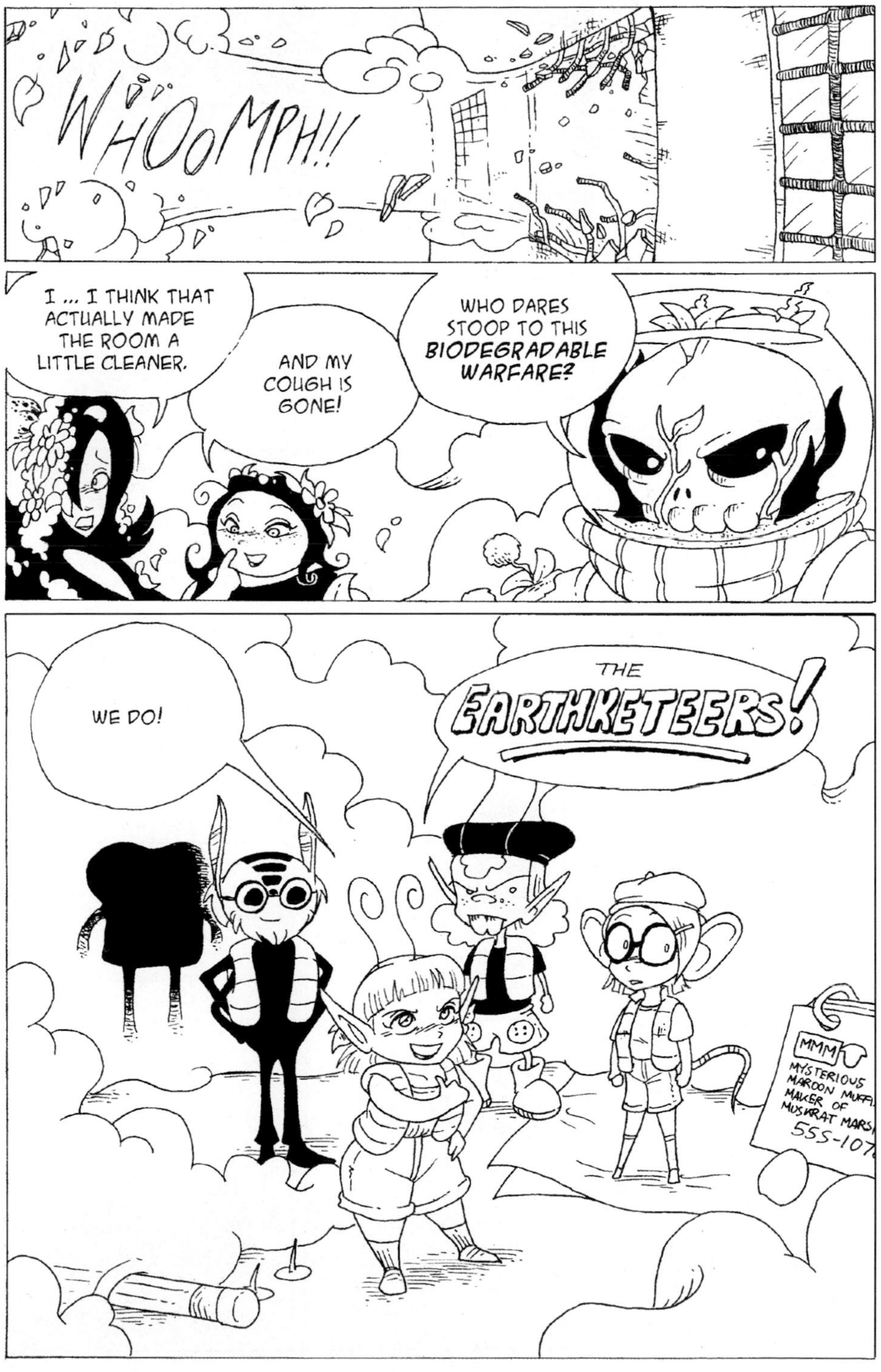
WHOOMPH!!
I ... I THINK THAT ACTUALLY MADE THE ROOM A LITTLE CLEANER.
AND MY COUGH IS GONE!
WHO DARES STOOP TO THIS BIODEGRADABLE WARFARE?
WE DO!
THE EARTHKETEERS!
MMM
MYSTERIOUS MAROON MUFFI MAKER OF MUSKRAT MARS
555-107

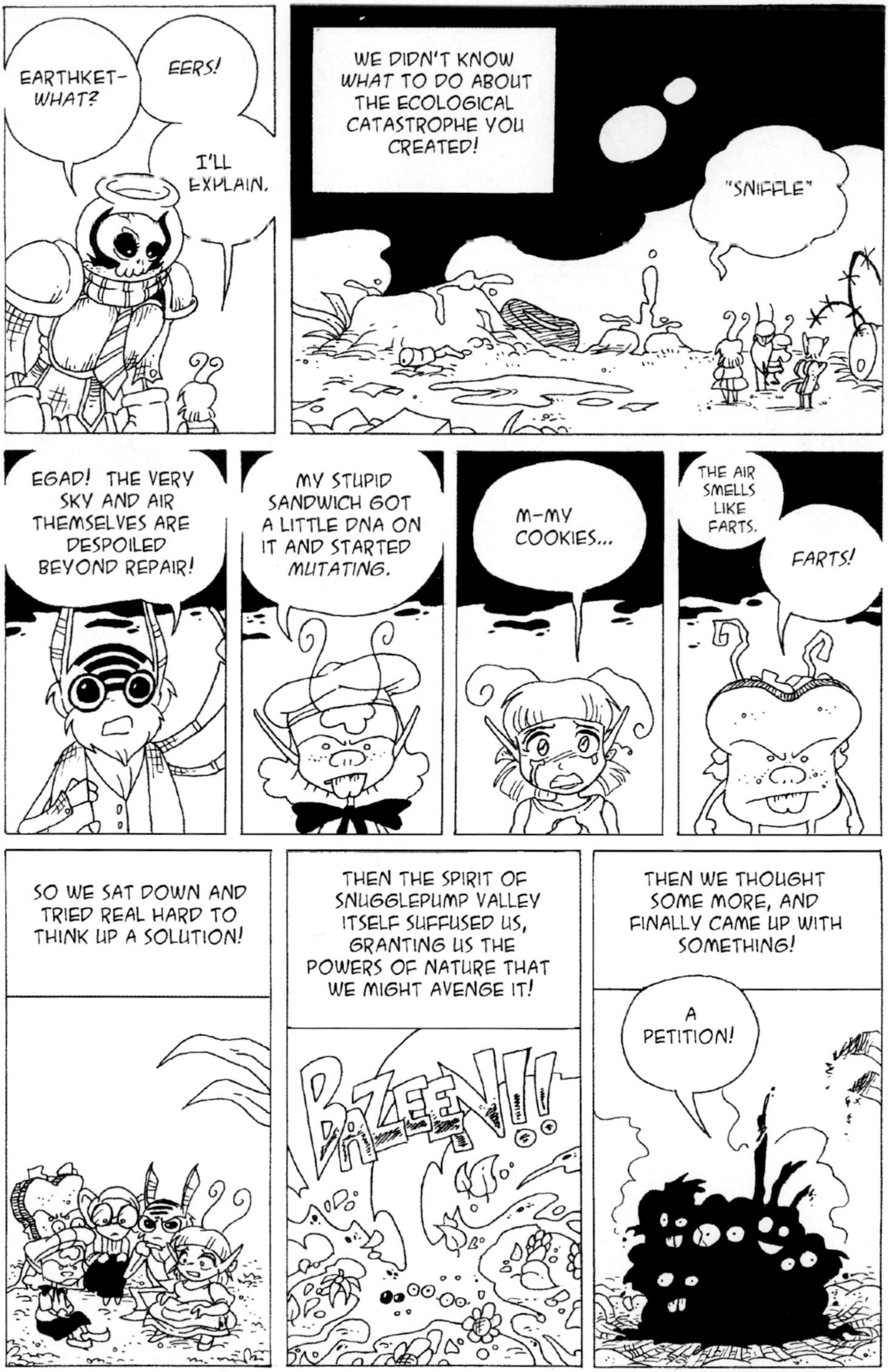
EARTHKET-WHAT?
EERS!
I'LL EXPLAIN.
WE DIDN'T KNOW WHAT TO DO ABOUT THE ECOLOGICAL CATASTROPHE YOU CREATED!
"SNIFFLE"
EGAD! THE VERY SKY AND AIR THEMSELVES ARE DESPOILED BEYOND REPAIR!
MY STUPID SANDWICH GOT A LITTLE DNA ON IT AND STARTED MUTATING.
M-MY COOKIES...
THE AIR SMELLS LIKE FARTS.
FARTS!
SO WE SAT DOWN AND TRIED REAL HARD TO THINK UP A SOLUTION!
THEN THE SPIRIT OF SNUGGLEPUMP VALLEY ITSELF SUFFUSED US, GRANTING US THE POWERS OF NATURE THAT WE MIGHT AVENGE IT!
BAZEEN!!!
THEN WE THOUGHT SOME MORE, AND FINALLY CAME UP WITH SOMETHING!
A PETITION!

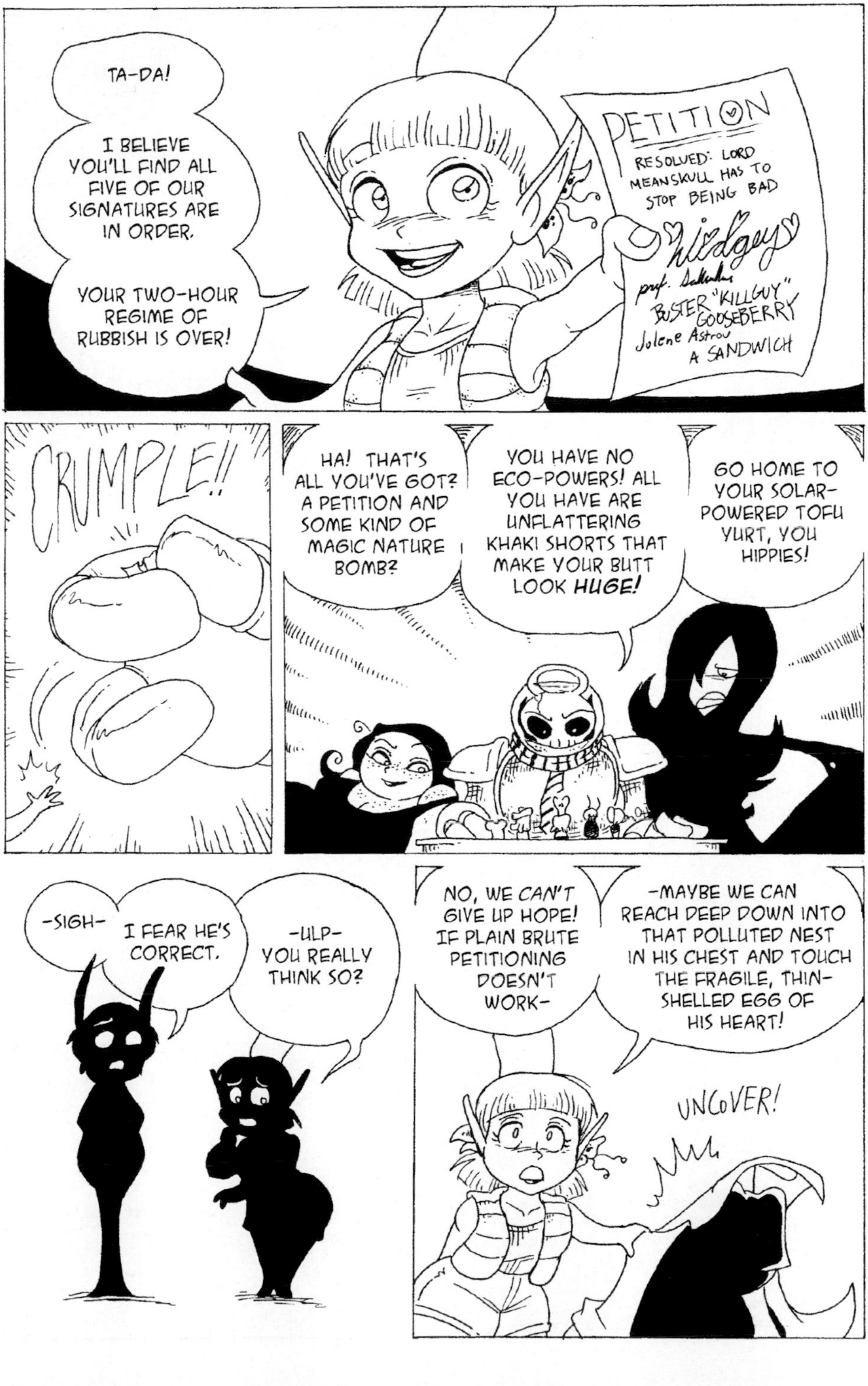
TA-DA!
I BELIEVE YOU'LL FIND ALL FIVE OF OUR SIGNATURES ARE IN ORDER.
YOUR TWO-HOUR REGIME OF RUBBISH IS OVER!
PETITION
RESOLVED: LORD MEANSKULL HAS TO STOP BEING BAD
BUSTER "KILLGUY" GOOSEBERRY
Jolene Astrou
A SANDWICH
CRUMPLE!!
HA! THAT'S ALL YOU'VE GOT? A PETITION AND SOME KIND OF MAGIC NATURE BOMB?
YOU HAVE NO ECO-POWERS! ALL YOU HAVE ARE UNFLATTERING KHAKI SHORTS THAT MAKE YOUR BUTT LOOK **HUGE!**
GO HOME TO YOUR SOLAR-POWERED TOFU YURT, YOU HIPPIES!
-SIGH-
I FEAR HE'S CORRECT.
-ULP- YOU REALLY THINK SO?
NO, WE *CAN'T* GIVE UP HOPE! IF PLAIN BRUTE PETITIONING DOESN'T WORK-
-MAYBE WE CAN REACH DEEP DOWN INTO THAT POLLUTED NEST IN HIS CHEST AND TOUCH THE FRAGILE, THIN-SHELLED EGG OF HIS HEART!
UNCOVER!

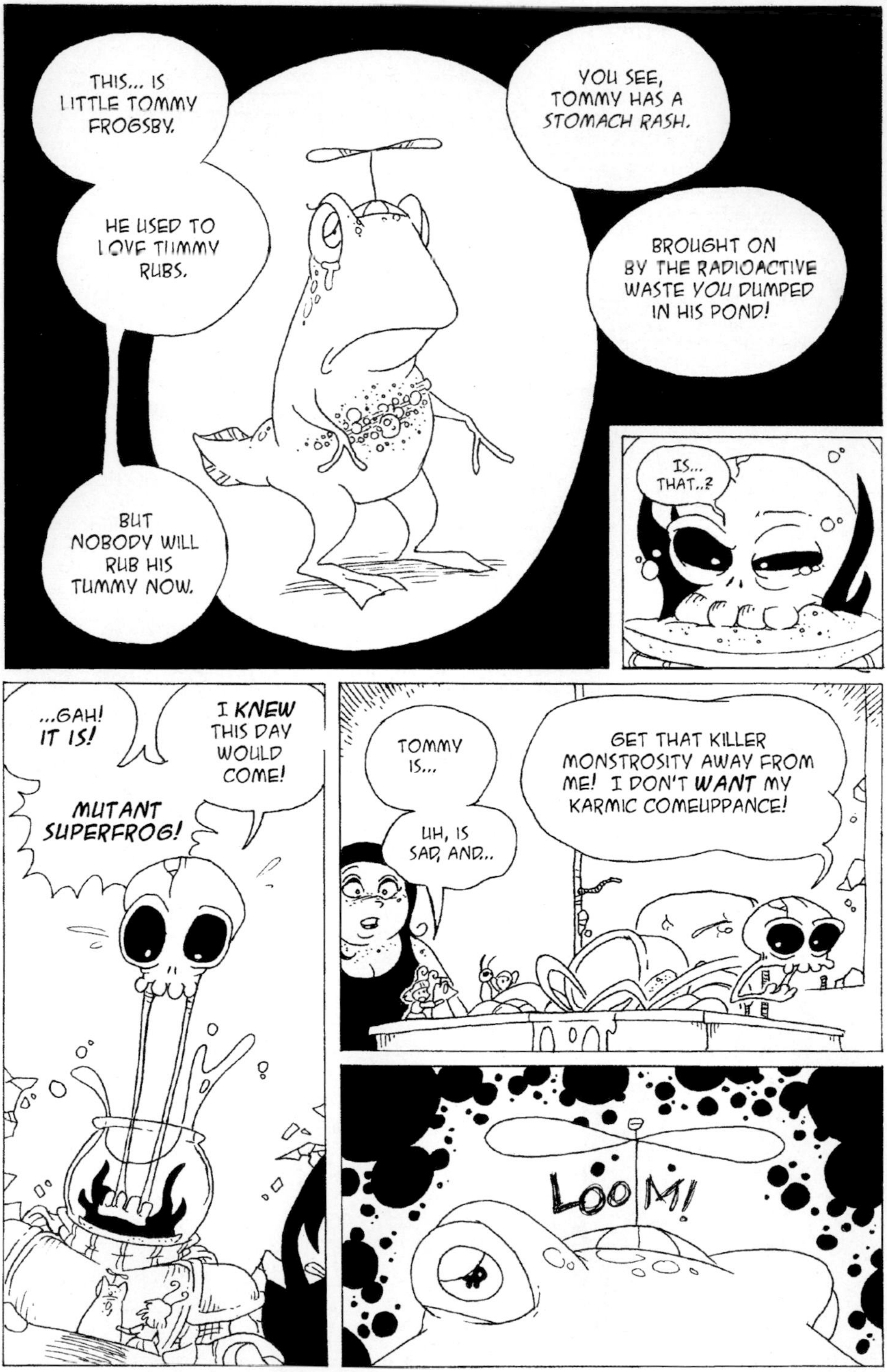

THIS... IS LITTLE TOMMY FROGSBY.
HE USED TO LOVE TUMMY RUBS.
BUT NOBODY WILL RUB HIS TUMMY NOW.
YOU SEE, TOMMY HAS A STOMACH RASH.
BROUGHT ON BY THE RADIOACTIVE WASTE YOU DUMPED IN HIS POND!
IS... THAT..?
...GAH! IT IS!
MUTANT SUPERFROG!
I KNEW THIS DAY WOULD COME!
TOMMY IS...
UH, IS SAD, AND...
GET THAT KILLER MONSTROSITY AWAY FROM ME! I DON'T WANT MY KARMIC COMEUPPANCE!
LOOM!

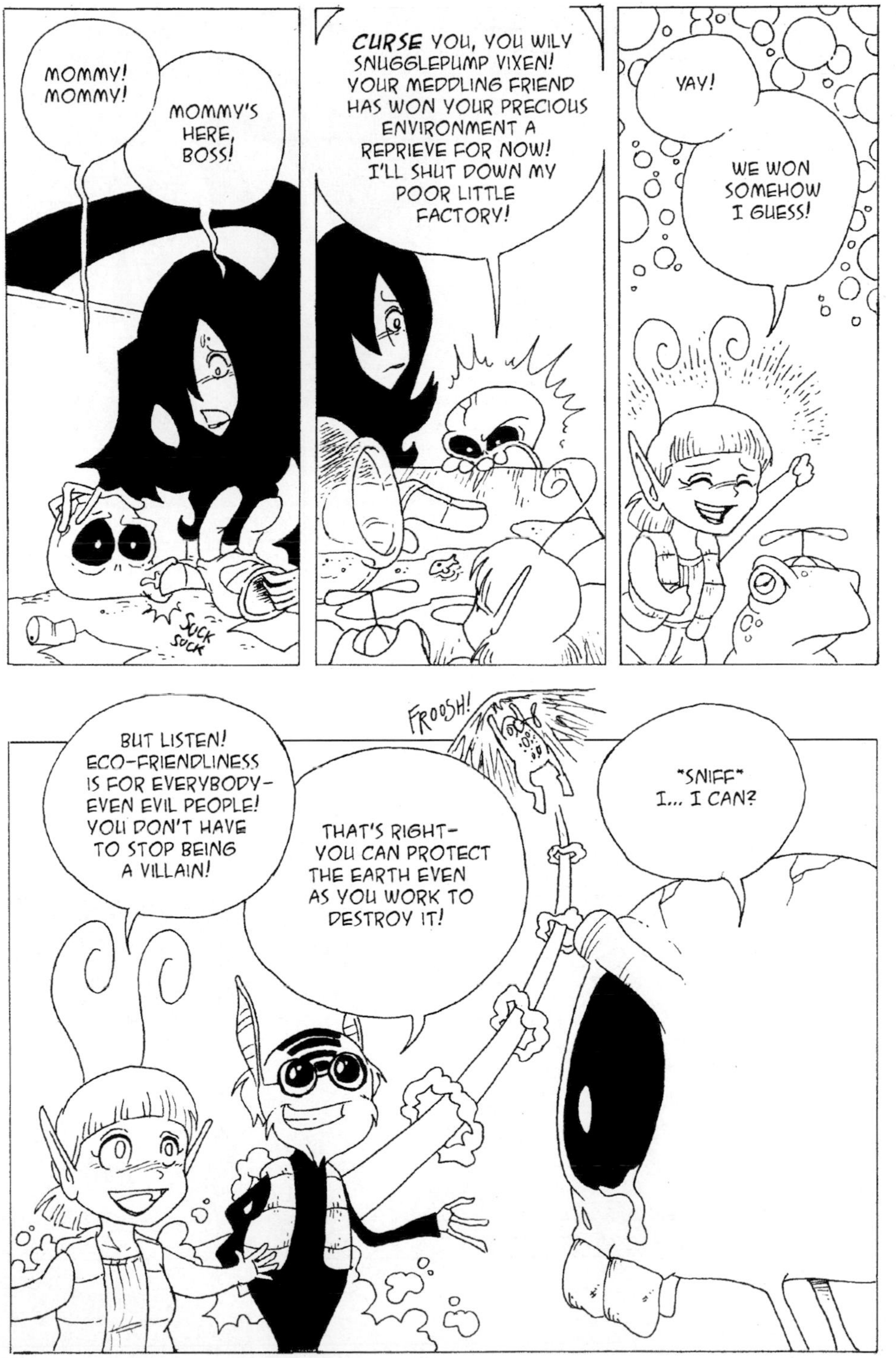
MOMMY! MOMMY!
MOMMY'S HERE, BOSS!
SUCK SUCK
CURSE YOU, YOU WILY SNUGGLEPUMP VIXEN! YOUR MEDDLING FRIEND HAS WON YOUR PRECIOUS ENVIRONMENT A REPRIEVE FOR NOW! I'LL SHUT DOWN MY POOR LITTLE FACTORY!
YAY!
WE WON SOMEHOW I GUESS!
FROOSH!
BUT LISTEN! ECO-FRIENDLINESS IS FOR EVERYBODY- EVEN EVIL PEOPLE! YOU DON'T HAVE TO STOP BEING A VILLAIN!
THAT'S RIGHT- YOU CAN PROTECT THE EARTH EVEN AS YOU WORK TO DESTROY IT!
SNIFF I... I CAN?

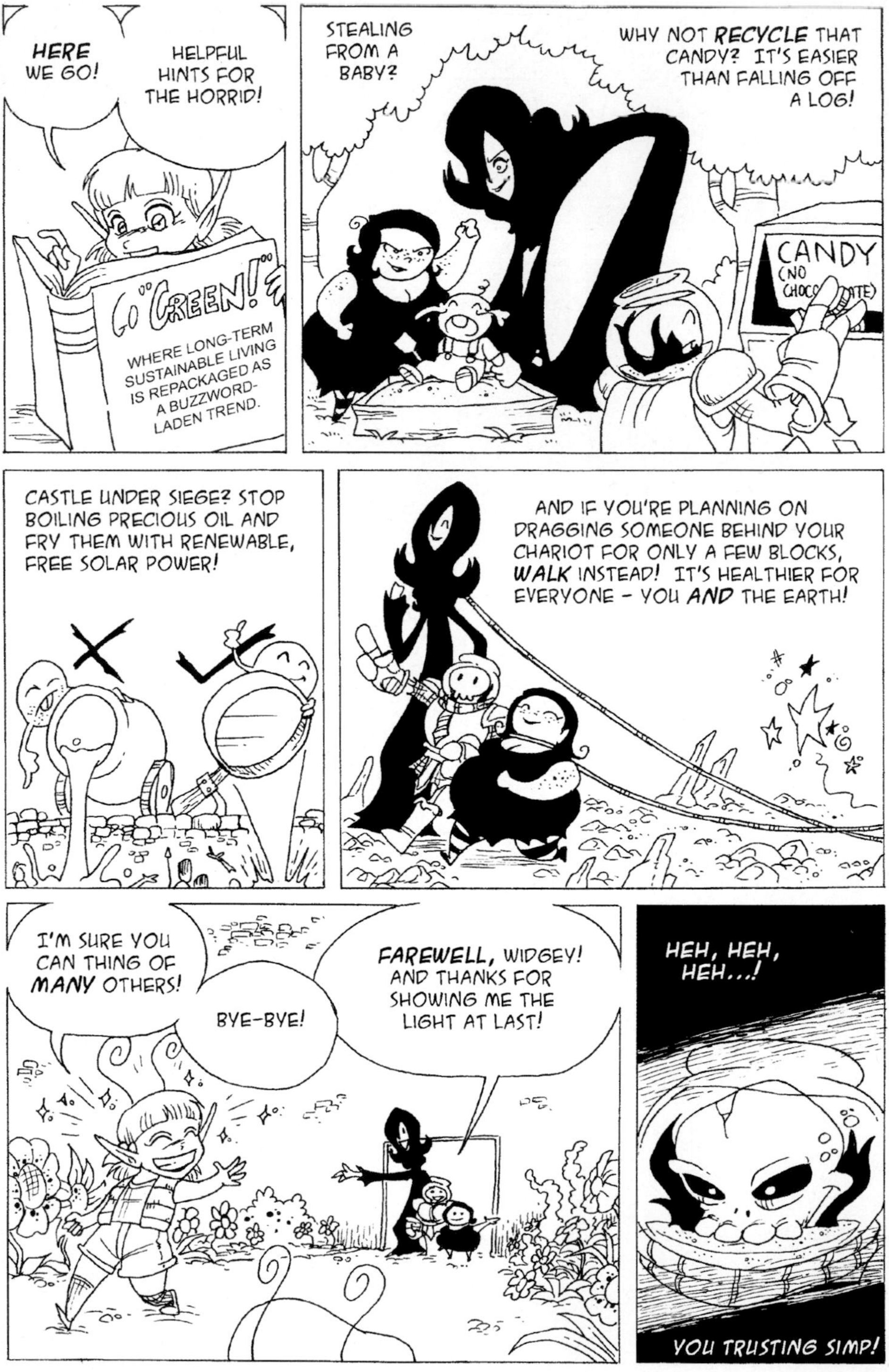
HERE WE GO!
HELPFUL HINTS FOR THE HORRID!
GO GREEN!
WHERE LONG-TERM SUSTAINABLE LIVING IS REPACKAGED AS A BUZZWORD-LADEN TREND.
STEALING FROM A BABY?
WHY NOT RECYCLE THAT CANDY? IT'S EASIER THAN FALLING OFF A LOG!
CANDY (NO CHOCO ATE)
CASTLE UNDER SIEGE? STOP BOILING PRECIOUS OIL AND FRY THEM WITH RENEWABLE, FREE SOLAR POWER!
AND IF YOU'RE PLANNING ON DRAGGING SOMEONE BEHIND YOUR CHARIOT FOR ONLY A FEW BLOCKS, WALK INSTEAD! IT'S HEALTHIER FOR EVERYONE - YOU AND THE EARTH!
I'M SURE YOU CAN THING OF MANY OTHERS!
BYE-BYE!
FAREWELL, WIDGEY! AND THANKS FOR SHOWING ME THE LIGHT AT LAST!
HEH, HEH, HEH...!
YOU TRUSTING SIMP!

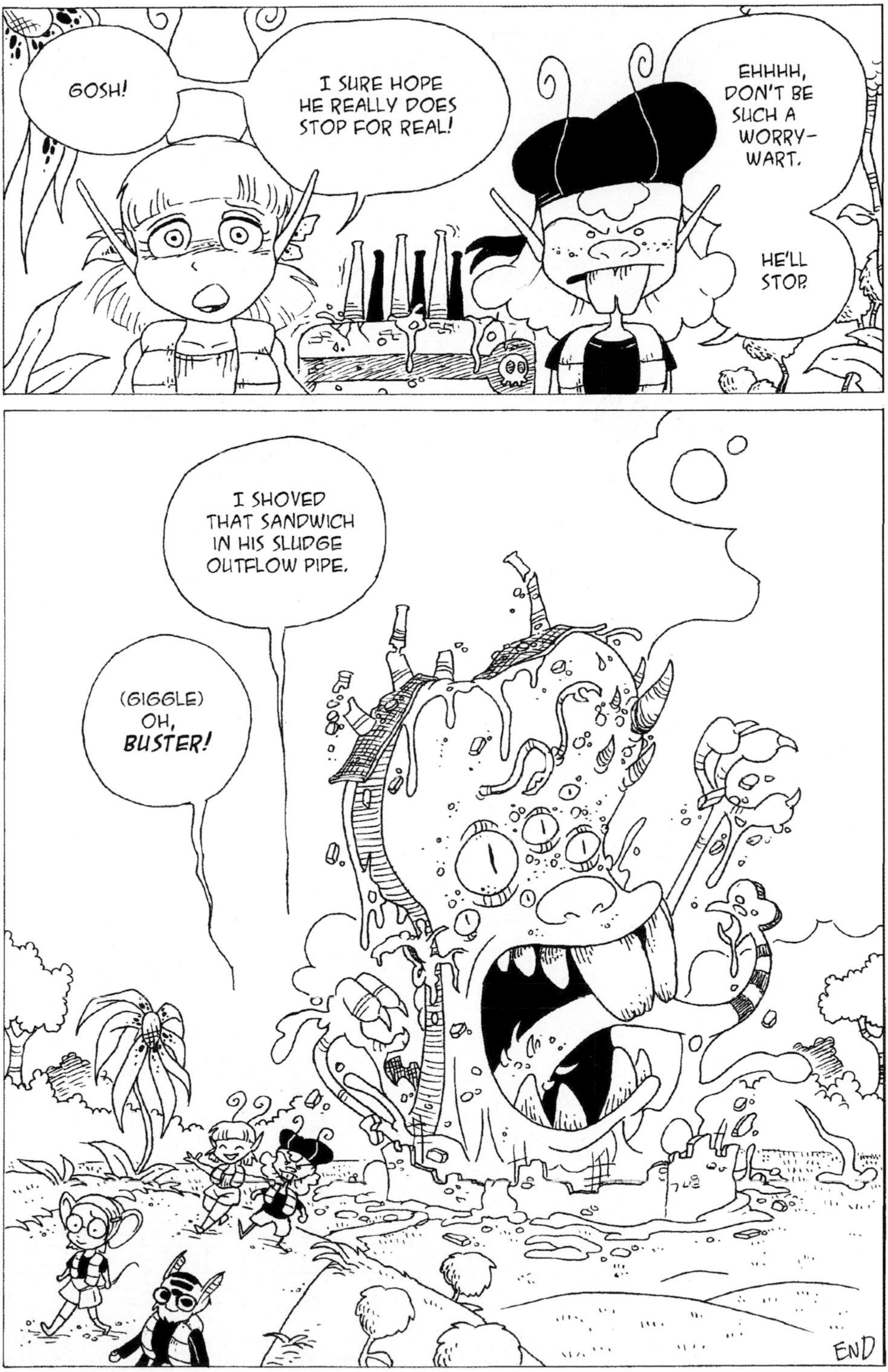
GOSH!
I SURE HOPE HE REALLY DOES STOP FOR REAL!
EHHHH, DON'T BE SUCH A WORRY-WART.
HE'LL STOP.
I SHOVED THAT SANDWICH IN HIS SLUDGE OUTFLOW PIPE.
(GIGGLE) OH, BUSTER!
END

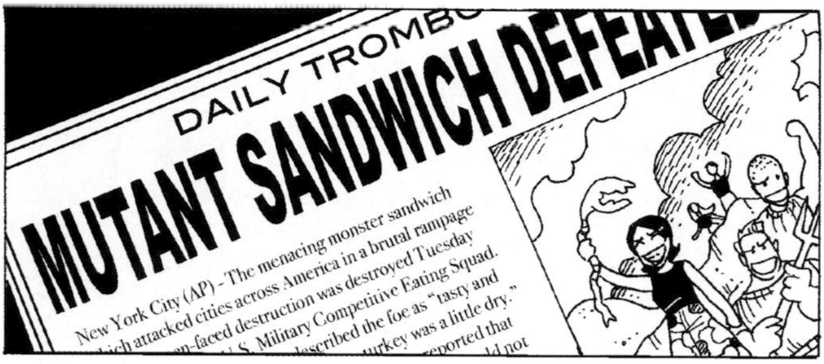
DAILY TROMBO
MUTANT SANDWICH DEFEATE
New York City (AP) - The menacing monster sandwich
attacked cities across America in a brutal rampage
faced destruction was destroyed Tuesday
Military Competitive Eating Squad.
described the foe as "tasty and
turkey was a little dry."
reported that

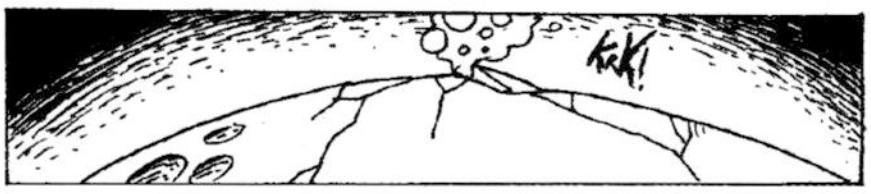
KRK!

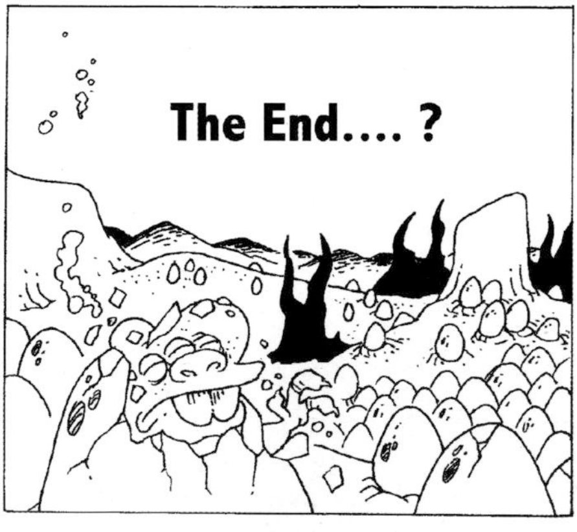
The End.... ?

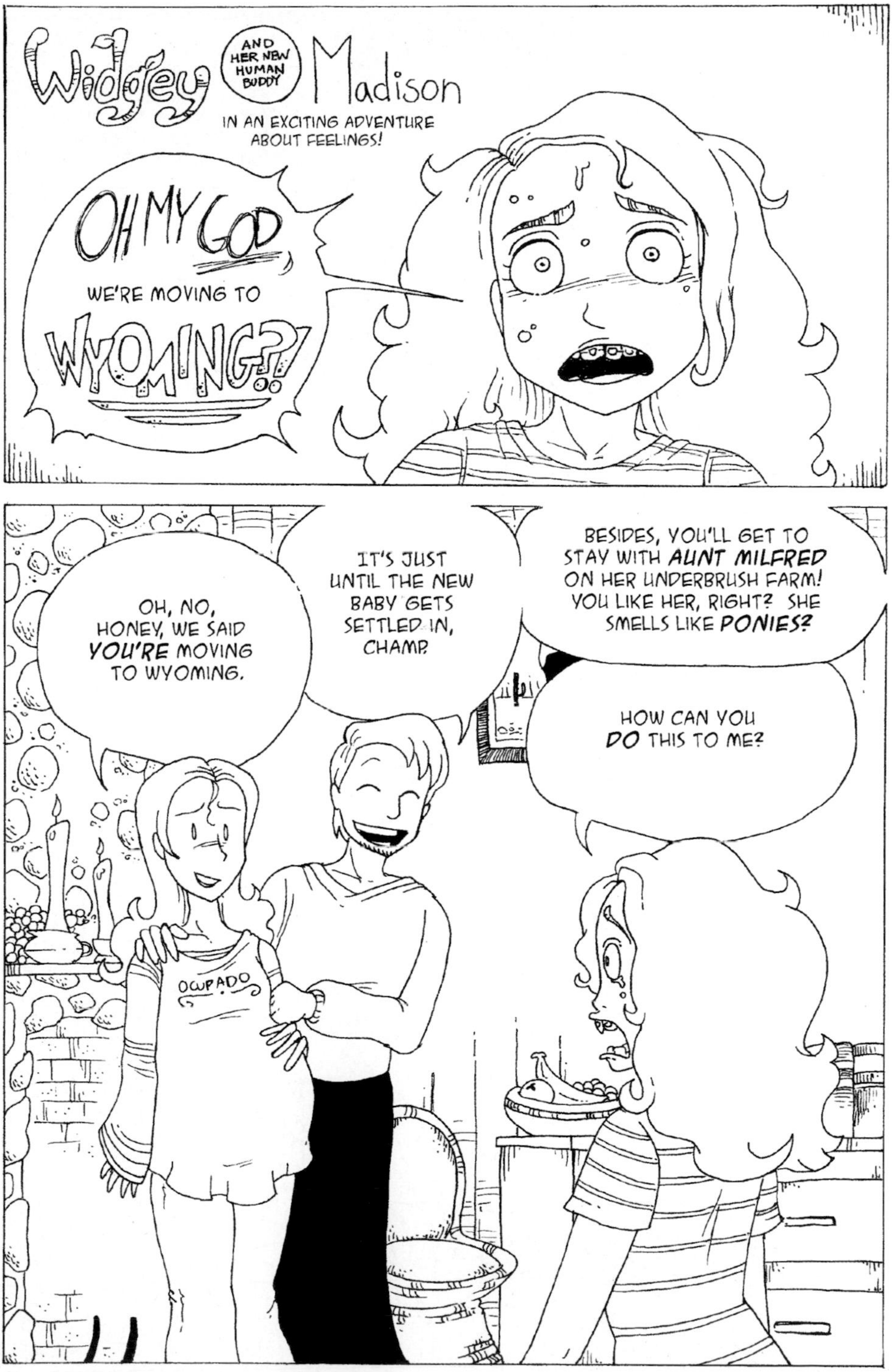
Widgey
AND HER NEW HUMAN BUDDY
Madison
IN AN EXCITING ADVENTURE ABOUT FEELINGS!
OH MY GOD WE'RE MOVING TO WYOMING?!
OH, NO, HONEY, WE SAID YOU'RE MOVING TO WYOMING.
IT'S JUST UNTIL THE NEW BABY GETS SETTLED IN, CHAMP.
BESIDES, YOU'LL GET TO STAY WITH AUNT MILFRED ON HER UNDERBRUSH FARM! YOU LIKE HER, RIGHT? SHE SMELLS LIKE PONIES?
HOW CAN YOU DO THIS TO ME?
OCUPADO

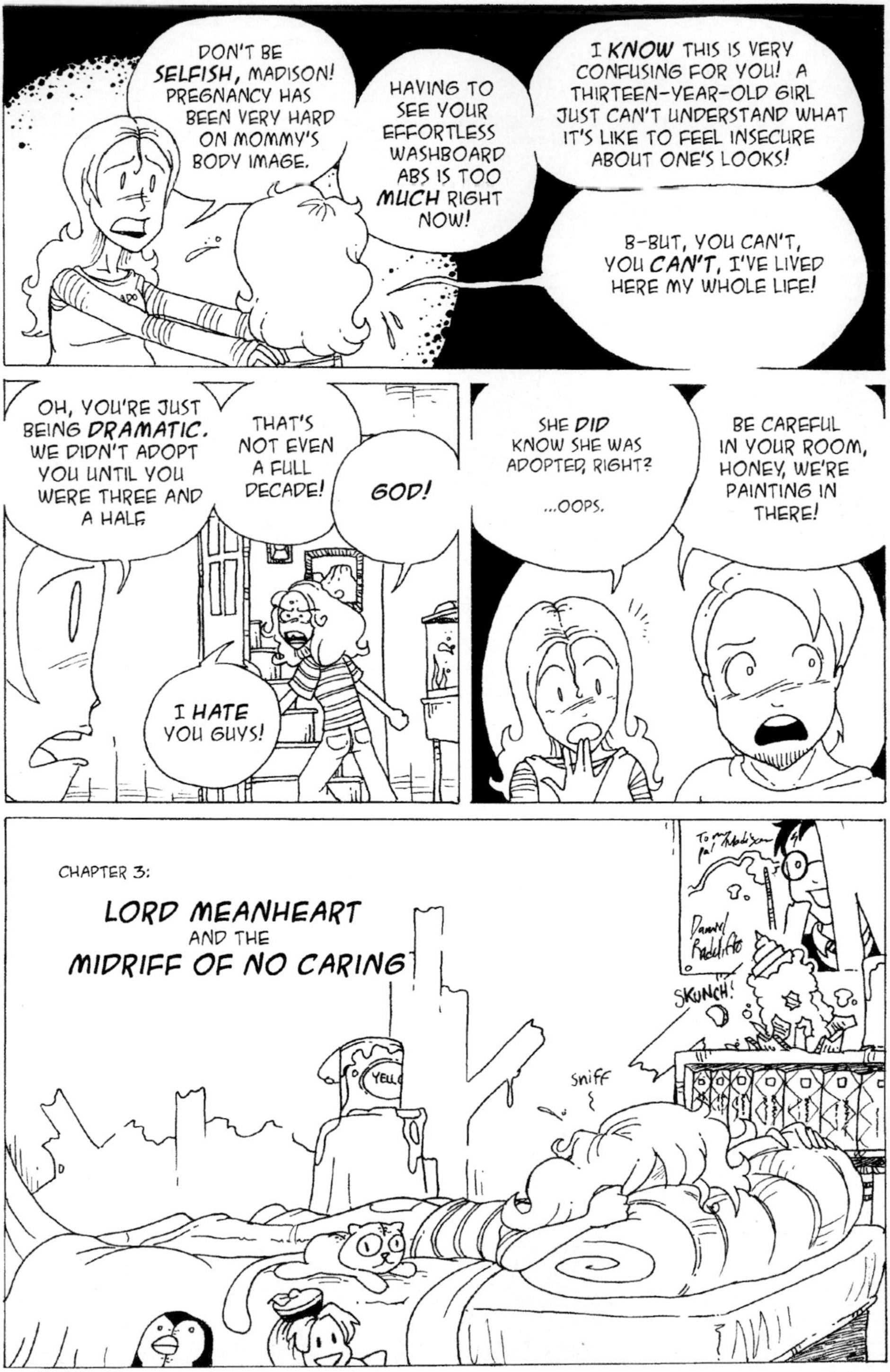
DON'T BE SELFISH, MADISON! PREGNANCY HAS BEEN VERY HARD ON MOMMY'S BODY IMAGE.
HAVING TO SEE YOUR EFFORTLESS WASHBOARD ABS IS TOO MUCH RIGHT NOW!
I KNOW THIS IS VERY CONFUSING FOR YOU! A THIRTEEN-YEAR-OLD GIRL JUST CAN'T UNDERSTAND WHAT IT'S LIKE TO FEEL INSECURE ABOUT ONE'S LOOKS!
B-BUT, YOU CAN'T, YOU CAN'T, I'VE LIVED HERE MY WHOLE LIFE!
OH, YOU'RE JUST BEING DRAMATIC. WE DIDN'T ADOPT YOU UNTIL YOU WERE THREE AND A HALF.
THAT'S NOT EVEN A FULL DECADE!
GOD!
I HATE YOU GUYS!
SHE DID KNOW SHE WAS ADOPTED, RIGHT?
...OOPS.
BE CAREFUL IN YOUR ROOM, HONEY, WE'RE PAINTING IN THERE!
CHAPTER 3:
LORD MEANHEART AND THE MIDRIFF OF NO CARING
SKUNCH!
YELLO
sniff

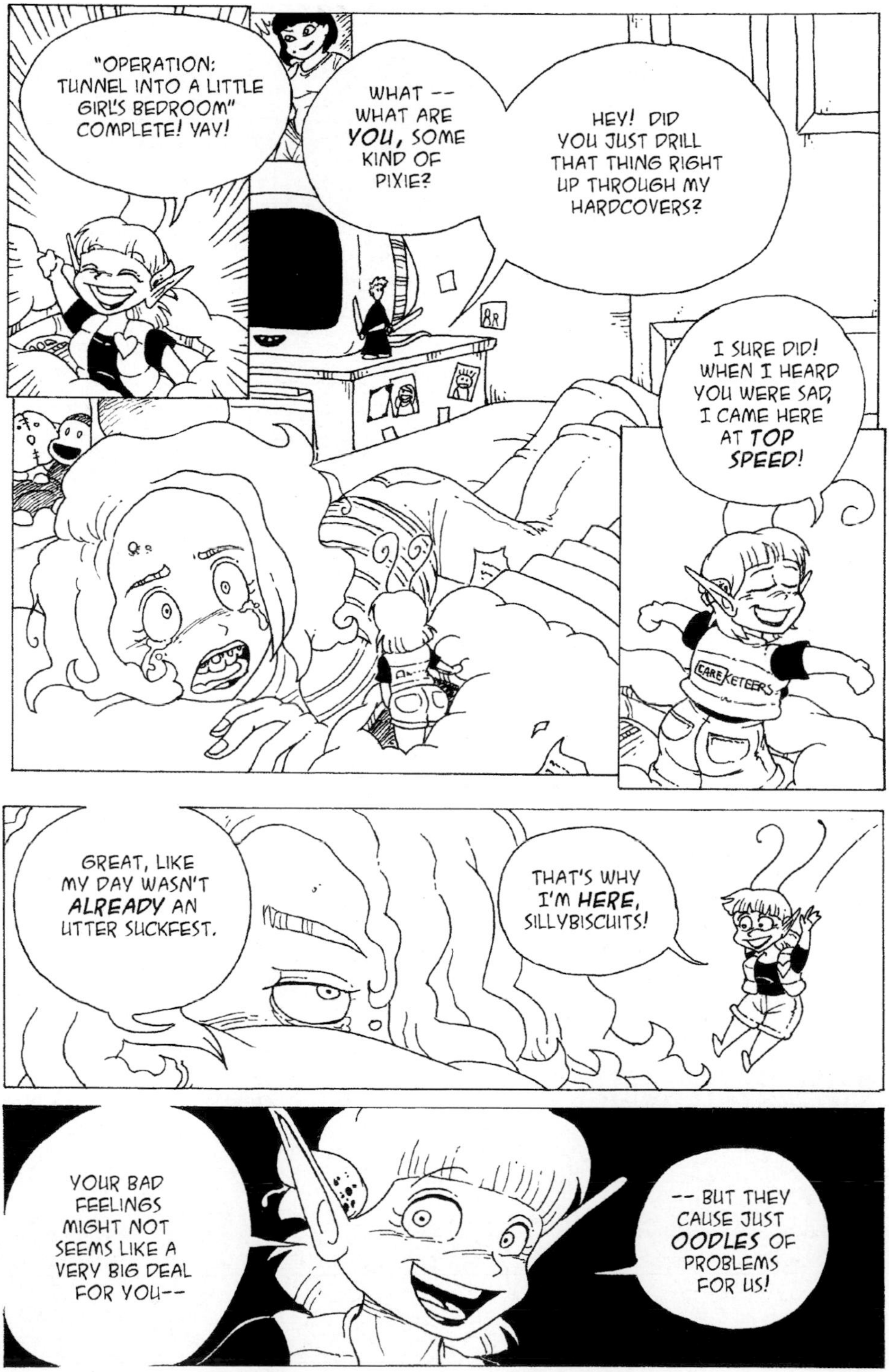
"OPERATION: TUNNEL INTO A LITTLE GIRL'S BEDROOM" COMPLETE! YAY!
WHAT -- WHAT ARE *YOU*, SOME KIND OF PIXIE?
HEY! DID YOU JUST DRILL THAT THING RIGHT UP THROUGH MY HARDCOVERS?
I SURE DID! WHEN I HEARD YOU WERE SAD, I CAME HERE AT *TOP SPEED*!
CAREKETEERS
GREAT, LIKE MY DAY WASN'T *ALREADY* AN UTTER SUCKFEST.
THAT'S WHY I'M *HERE*, SILLYBISCUITS!
YOUR BAD FEELINGS MIGHT NOT SEEMS LIKE A VERY BIG DEAL FOR YOU--
-- BUT THEY CAUSE JUST *OODLES* OF PROBLEMS FOR US!

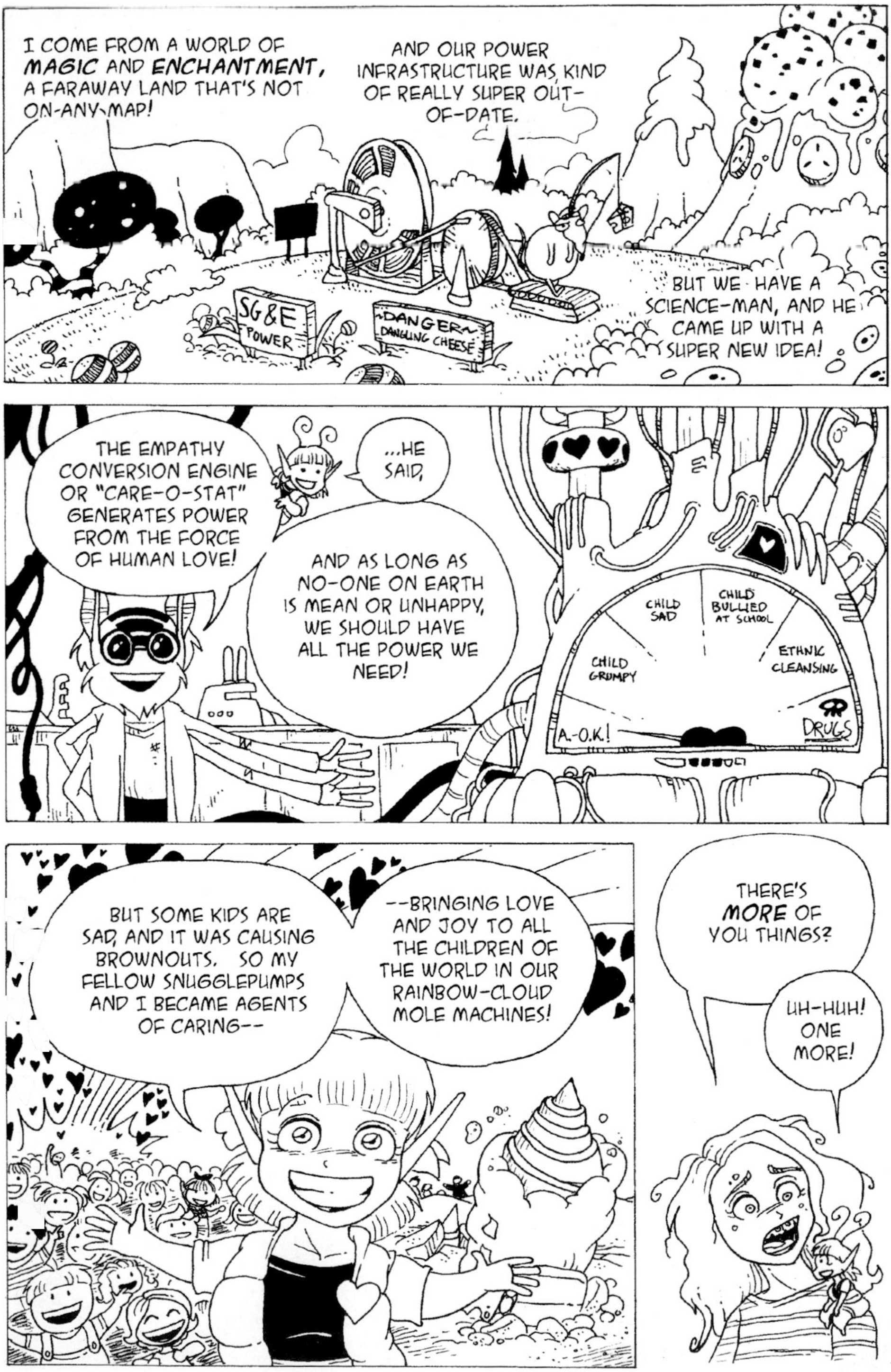
I COME FROM A WORLD OF MAGIC AND ENCHANTMENT, A FARAWAY LAND THAT'S NOT ON-ANY-MAP!
AND OUR POWER INFRASTRUCTURE WAS, KIND OF REALLY SUPER OUT-OF-DATE.
SG&E POWER
DANGER DANGLING CHEESE
BUT WE HAVE A SCIENCE-MAN, AND HE CAME UP WITH A SUPER NEW IDEA!
THE EMPATHY CONVERSION ENGINE OR "CARE-O-STAT" GENERATES POWER FROM THE FORCE OF HUMAN LOVE!
...HE SAID,
AND AS LONG AS NO-ONE ON EARTH IS MEAN OR UNHAPPY, WE SHOULD HAVE ALL THE POWER WE NEED!
A.-O.K.!
CHILD GRUMPY
CHILD SAD
CHILD BULLIED AT SCHOOL
ETHNIC CLEANSING
DRUGS
BUT SOME KIDS ARE SAD, AND IT WAS CAUSING BROWNOUTS. SO MY FELLOW SNUGGLEPUMPS AND I BECAME AGENTS OF CARING--
--BRINGING LOVE AND JOY TO ALL THE CHILDREN OF THE WORLD IN OUR RAINBOW-CLOUD MOLE MACHINES!
THERE'S MORE OF YOU THINGS?
UH-HUH! ONE MORE!

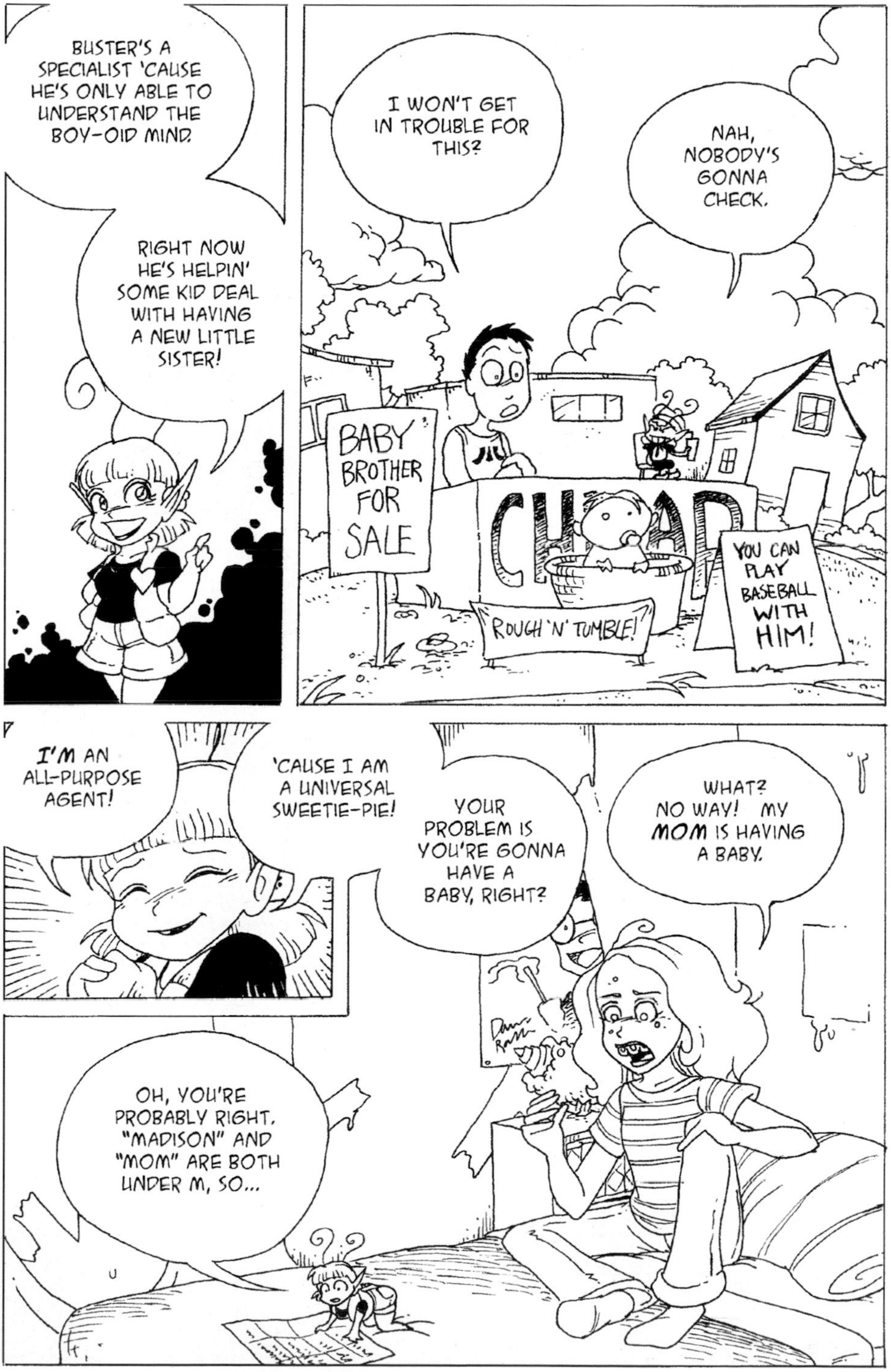
BUSTER'S A SPECIALIST 'CAUSE HE'S ONLY ABLE TO UNDERSTAND THE BOY-OID MIND.
RIGHT NOW HE'S HELPIN' SOME KID DEAL WITH HAVING A NEW LITTLE SISTER!
I WON'T GET IN TROUBLE FOR THIS?
NAH, NOBODY'S GONNA CHECK.
BABY BROTHER FOR SALE
CHEAP
ROUGH 'N' TUMBLE!
YOU CAN PLAY BASEBALL WITH HIM!
I'M AN ALL-PURPOSE AGENT!
'CAUSE I AM A UNIVERSAL SWEETIE-PIE!
YOUR PROBLEM IS YOU'RE GONNA HAVE A BABY, RIGHT?
WHAT? NO WAY! MY MOM IS HAVING A BABY.
OH, YOU'RE PROBABLY RIGHT. "MADISON" AND "MOM" ARE BOTH UNDER M, SO...

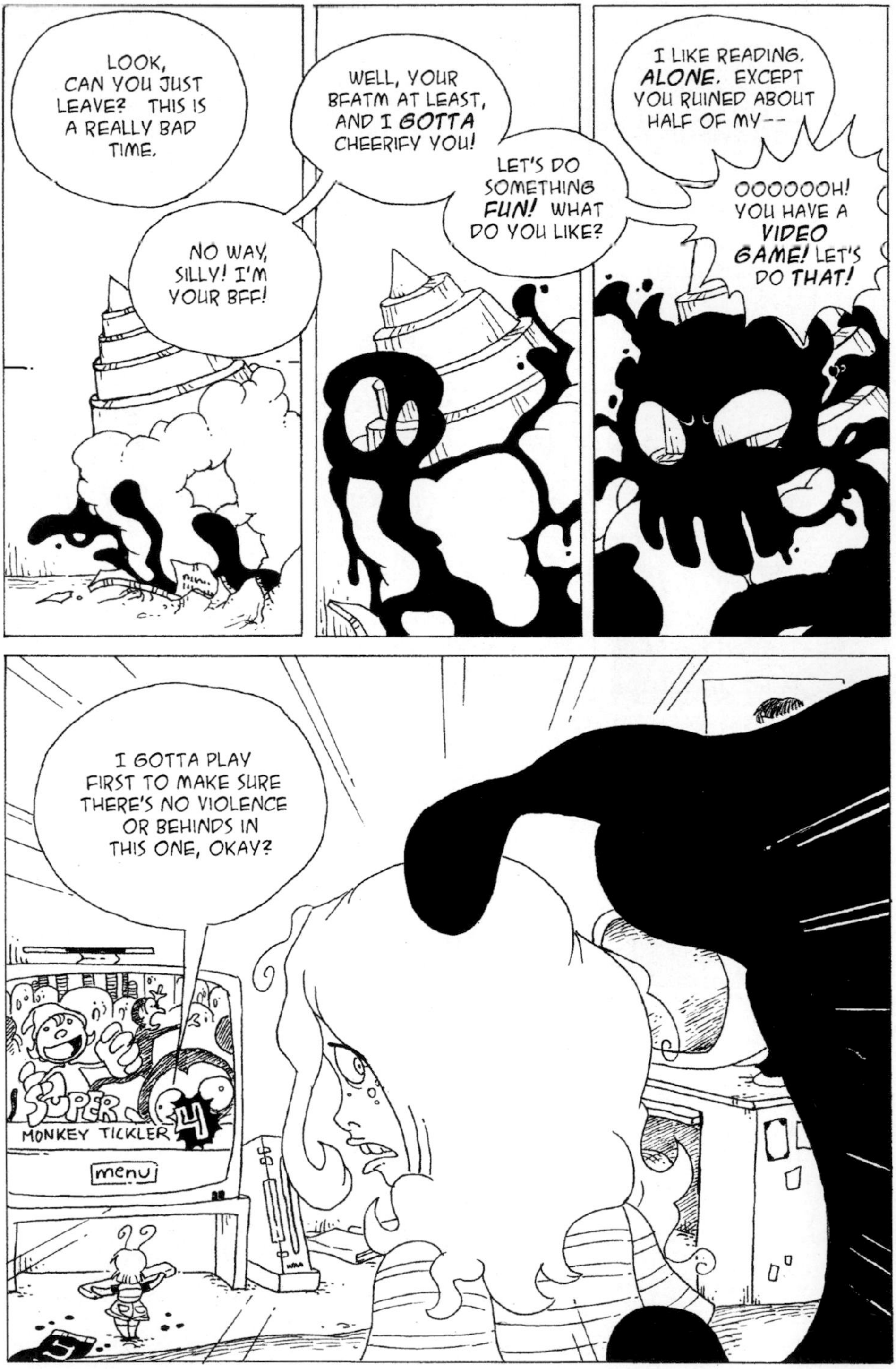
LOOK, CAN YOU JUST LEAVE? THIS IS A REALLY BAD TIME.
NO WAY, SILLY! I'M YOUR BFF!
WELL, YOUR BFATM AT LEAST, AND I GOTTA CHEERIFY YOU!
LET'S DO SOMETHING FUN! WHAT DO YOU LIKE?
I LIKE READING. ALONE. EXCEPT YOU RUINED ABOUT HALF OF MY--
OOOOOOH! YOU HAVE A VIDEO GAME! LET'S DO THAT!
I GOTTA PLAY FIRST TO MAKE SURE THERE'S NO VIOLENCE OR BEHINDS IN THIS ONE, OKAY?
SUPER MONKEY TICKLER 4
menu

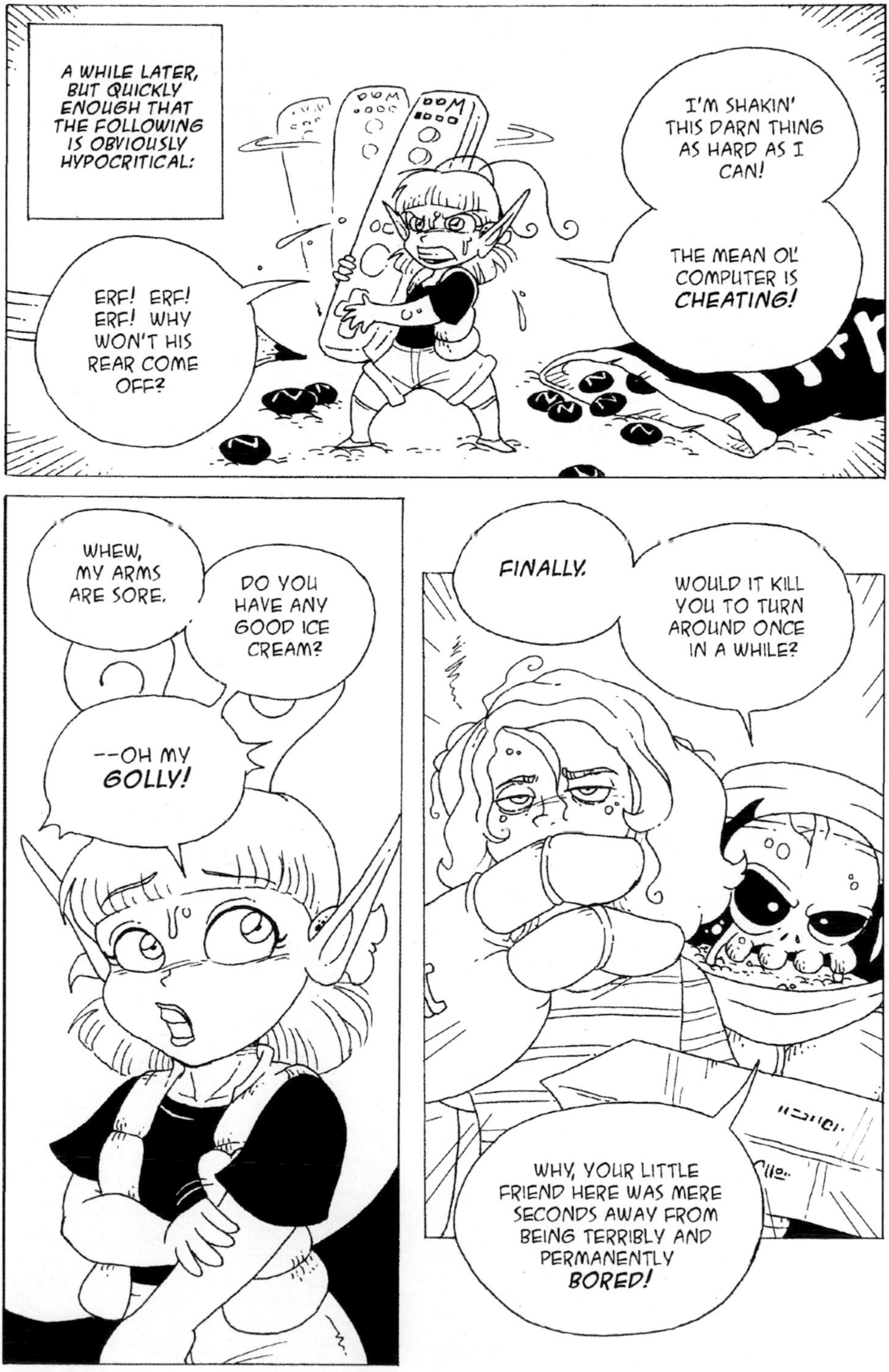
A WHILE LATER, BUT QUICKLY ENOUGH THAT THE FOLLOWING IS OBVIOUSLY HYPOCRITICAL:
ERF! ERF! ERF! WHY WON'T HIS REAR COME OFF?
I'M SHAKIN' THIS DARN THING AS HARD AS I CAN!
THE MEAN OL' COMPUTER IS CHEATING!
WHEW, MY ARMS ARE SORE.
DO YOU HAVE ANY GOOD ICE CREAM?
--OH MY GOLLY!
FINALLY.
WOULD IT KILL YOU TO TURN AROUND ONCE IN A WHILE?
WHY, YOUR LITTLE FRIEND HERE WAS MERE SECONDS AWAY FROM BEING TERRIBLY AND PERMANENTLY BORED!

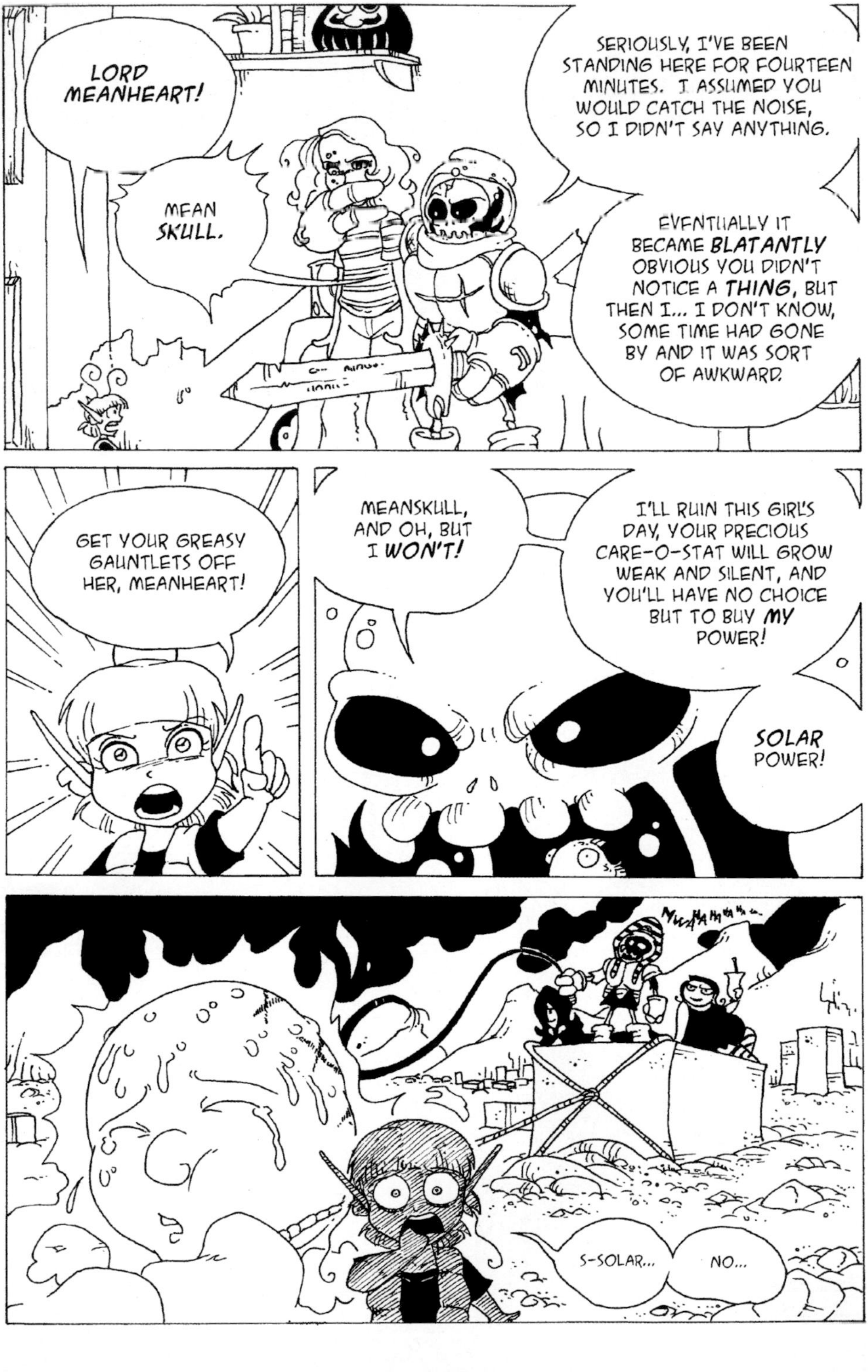
LORD MEANHEART!
MEAN SKULL.
SERIOUSLY, I'VE BEEN STANDING HERE FOR FOURTEEN MINUTES. I ASSUMED YOU WOULD CATCH THE NOISE, SO I DIDN'T SAY ANYTHING.
EVENTUALLY IT BECAME BLATANTLY OBVIOUS YOU DIDN'T NOTICE A THING, BUT THEN I... I DON'T KNOW, SOME TIME HAD GONE BY AND IT WAS SORT OF AWKWARD.
GET YOUR GREASY GAUNTLETS OFF HER, MEANHEART!
MEANSKULL, AND OH, BUT I WON'T!
I'LL RUIN THIS GIRL'S DAY, YOUR PRECIOUS CARE-O-STAT WILL GROW WEAK AND SILENT, AND YOU'LL HAVE NO CHOICE BUT TO BUY MY POWER!
SOLAR POWER!
MWAHAHAHAHAHA...
S-SOLAR...
NO...

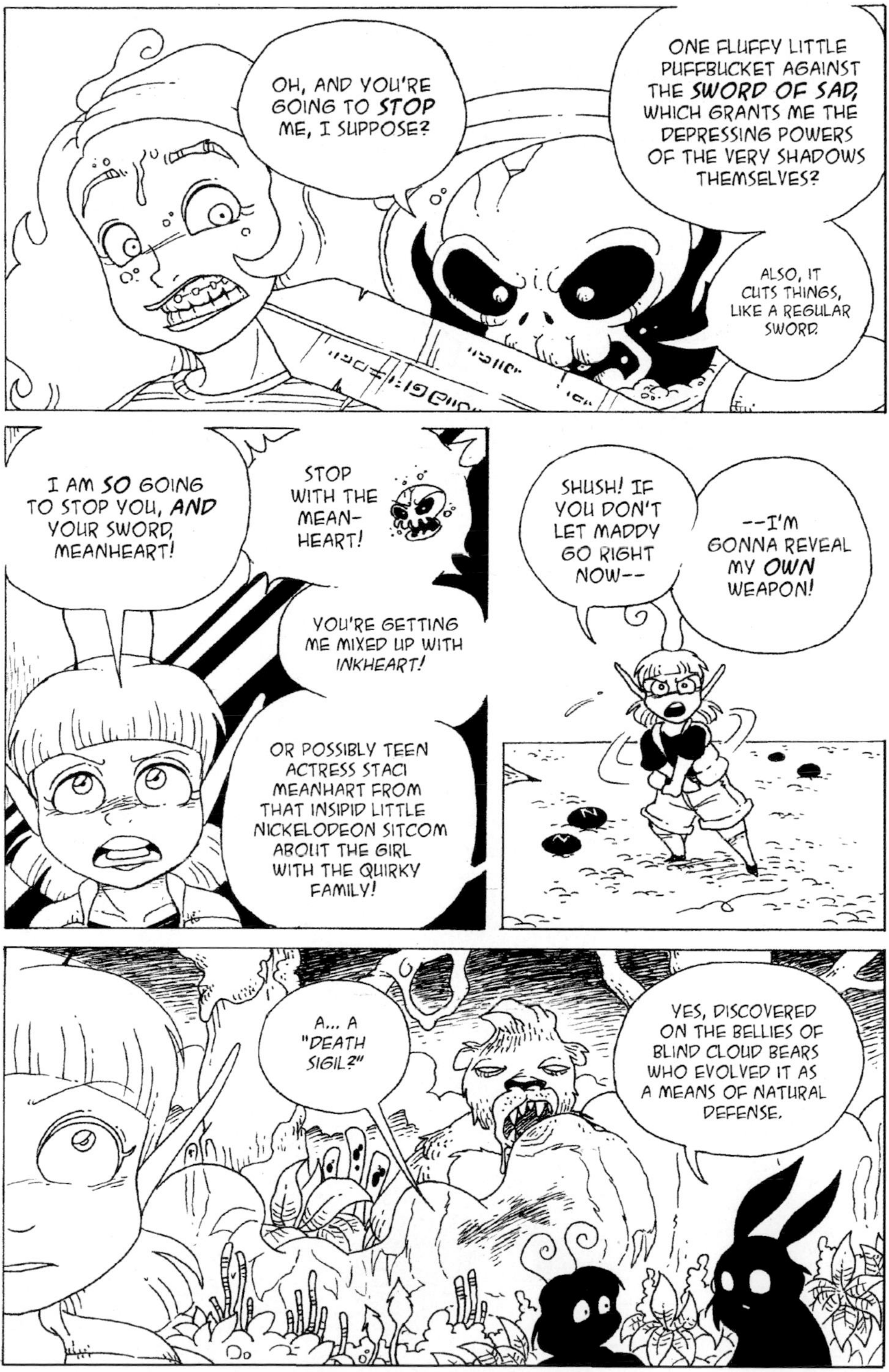
OH, AND YOU'RE GOING TO STOP ME, I SUPPOSE?
ONE FLUFFY LITTLE PUFFBUCKET AGAINST THE SWORD OF SAD, WHICH GRANTS ME THE DEPRESSING POWERS OF THE VERY SHADOWS THEMSELVES?
ALSO, IT CUTS THINGS, LIKE A REGULAR SWORD.
I AM SO GOING TO STOP YOU, AND YOUR SWORD, MEANHEART!
STOP WITH THE MEAN-HEART!
YOU'RE GETTING ME MIXED UP WITH INKHEART!
OR POSSIBLY TEEN ACTRESS STACI MEANHART FROM THAT INSIPID LITTLE NICKELODEON SITCOM ABOUT THE GIRL WITH THE QUIRKY FAMILY!
SHUSH! IF YOU DON'T LET MADDY GO RIGHT NOW--
--I'M GONNA REVEAL MY OWN WEAPON!
A... A "DEATH SIGIL?"
YES, DISCOVERED ON THE BELLIES OF BLIND CLOUD BEARS WHO EVOLVED IT AS A MEANS OF NATURAL DEFENSE.

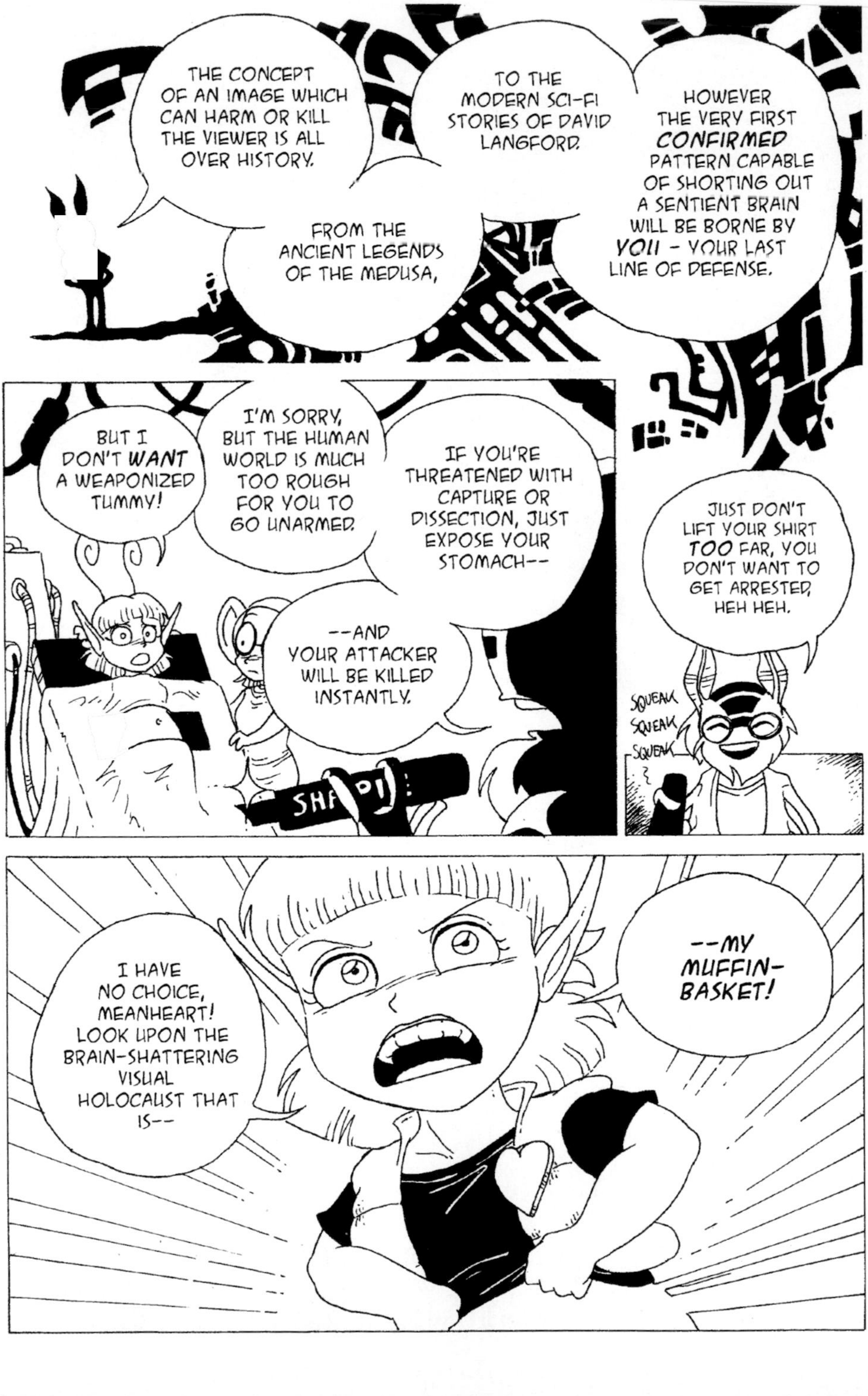
THE CONCEPT OF AN IMAGE WHICH CAN HARM OR KILL THE VIEWER IS ALL OVER HISTORY.
FROM THE ANCIENT LEGENDS OF THE MEDUSA,
TO THE MODERN SCI-FI STORIES OF DAVID LANGFORD.
HOWEVER THE VERY FIRST CONFIRMED PATTERN CAPABLE OF SHORTING OUT A SENTIENT BRAIN WILL BE BORNE BY YOU - YOUR LAST LINE OF DEFENSE.
BUT I DON'T WANT A WEAPONIZED TUMMY!
I'M SORRY, BUT THE HUMAN WORLD IS MUCH TOO ROUGH FOR YOU TO GO UNARMED.
IF YOU'RE THREATENED WITH CAPTURE OR DISSECTION, JUST EXPOSE YOUR STOMACH--
--AND YOUR ATTACKER WILL BE KILLED INSTANTLY.
JUST DON'T LIFT YOUR SHIRT TOO FAR, YOU DON'T WANT TO GET ARRESTED, HEH HEH.
SQUEAK SQUEAK SQUEAK
I HAVE NO CHOICE, MEANHEART! LOOK UPON THE BRAIN-SHATTERING VISUAL HOLOCAUST THAT IS--
--MY MUFFIN-BASKET!

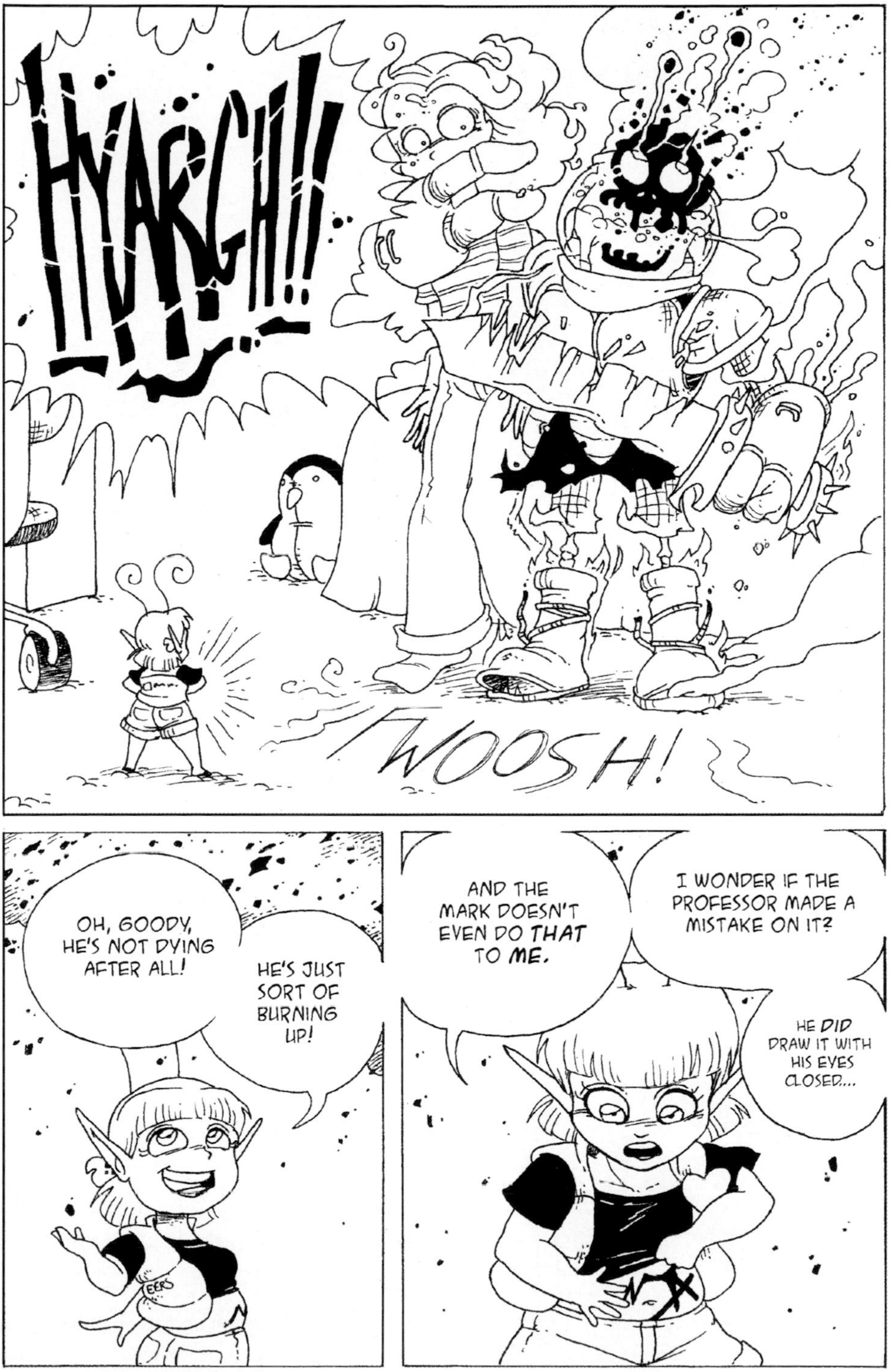
HYARGH!!
WOOSH!
OH, GOODY, HE'S NOT DYING AFTER ALL!
HE'S JUST SORT OF BURNING UP!
AND THE MARK DOESN'T EVEN DO THAT TO ME.
I WONDER IF THE PROFESSOR MADE A MISTAKE ON IT?
HE DID DRAW IT WITH HIS EYES CLOSED...

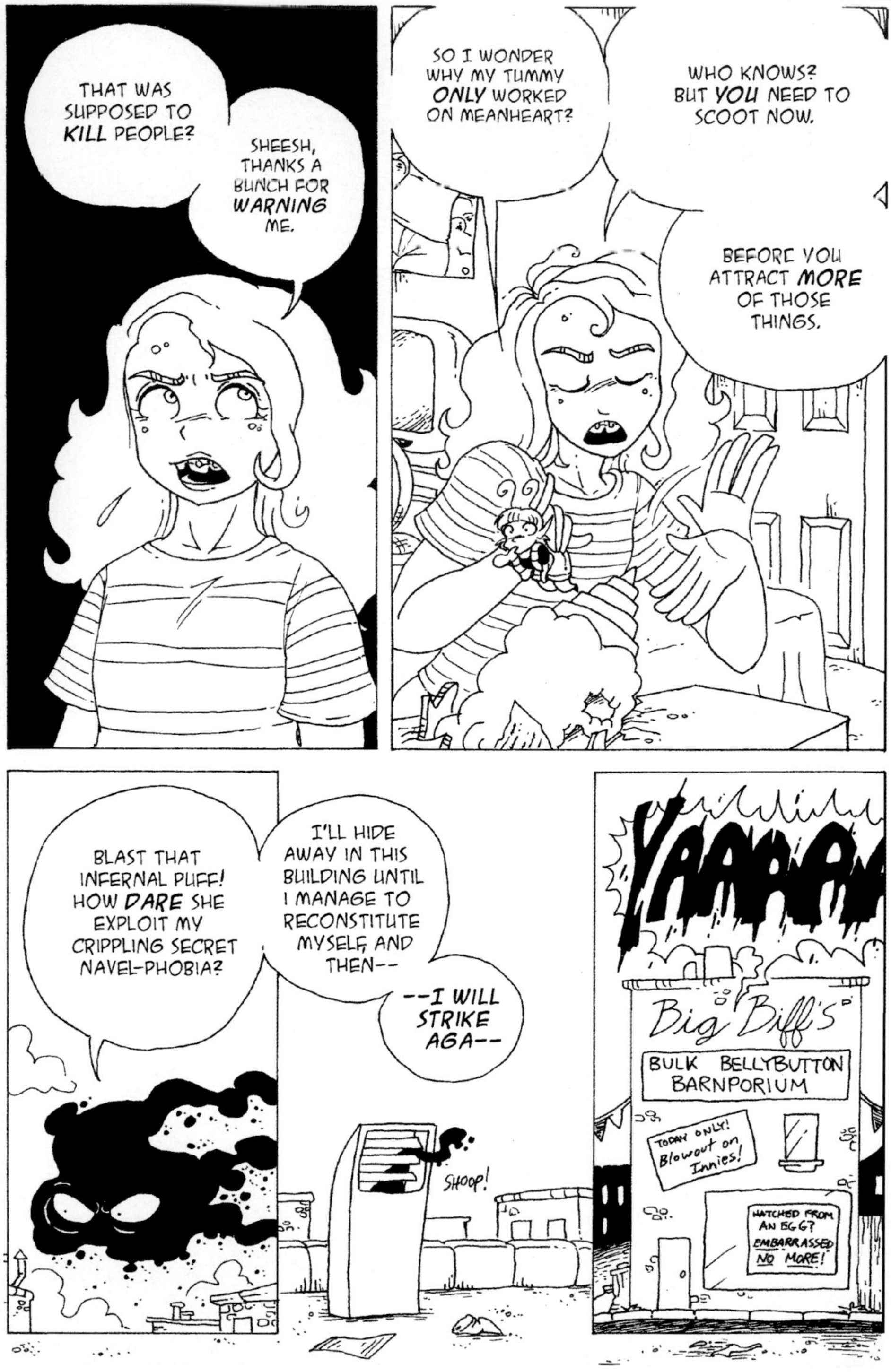
THAT WAS SUPPOSED TO KILL PEOPLE?
SHEESH, THANKS A BUNCH FOR WARNING ME.
SO I WONDER WHY MY TUMMY ONLY WORKED ON MEANHEART?
WHO KNOWS? BUT YOU NEED TO SCOOT NOW.
BEFORE YOU ATTRACT MORE OF THOSE THINGS.
BLAST THAT INFERNAL PUFF! HOW DARE SHE EXPLOIT MY CRIPPLING SECRET NAVEL-PHOBIA?
I'LL HIDE AWAY IN THIS BUILDING UNTIL I MANAGE TO RECONSTITUTE MYSELF AND THEN--
--I WILL STRIKE AGA--
SHOOP!
YAAAAA
Big Biff's
BULK BELLYBUTTON BARNPORIUM
TODAY ONLY! Blowout on Innies!
HATCHED FROM AN EGG? EMBARRASSED NO MORE!

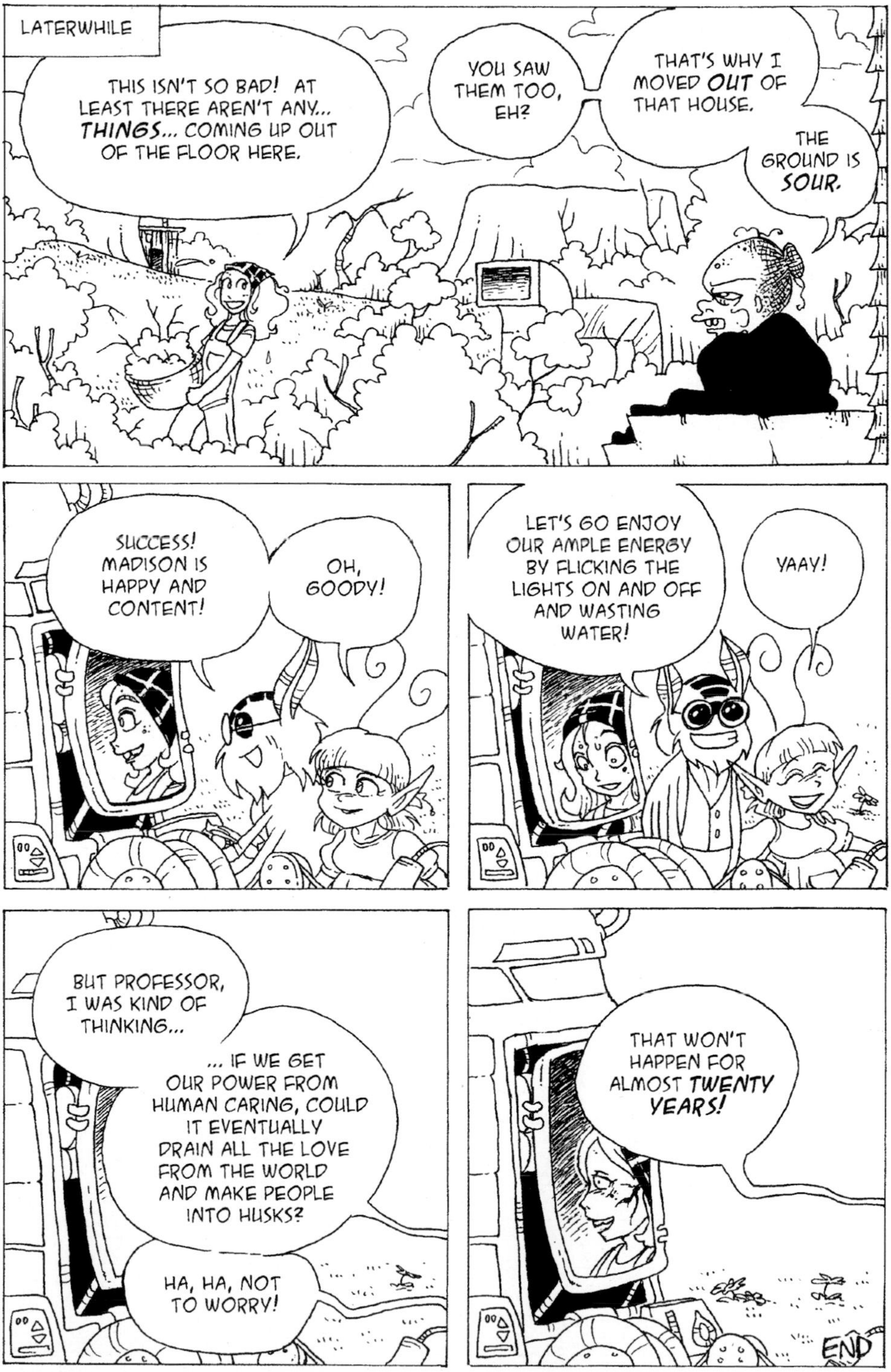
LATERWHILE
THIS ISN'T SO BAD! AT LEAST THERE AREN'T ANY... THINGS... COMING UP OUT OF THE FLOOR HERE.
YOU SAW THEM TOO, EH?
THAT'S WHY I MOVED OUT OF THAT HOUSE.
THE GROUND IS SOUR.
SUCCESS! MADISON IS HAPPY AND CONTENT!
OH, GOODY!
LET'S GO ENJOY OUR AMPLE ENERGY BY FLICKING THE LIGHTS ON AND OFF AND WASTING WATER!
YAAY!
BUT PROFESSOR, I WAS KIND OF THINKING...
... IF WE GET OUR POWER FROM HUMAN CARING, COULD IT EVENTUALLY DRAIN ALL THE LOVE FROM THE WORLD AND MAKE PEOPLE INTO HUSKS?
HA, HA, NOT TO WORRY!
THAT WON'T HAPPEN FOR ALMOST TWENTY YEARS!
END

PERFECTED AT LAST:
the KILLING IMAGE!

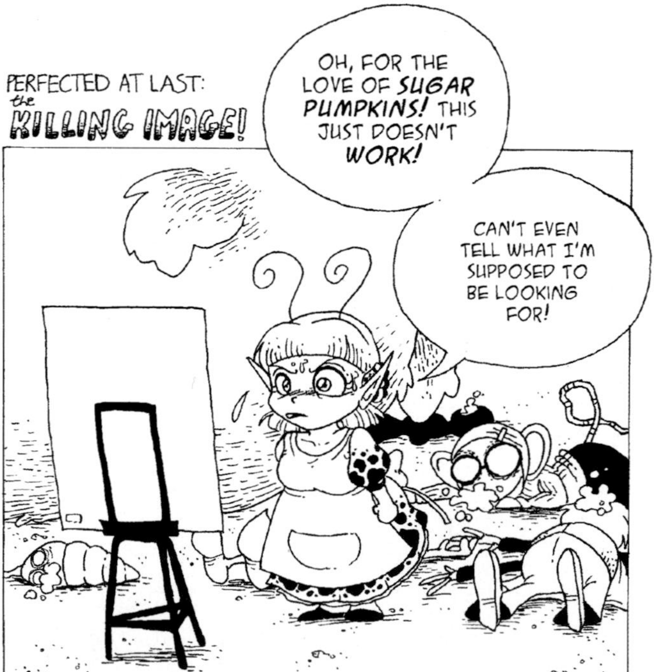
OH, FOR THE LOVE OF SUGAR PUMPKINS! THIS JUST DOESN'T WORK!
CAN'T EVEN TELL WHAT I'M SUPPOSED TO BE LOOKING FOR!

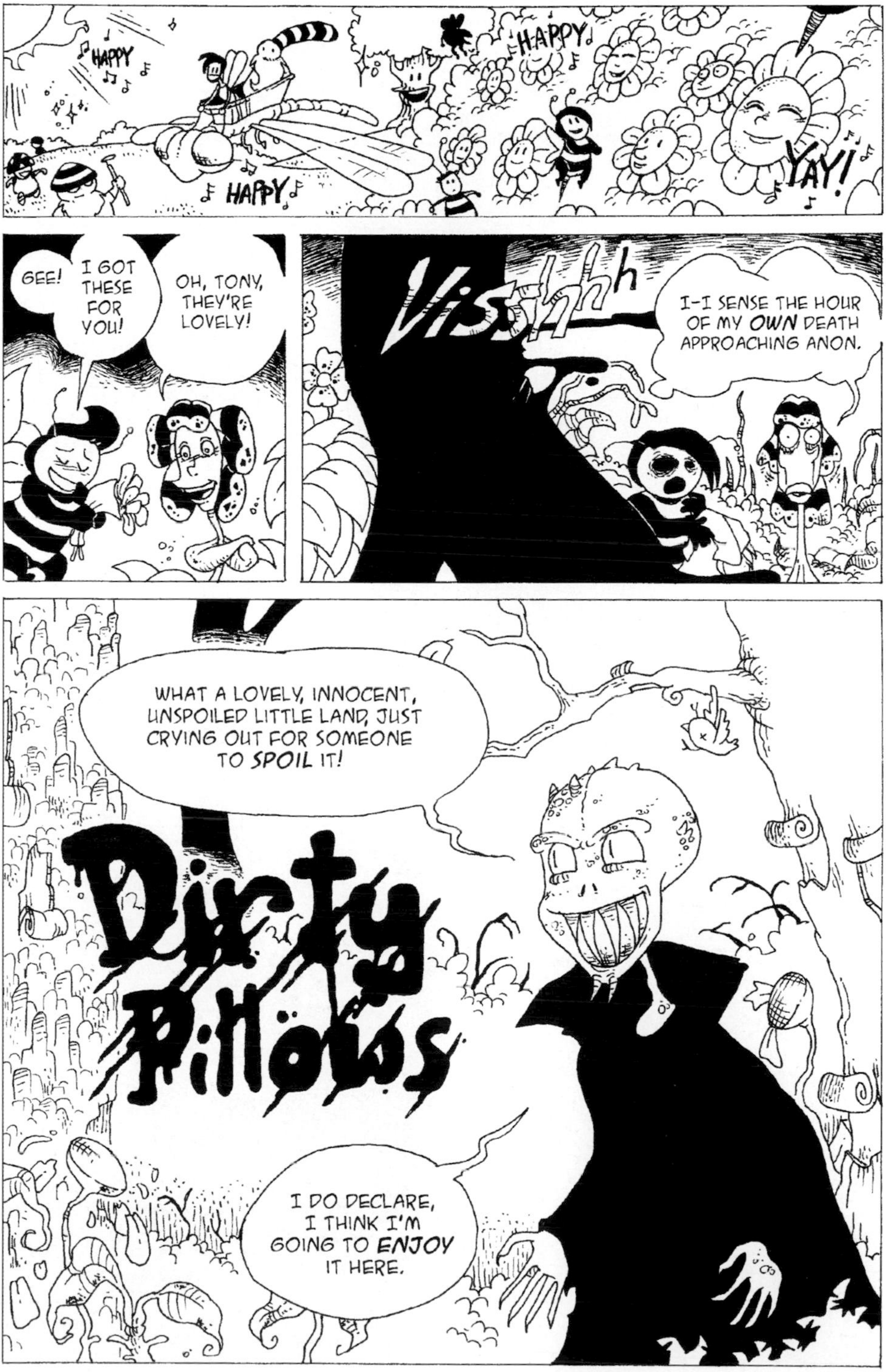

HAPPY
HAPPY
HAPPY
YAY!
GEE!
I GOT THESE FOR YOU!
OH, TONY, THEY'RE LOVELY!
Visshhh
I-I SENSE THE HOUR OF MY *OWN* DEATH APPROACHING ANON.
WHAT A LOVELY, INNOCENT, UNSPOILED LITTLE LAND, JUST CRYING OUT FOR SOMEONE TO *SPOIL* IT!
Dirty Pillöws
I DO DECLARE, I THINK I'M GOING TO *ENJOY* IT HERE.

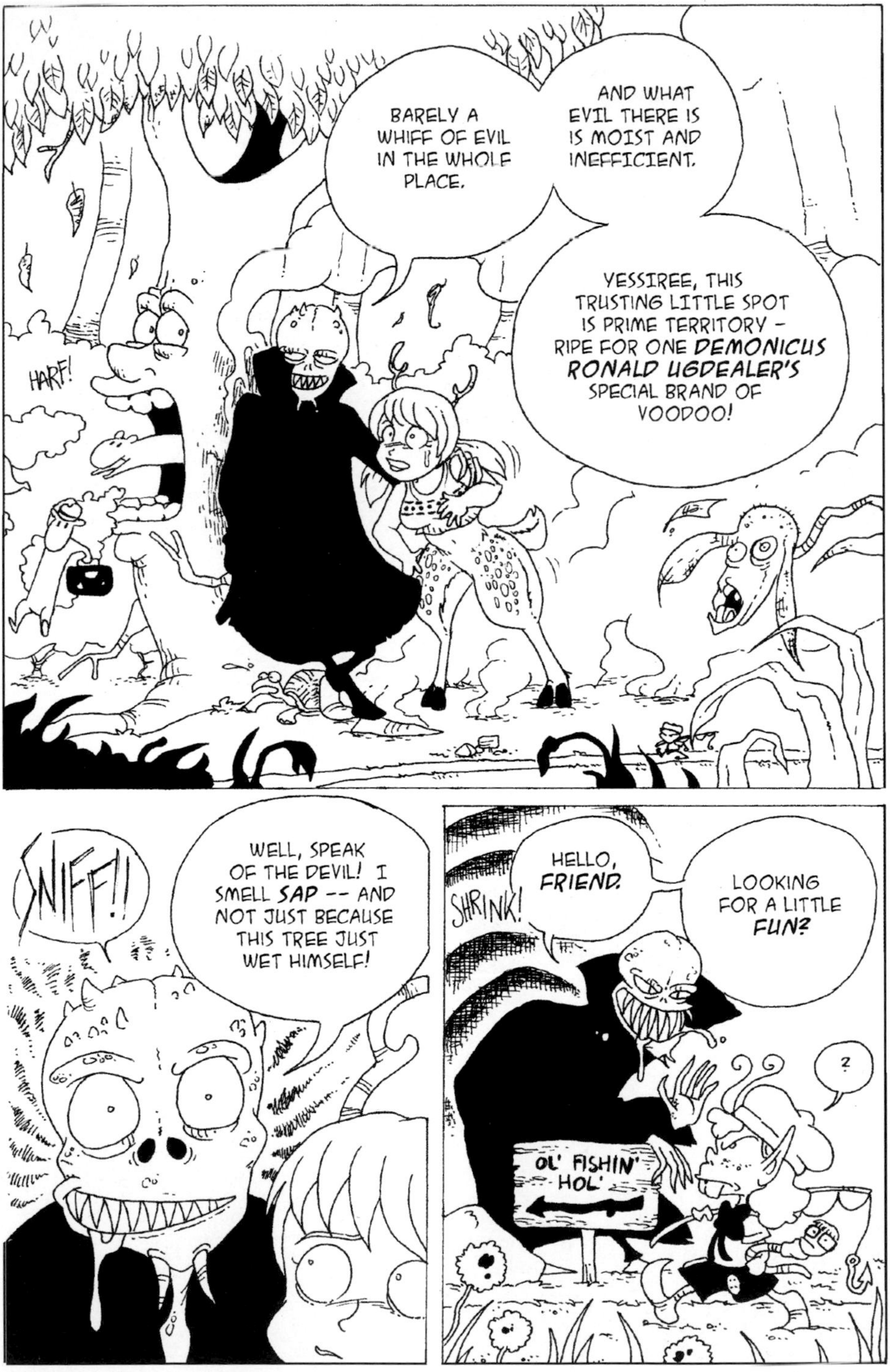
BARELY A WHIFF OF EVIL IN THE WHOLE PLACE.
AND WHAT EVIL THERE IS IS MOIST AND INEFFICIENT.
YESSIREE, THIS TRUSTING LITTLE SPOT IS PRIME TERRITORY - RIPE FOR ONE DEMONICUS RONALD UGDEALER'S SPECIAL BRAND OF VOODOO!
HARF!
SNIFF!!
WELL, SPEAK OF THE DEVIL! I SMELL SAP -- AND NOT JUST BECAUSE THIS TREE JUST WET HIMSELF!
SHRINK!
HELLO, FRIEND.
LOOKING FOR A LITTLE FUN?
?
OL' FISHIN' HOL'

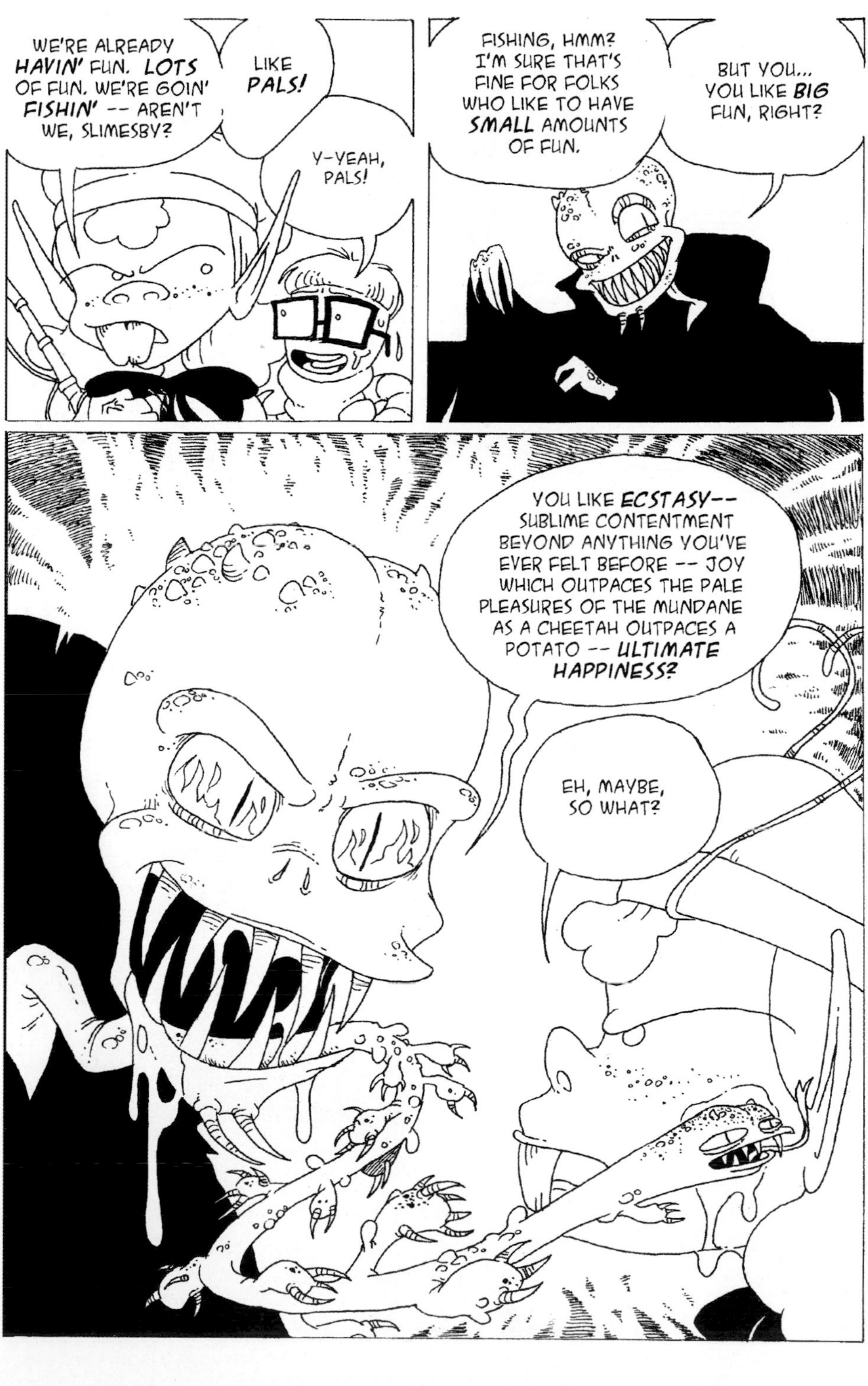
WE'RE ALREADY HAVIN' FUN. LOTS OF FUN. WE'RE GOIN' FISHIN' -- AREN'T WE, SLIMESBY?
LIKE PALS!
Y-YEAH, PALS!
FISHING, HMM? I'M SURE THAT'S FINE FOR FOLKS WHO LIKE TO HAVE SMALL AMOUNTS OF FUN.
BUT YOU... YOU LIKE BIG FUN, RIGHT?
YOU LIKE ECSTASY-- SUBLIME CONTENTMENT BEYOND ANYTHING YOU'VE EVER FELT BEFORE -- JOY WHICH OUTPACES THE PALE PLEASURES OF THE MUNDANE AS A CHEETAH OUTPACES A POTATO -- ULTIMATE HAPPINESS?
EH, MAYBE, SO WHAT?

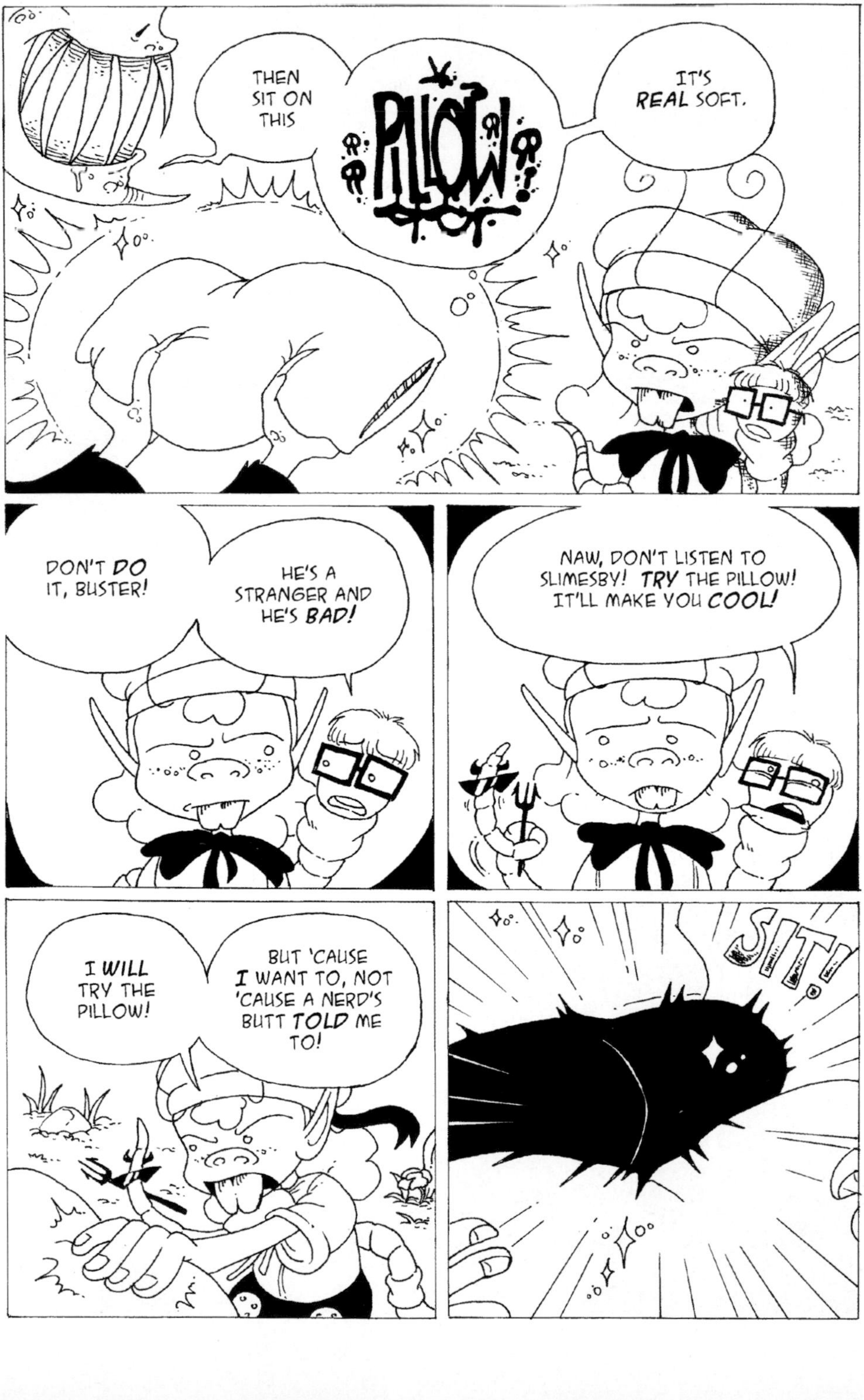
THEN SIT ON THIS
PILLOW!
IT'S REAL SOFT.
DON'T DO IT, BUSTER!
HE'S A STRANGER AND HE'S BAD!
NAW, DON'T LISTEN TO SLIMESBY! TRY THE PILLOW! IT'LL MAKE YOU COOL!
I WILL TRY THE PILLOW!
BUT 'CAUSE I WANT TO, NOT 'CAUSE A NERD'S BUTT TOLD ME TO!
SIT!

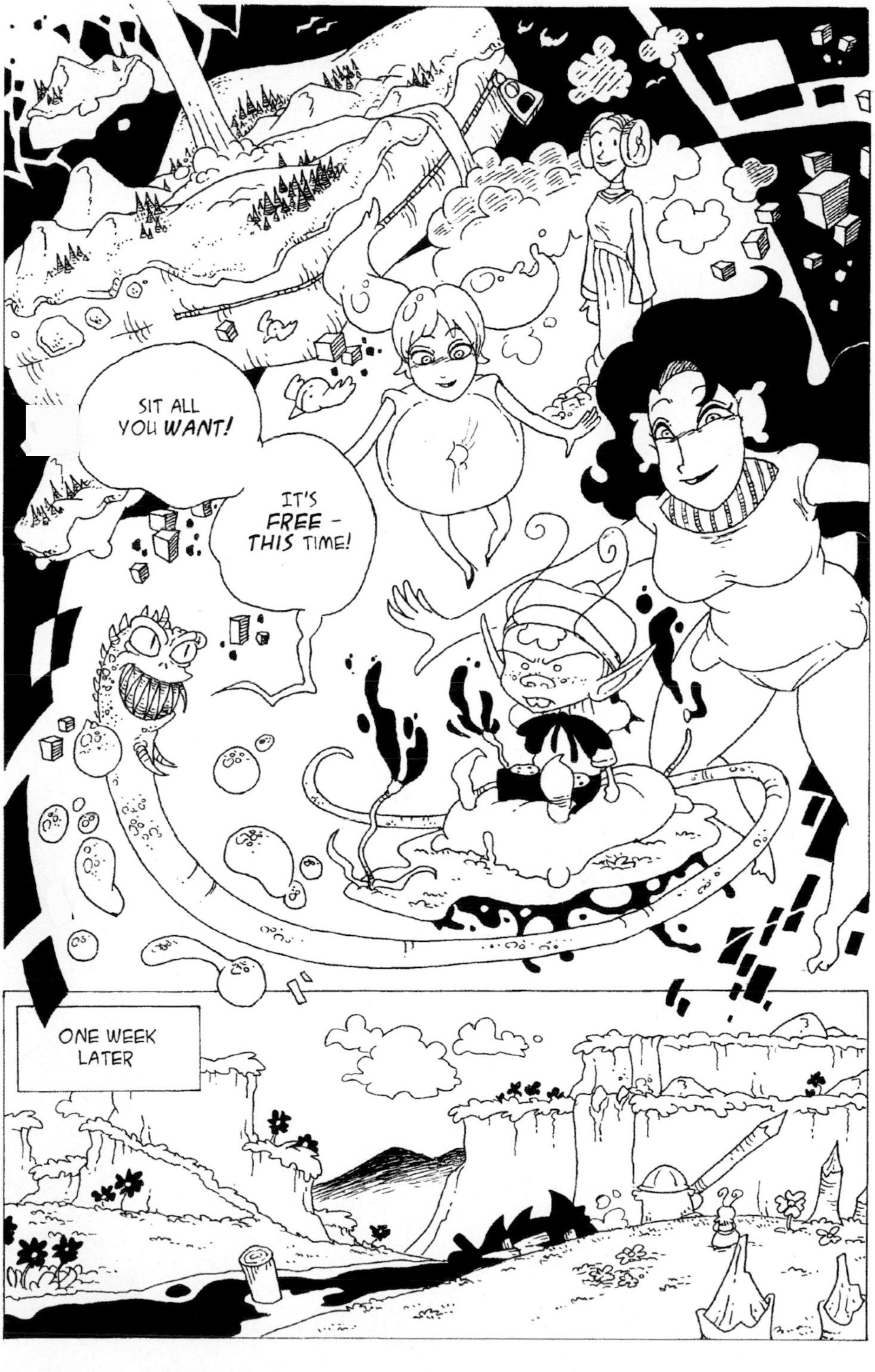
SIT ALL YOU WANT!
IT'S FREE - THIS TIME!
ONE WEEK LATER

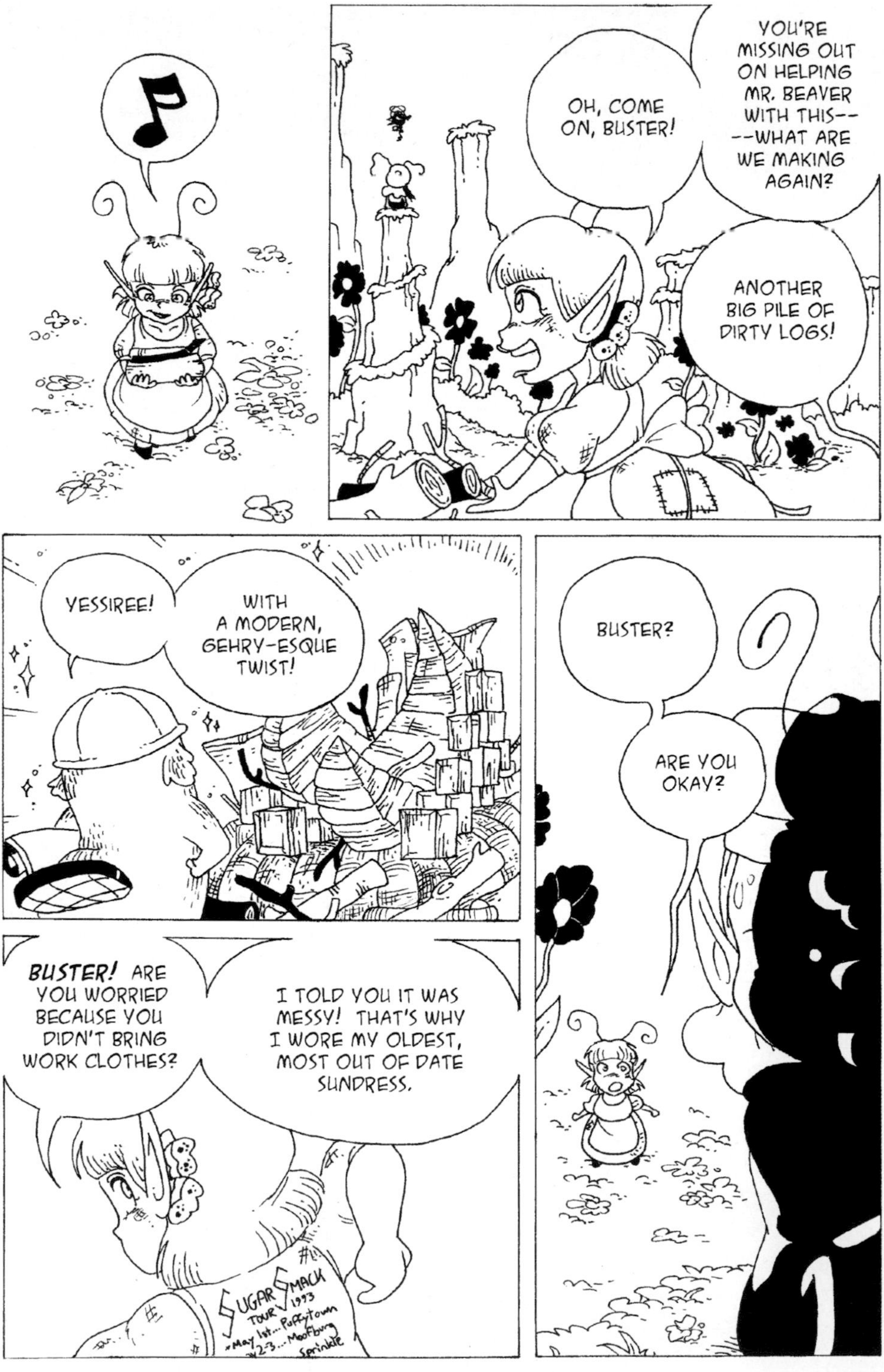
OH, COME ON, BUSTER!
YOU'RE MISSING OUT ON HELPING MR. BEAVER WITH THIS--
--WHAT ARE WE MAKING AGAIN?
ANOTHER BIG PILE OF DIRTY LOGS!
YESSIREE!
WITH A MODERN, GEHRY-ESQUE TWIST!
BUSTER?
ARE YOU OKAY?
BUSTER! ARE YOU WORRIED BECAUSE YOU DIDN'T BRING WORK CLOTHES?
I TOLD YOU IT WAS MESSY! THAT'S WHY I WORE MY OLDEST, MOST OUT OF DATE SUNDRESS.
SUGAR SMACK 1993 TOUR
May 1st... Puffytown
2-3... Moofburg
Sprinkle

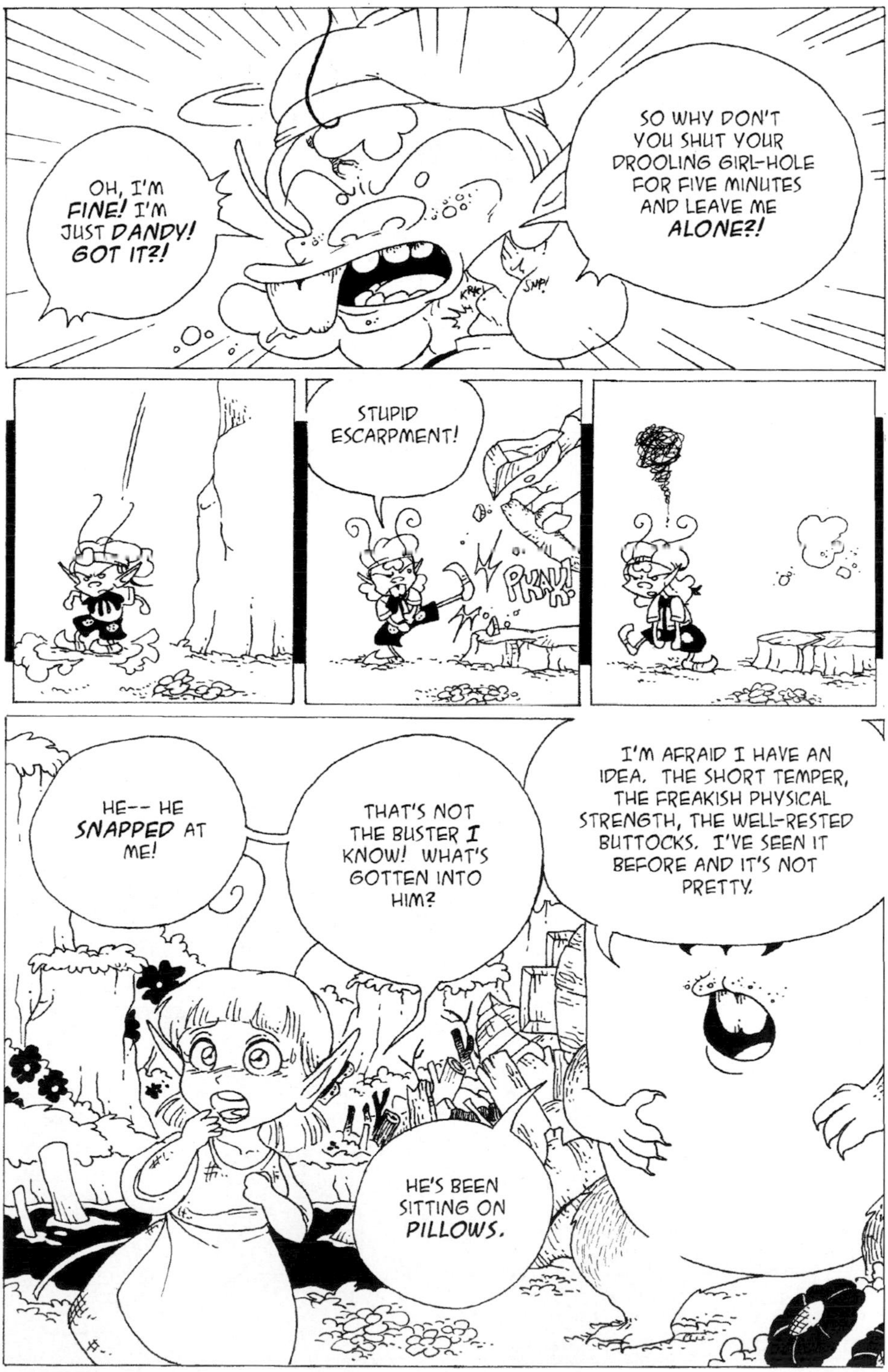
OH, I'M FINE! I'M JUST DANDY! GOT IT?!
SO WHY DON'T YOU SHUT YOUR DROOLING GIRL-HOLE FOR FIVE MINUTES AND LEAVE ME ALONE?!
STUPID ESCARPMENT!
PKRAK!
HE-- HE SNAPPED AT ME!
THAT'S NOT THE BUSTER I KNOW! WHAT'S GOTTEN INTO HIM?
I'M AFRAID I HAVE AN IDEA. THE SHORT TEMPER, THE FREAKISH PHYSICAL STRENGTH, THE WELL-RESTED BUTTOCKS. I'VE SEEN IT BEFORE AND IT'S NOT PRETTY.
HE'S BEEN SITTING ON PILLOWS.

YES, *PILLOWS*. NOBODY WANTS TO ACCEPT THAT SOMEBODY THEY CARE ABOUT IS A WILLING SLAVE TO THE FLUFFYSOFT TUSHIE-SEDUCTRESS THAT HAS SCOURGED CIVILIZATION SINCE FIRST A CURIOUS CAVEMAN STUFFED A SHEEP'S BLADDER WITH LEAVES AND SAT ON IT.

BUT WE MUST SUCK THE TEARS LIKE SALTY BOOGERS BACK INTO THE NOSES OF OUR EYES, AND FACE REALITY CLEAR-HEADED!

WE MUST ARM OURSELVES WITH THE GREATEST WEAPON OF ALL – *THE TRUTH!*

AND TO SAVE OUR ERSTWHILE FRIENDS, WE MUST TRACK THEM LIKE ANIMALS INTO THE DARK PLACES OF THIS WORLD...

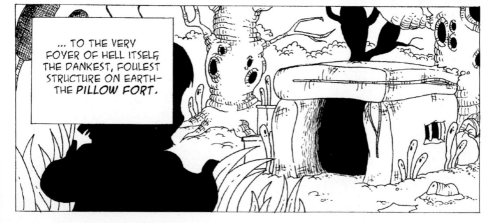

... TO THE VERY FOYER OF HELL ITSELF, THE DANKEST, FOULEST STRUCTURE ON EARTH— THE *PILLOW FORT.*

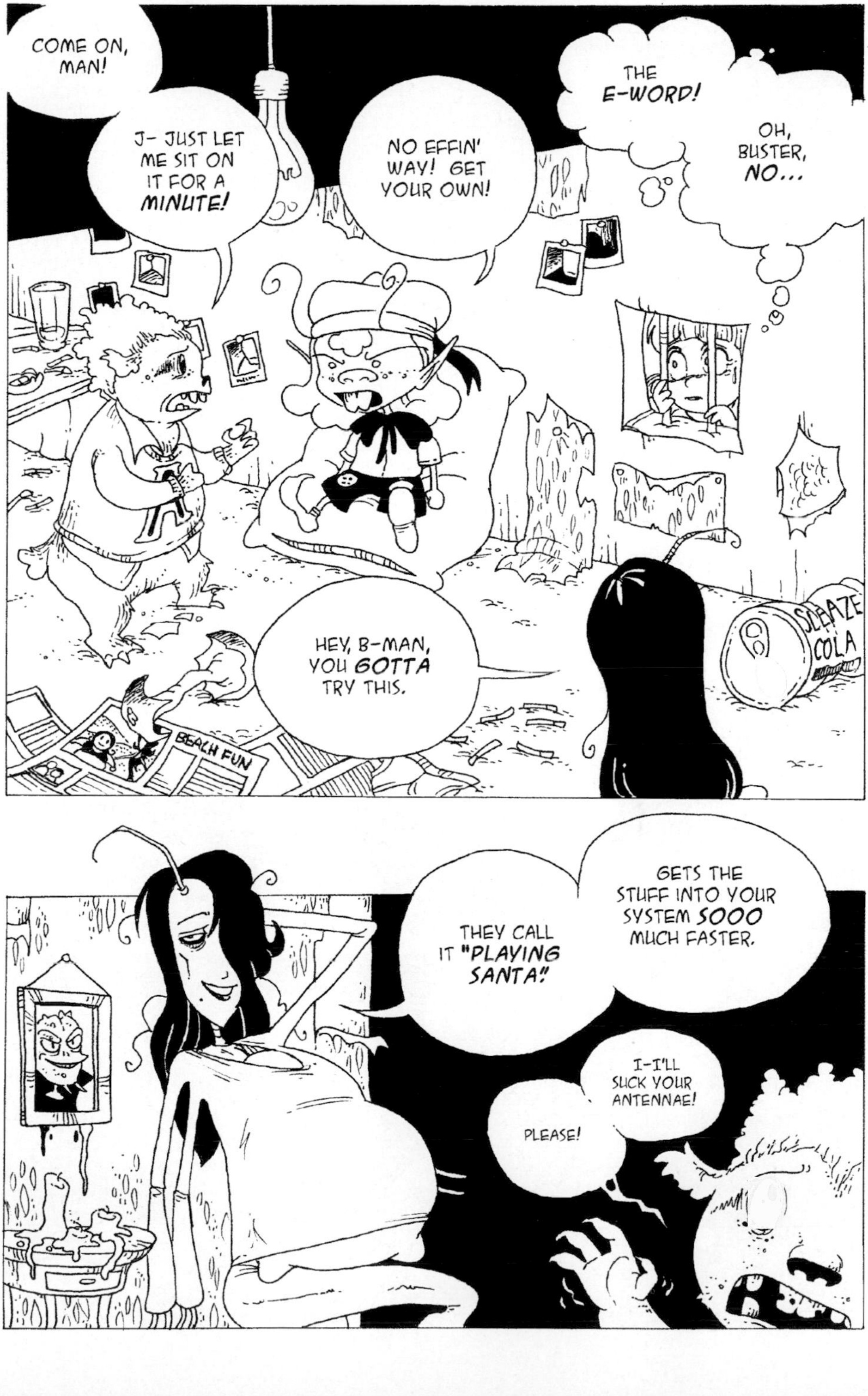

COME ON, MAN!
J- JUST LET ME SIT ON IT FOR A MINUTE!
NO EFFIN' WAY! GET YOUR OWN!
THE E-WORD!
OH, BUSTER, NO...
SLEAZE COLA
BEACH FUN
HEY, B-MAN, YOU GOTTA TRY THIS.
THEY CALL IT "PLAYING SANTA!"
GETS THE STUFF INTO YOUR SYSTEM SOOO MUCH FASTER.
I-I'LL SUCK YOUR ANTENNAE!
PLEASE!

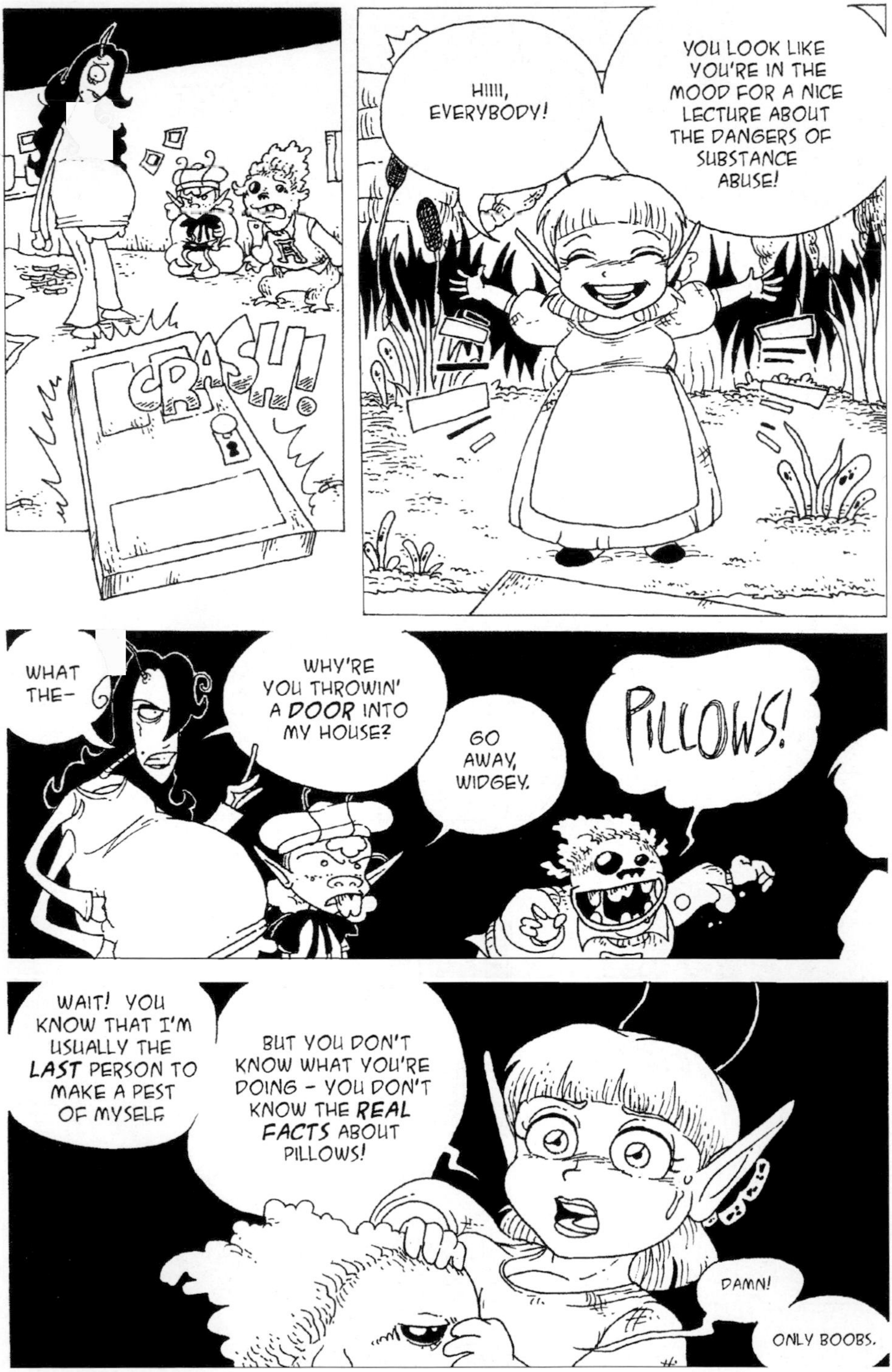
CRASH!
HIIII, EVERYBODY!
YOU LOOK LIKE YOU'RE IN THE MOOD FOR A NICE LECTURE ABOUT THE DANGERS OF SUBSTANCE ABUSE!
WHAT THE-
WHY'RE YOU THROWIN' A DOOR INTO MY HOUSE?
GO AWAY, WIDGEY.
PILLOWS!
WAIT! YOU KNOW THAT I'M USUALLY THE LAST PERSON TO MAKE A PEST OF MYSELF.
BUT YOU DON'T KNOW WHAT YOU'RE DOING - YOU DON'T KNOW THE REAL FACTS ABOUT PILLOWS!
DAMN!
ONLY BOOBS.

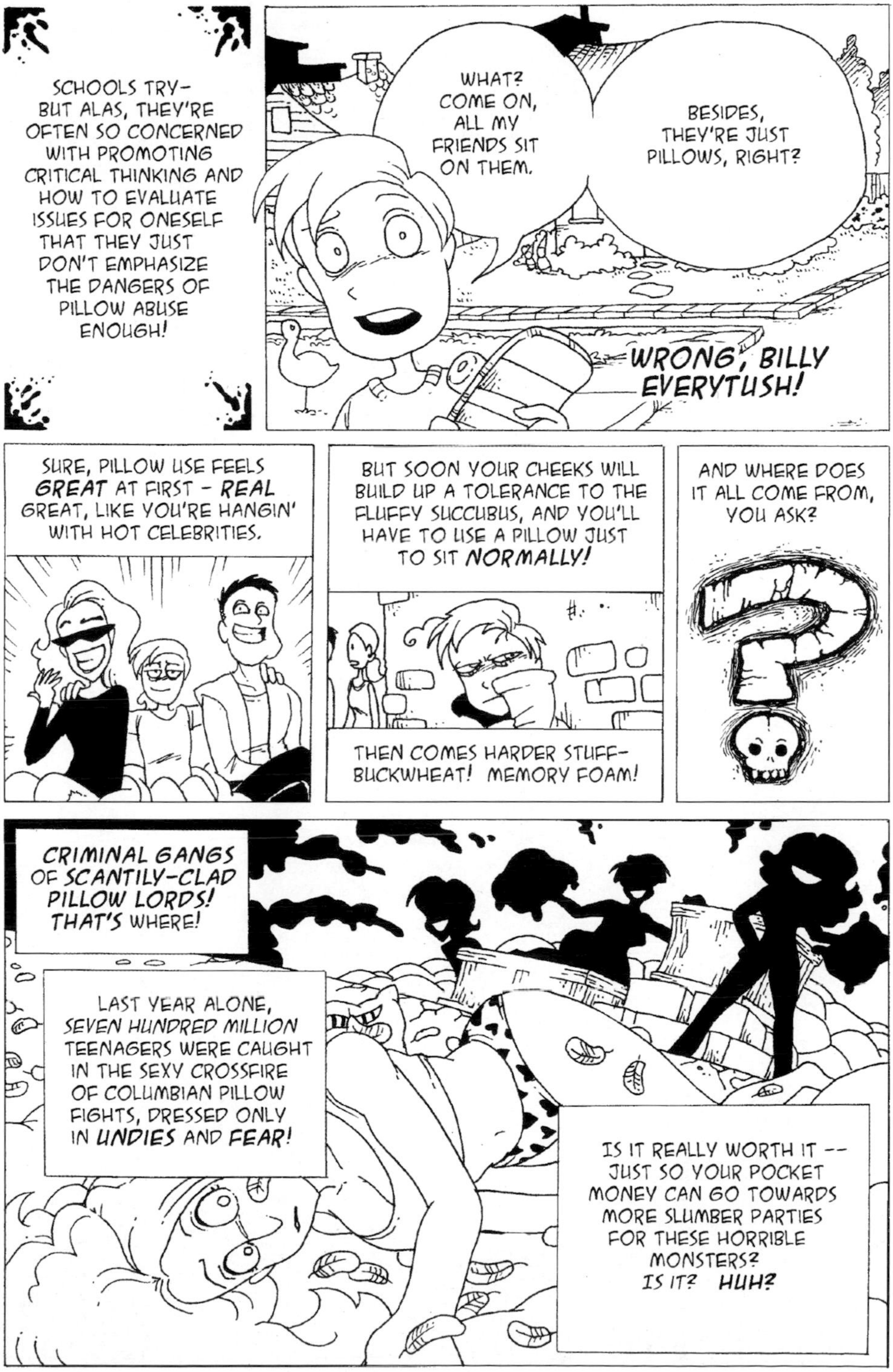
SCHOOLS TRY- BUT ALAS, THEY'RE OFTEN SO CONCERNED WITH PROMOTING CRITICAL THINKING AND HOW TO EVALUATE ISSUES FOR ONESELF THAT THEY JUST DON'T EMPHASIZE THE DANGERS OF PILLOW ABUSE ENOUGH!
WHAT? COME ON, ALL MY FRIENDS SIT ON THEM.
BESIDES, THEY'RE JUST PILLOWS, RIGHT?
WRONG, BILLY EVERYTUSH!
SURE, PILLOW USE FEELS GREAT AT FIRST - REAL GREAT, LIKE YOU'RE HANGIN' WITH HOT CELEBRITIES.
BUT SOON YOUR CHEEKS WILL BUILD UP A TOLERANCE TO THE FLUFFY SUCCUBUS, AND YOU'LL HAVE TO USE A PILLOW JUST TO SIT NORMALLY!
THEN COMES HARDER STUFF- BUCKWHEAT! MEMORY FOAM!
AND WHERE DOES IT ALL COME FROM, YOU ASK?
CRIMINAL GANGS OF SCANTILY-CLAD PILLOW LORDS! THAT'S WHERE!
LAST YEAR ALONE, SEVEN HUNDRED MILLION TEENAGERS WERE CAUGHT IN THE SEXY CROSSFIRE OF COLUMBIAN PILLOW FIGHTS, DRESSED ONLY IN UNDIES AND FEAR!
IS IT REALLY WORTH IT -- JUST SO YOUR POCKET MONEY CAN GO TOWARDS MORE SLUMBER PARTIES FOR THESE HORRIBLE MONSTERS? IS IT? HUH?

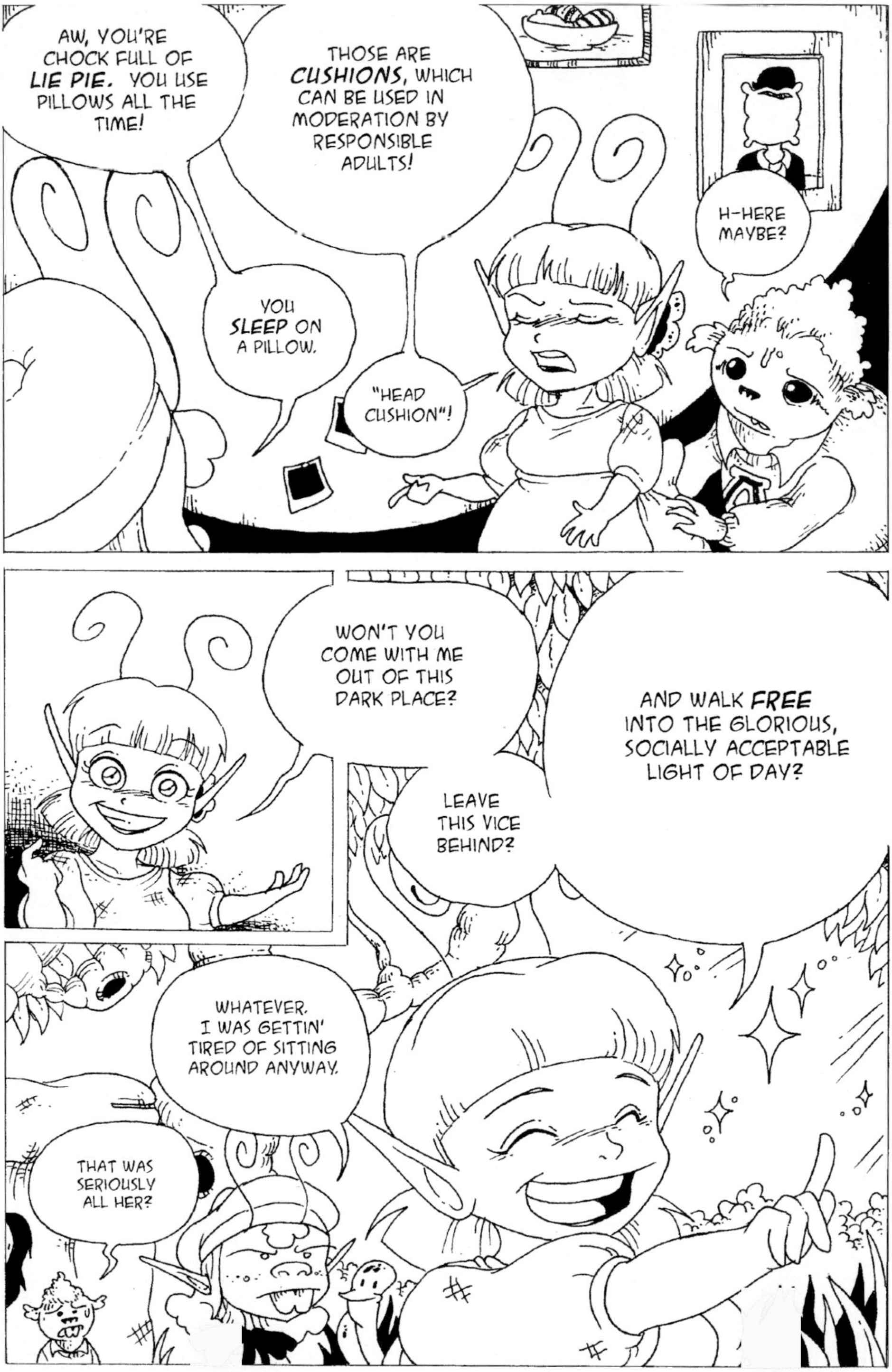

AW, YOU'RE CHOCK FULL OF **LIE PIE.** YOU USE PILLOWS ALL THE TIME!
THOSE ARE **CUSHIONS**, WHICH CAN BE USED IN MODERATION BY RESPONSIBLE ADULTS!
H-HERE MAYBE?
YOU **SLEEP** ON A PILLOW.
"HEAD CUSHION"!
WON'T YOU COME WITH ME OUT OF THIS DARK PLACE?
LEAVE THIS VICE BEHIND?
AND WALK **FREE** INTO THE GLORIOUS, SOCIALLY ACCEPTABLE LIGHT OF DAY?
WHATEVER. I WAS GETTIN' TIRED OF SITTING AROUND ANYWAY.
THAT WAS SERIOUSLY ALL HER?

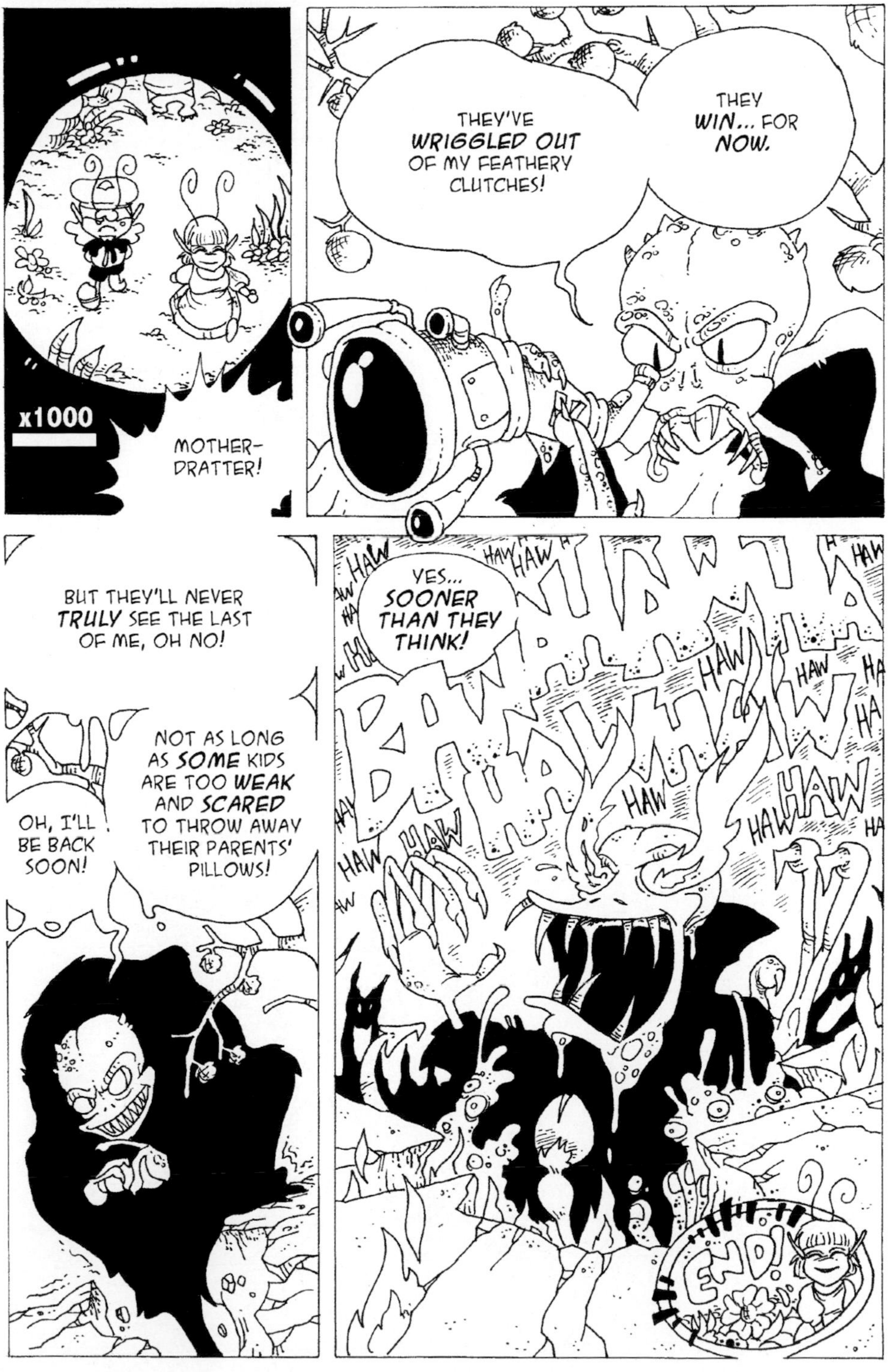
x1000
MOTHER-DRATTER!
THEY'VE WRIGGLED OUT OF MY FEATHERY CLUTCHES!
THEY WIN... FOR NOW.
BUT THEY'LL NEVER TRULY SEE THE LAST OF ME, OH NO!
NOT AS LONG AS SOME KIDS ARE TOO WEAK AND SCARED TO THROW AWAY THEIR PARENTS' PILLOWS!
OH, I'LL BE BACK SOON!
YES... SOONER THAN THEY THINK!
BWAHAHAHAW
HAW HAW HAW HAW HAW HAW HAW HAW HAW
END!

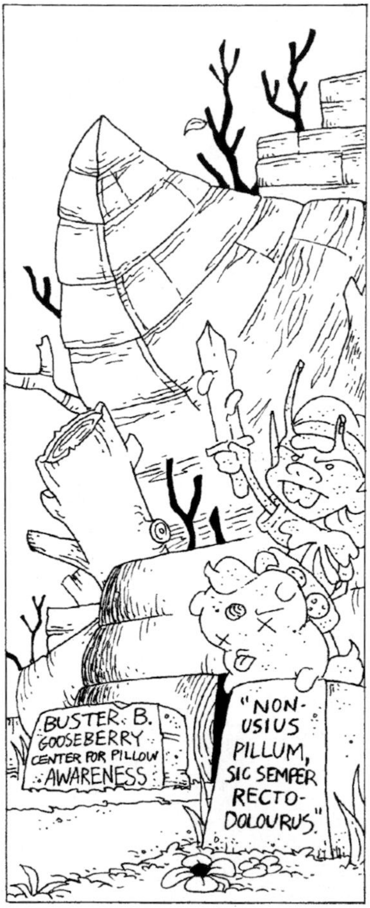
BUSTER B. GOOSEBERRY CENTER FOR PILLOW AWARENESS
"NON-USIUS PILLUM, SIC SEMPER RECTO-DOLOURUS."

A BITTER HARVEST

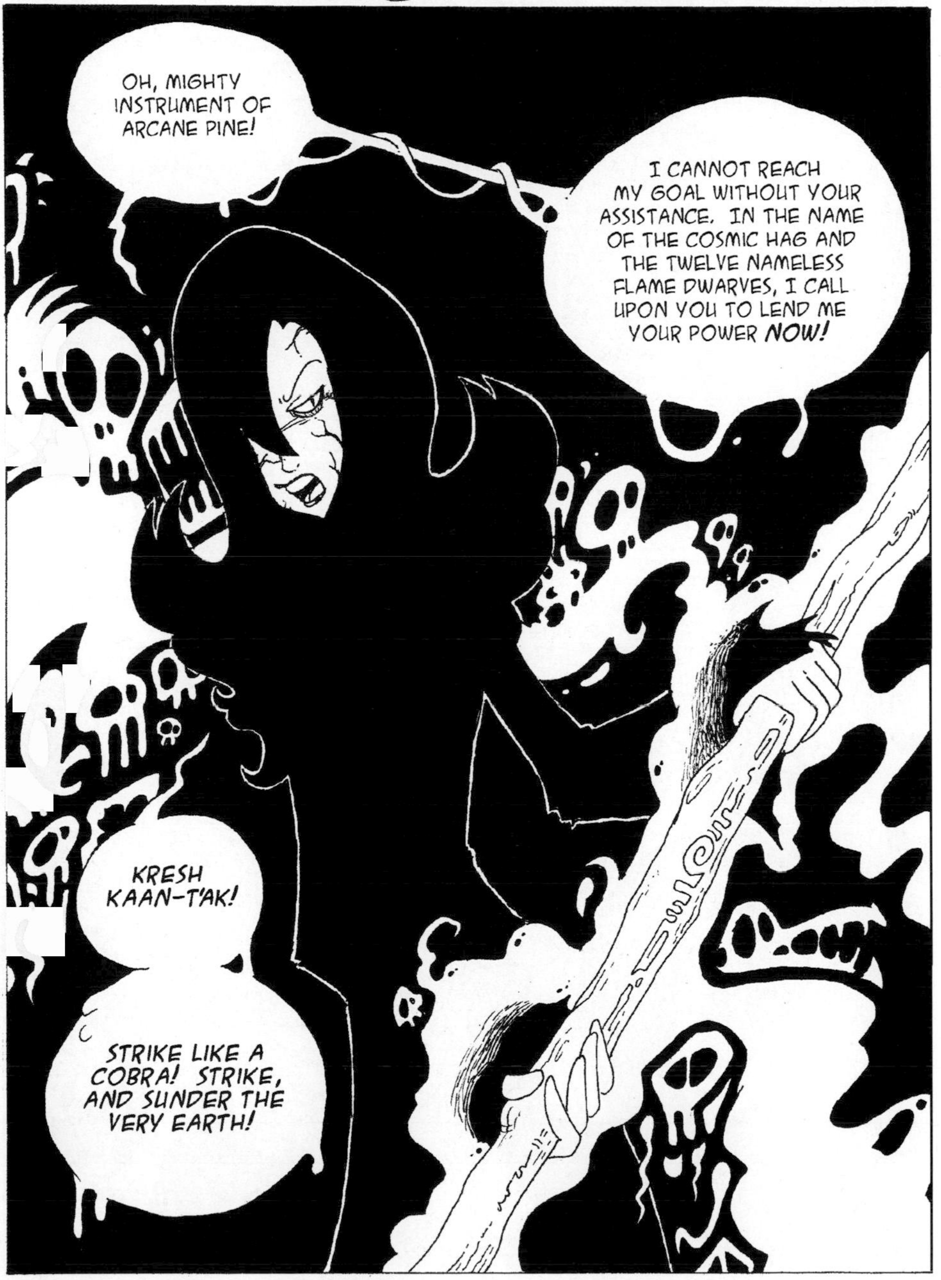
OH, MIGHTY INSTRUMENT OF ARCANE PINE!
I CANNOT REACH MY GOAL WITHOUT YOUR ASSISTANCE. IN THE NAME OF THE COSMIC HAG AND THE TWELVE NAMELESS FLAME DWARVES, I CALL UPON YOU TO LEND ME YOUR POWER *NOW!*
KRESH KAAN-T'AK!
STRIKE LIKE A COBRA! STRIKE, AND SUNDER THE VERY EARTH!

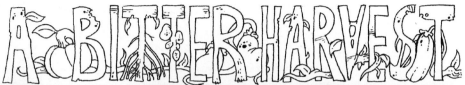

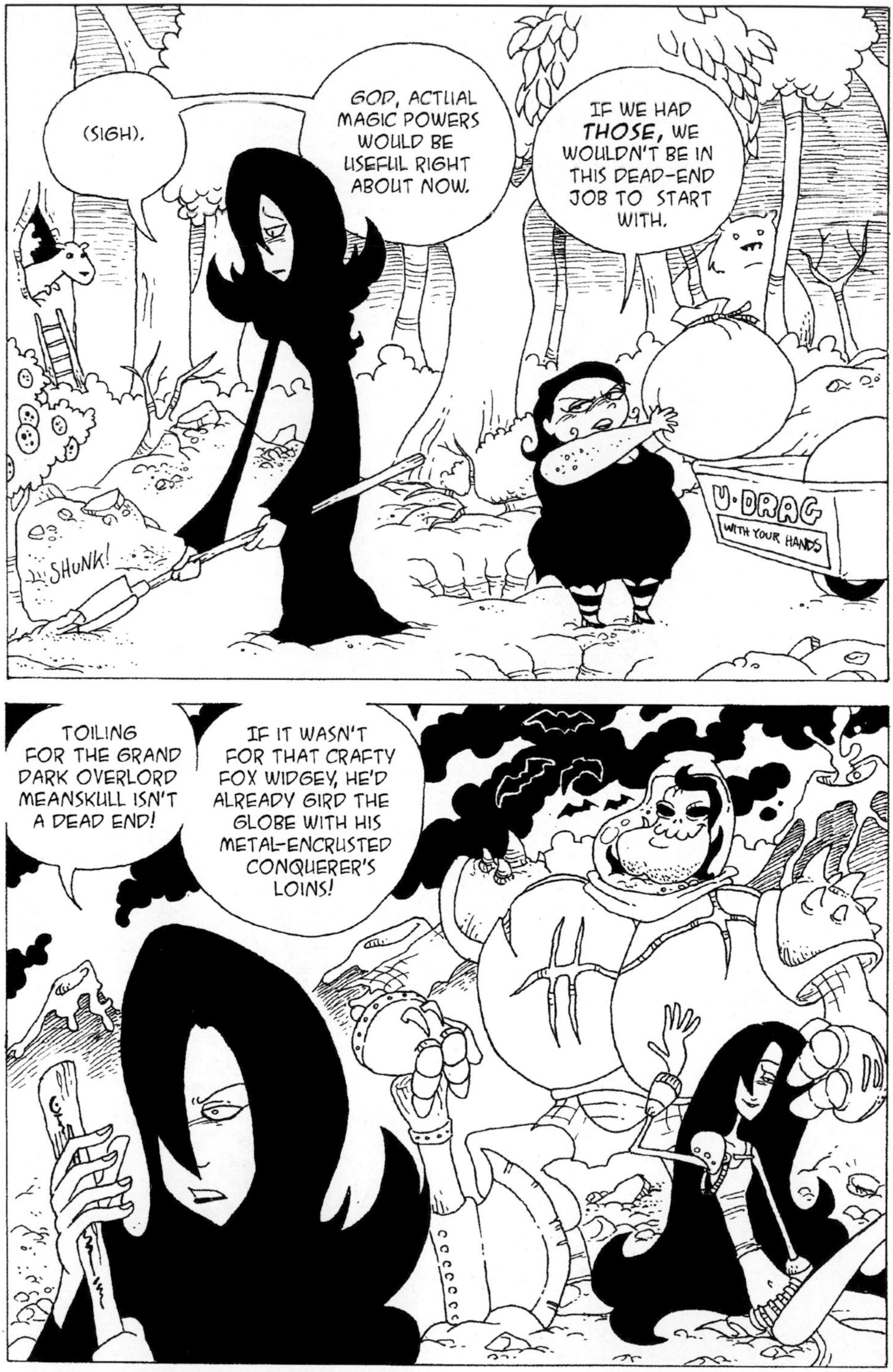
(SIGH).
GOD, ACTUAL MAGIC POWERS WOULD BE USEFUL RIGHT ABOUT NOW.
IF WE HAD THOSE, WE WOULDN'T BE IN THIS DEAD-END JOB TO START WITH.
SHUNK!
U-DRAG
WITH YOUR HANDS
TOILING FOR THE GRAND DARK OVERLORD MEANSKULL ISN'T A DEAD END!
IF IT WASN'T FOR THAT CRAFTY FOX WIDGEY, HE'D ALREADY GIRD THE GLOBE WITH HIS METAL-ENCRUSTED CONQUERER'S LOINS!

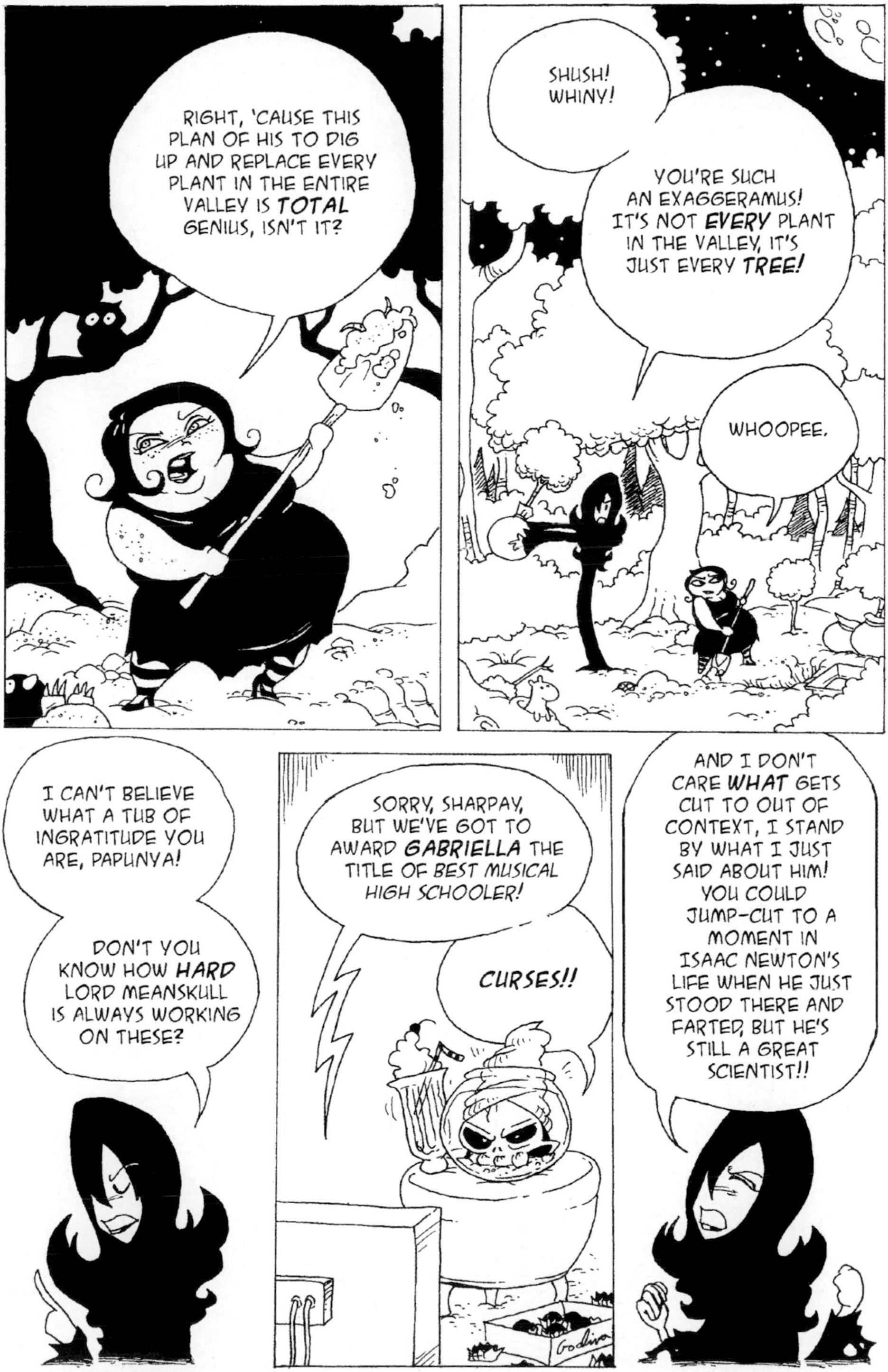
RIGHT, 'CAUSE THIS PLAN OF HIS TO DIG UP AND REPLACE EVERY PLANT IN THE ENTIRE VALLEY IS **TOTAL** GENIUS, ISN'T IT?
SHUSH! WHINY!
YOU'RE SUCH AN EXAGGERAMUS! IT'S NOT **EVERY** PLANT IN THE VALLEY, IT'S JUST EVERY **TREE!**
WHOOPEE.
I CAN'T BELIEVE WHAT A TUB OF INGRATITUDE YOU ARE, PAPUNYA!
DON'T YOU KNOW HOW **HARD** LORD MEANSKULL IS ALWAYS WORKING ON THESE?
SORRY, SHARPAY, BUT WE'VE GOT TO AWARD **GABRIELLA** THE TITLE OF *BEST MUSICAL HIGH SCHOOLER!*
CURSES!!
Godiva
AND I DON'T CARE **WHAT** GETS CUT TO OUT OF CONTEXT, I STAND BY WHAT I JUST SAID ABOUT HIM! YOU COULD JUMP-CUT TO A MOMENT IN ISAAC NEWTON'S LIFE WHEN HE JUST STOOD THERE AND FARTED, BUT HE'S STILL A GREAT SCIENTIST!!

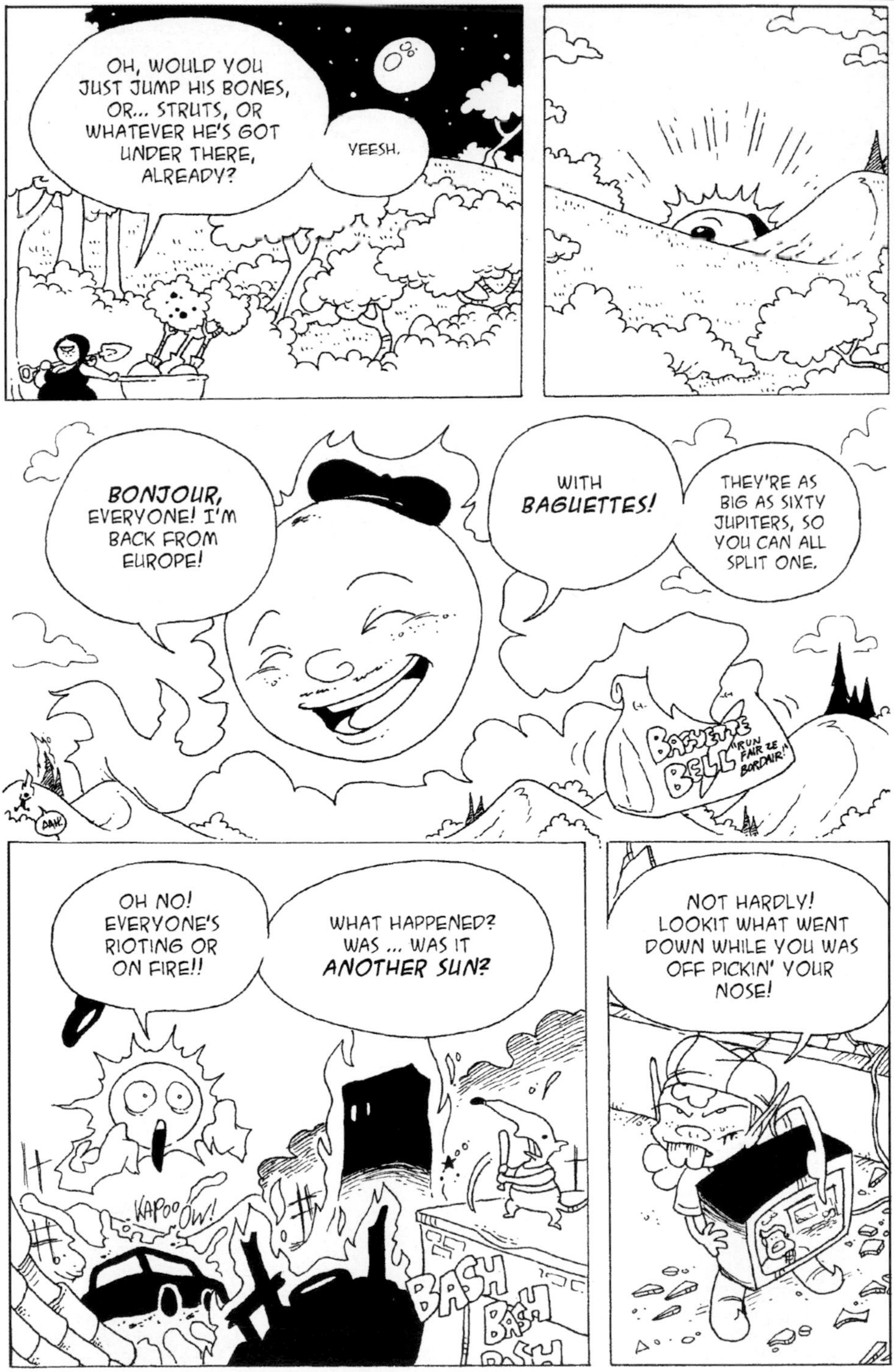
OH, WOULD YOU JUST JUMP HIS BONES, OR... STRUTS, OR WHATEVER HE'S GOT UNDER THERE, ALREADY?
YEESH.
BONJOUR, EVERYONE! I'M BACK FROM EUROPE!
WITH BAGUETTES!
THEY'RE AS BIG AS SIXTY JUPITERS, SO YOU CAN ALL SPLIT ONE.
BAGUETTE BELL
"RUN FAIR ZE BORDAIR!"
AAH.
OH NO! EVERYONE'S RIOTING OR ON FIRE!!
WHAT HAPPENED? WAS ... WAS IT ANOTHER SUN?
KAPOOOW!
BASH
BASH
BASH
NOT HARDLY! LOOKIT WHAT WENT DOWN WHILE YOU WAS OFF PICKIN' YOUR NOSE!

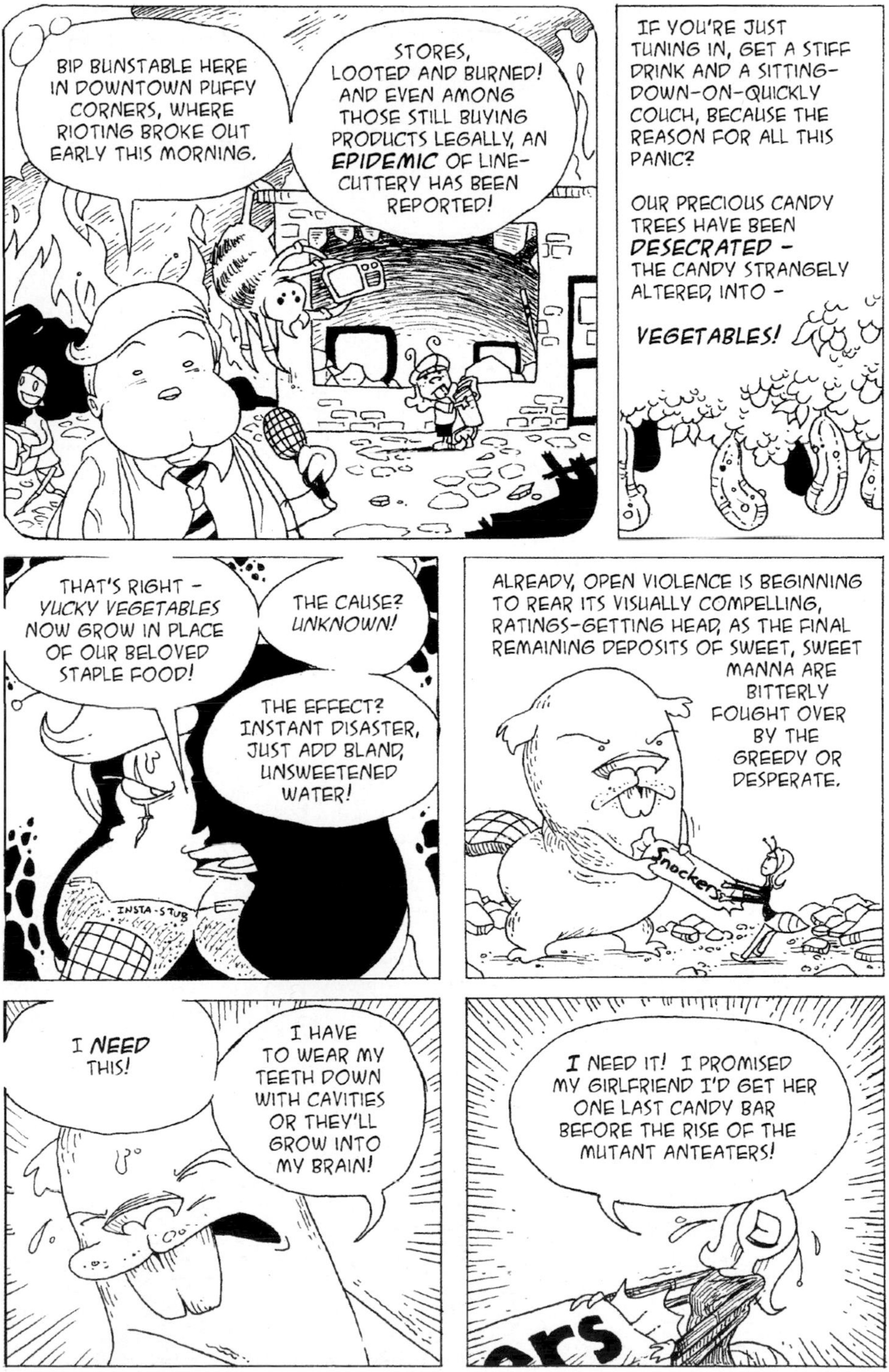
BIP BUNSTABLE HERE IN DOWNTOWN PUFFY CORNERS, WHERE RIOTING BROKE OUT EARLY THIS MORNING.
STORES, LOOTED AND BURNED! AND EVEN AMONG THOSE STILL BUYING PRODUCTS LEGALLY, AN EPIDEMIC OF LINE-CUTTERY HAS BEEN REPORTED!
IF YOU'RE JUST TUNING IN, GET A STIFF DRINK AND A SITTING-DOWN-ON-QUICKLY COUCH, BECAUSE THE REASON FOR ALL THIS PANIC?
OUR PRECIOUS CANDY TREES HAVE BEEN DESECRATED - THE CANDY STRANGELY ALTERED, INTO -
VEGETABLES!
THAT'S RIGHT - YUCKY VEGETABLES NOW GROW IN PLACE OF OUR BELOVED STAPLE FOOD!
THE CAUSE? UNKNOWN!
THE EFFECT? INSTANT DISASTER, JUST ADD BLAND, UNSWEETENED WATER!
INSTA-STUB
ALREADY, OPEN VIOLENCE IS BEGINNING TO REAR ITS VISUALLY COMPELLING, RATINGS-GETTING HEAD, AS THE FINAL REMAINING DEPOSITS OF SWEET, SWEET MANNA ARE BITTERLY FOUGHT OVER BY THE GREEDY OR DESPERATE.
Snockers
I NEED THIS!
I HAVE TO WEAR MY TEETH DOWN WITH CAVITIES OR THEY'LL GROW INTO MY BRAIN!
I NEED IT! I PROMISED MY GIRLFRIEND I'D GET HER ONE LAST CANDY BAR BEFORE THE RISE OF THE MUTANT ANTEATERS!
ers

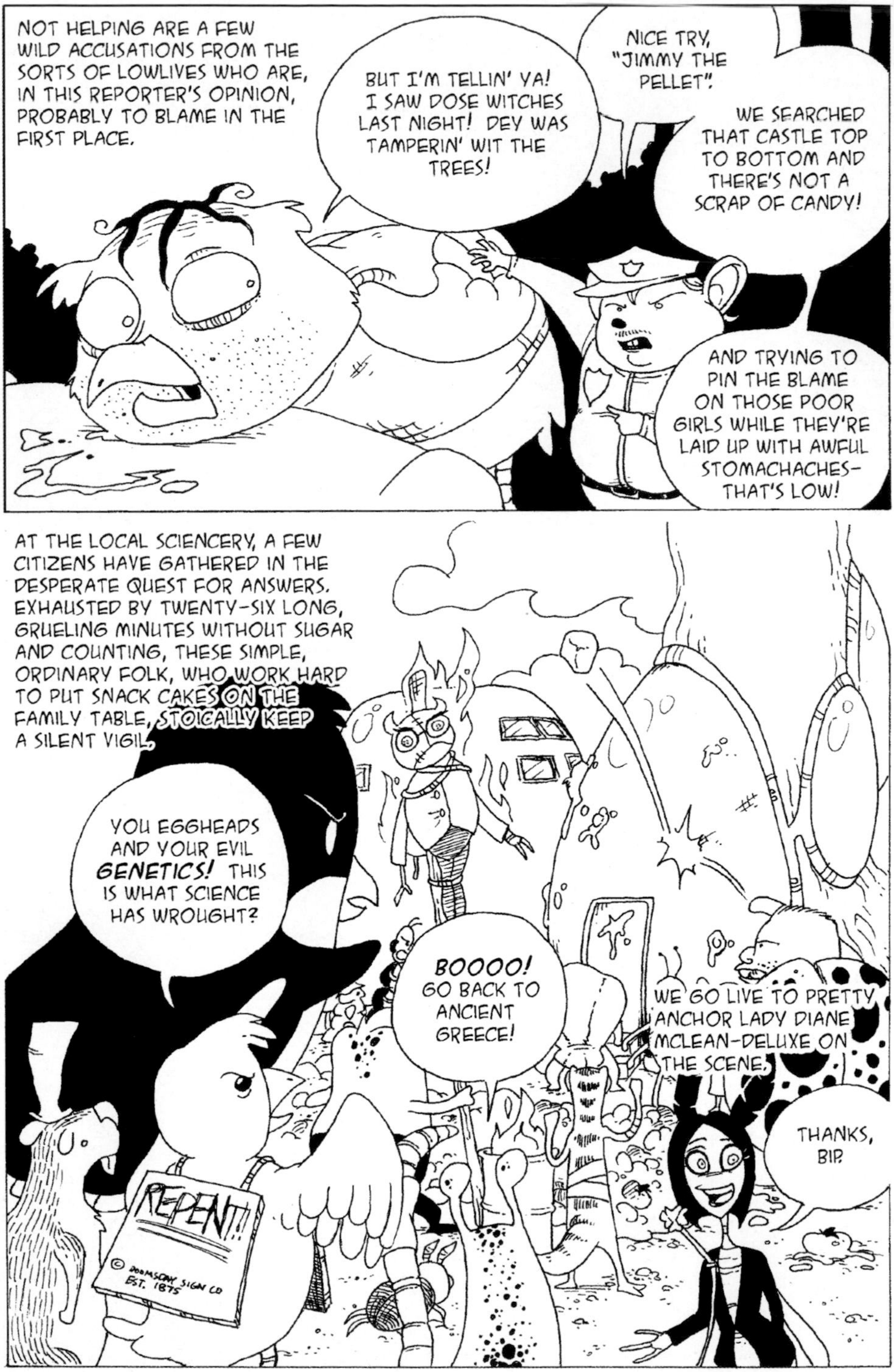
NOT HELPING ARE A FEW WILD ACCUSATIONS FROM THE SORTS OF LOWLIVES WHO ARE, IN THIS REPORTER'S OPINION, PROBABLY TO BLAME IN THE FIRST PLACE.
BUT I'M TELLIN' YA! I SAW DOSE WITCHES LAST NIGHT! DEY WAS TAMPERIN' WIT THE TREES!
NICE TRY, "JIMMY THE PELLET".
WE SEARCHED THAT CASTLE TOP TO BOTTOM AND THERE'S NOT A SCRAP OF CANDY!
AND TRYING TO PIN THE BLAME ON THOSE POOR GIRLS WHILE THEY'RE LAID UP WITH AWFUL STOMACHACHES– THAT'S LOW!
AT THE LOCAL SCIENCERY, A FEW CITIZENS HAVE GATHERED IN THE DESPERATE QUEST FOR ANSWERS. EXHAUSTED BY TWENTY-SIX LONG, GRUELING MINUTES WITHOUT SUGAR AND COUNTING, THESE SIMPLE, ORDINARY FOLK, WHO WORK HARD TO PUT SNACK CAKES ON THE FAMILY TABLE, STOICALLY KEEP A SILENT VIGIL.
YOU EGGHEADS AND YOUR EVIL *GENETICS!* THIS IS WHAT SCIENCE HAS WROUGHT?
REPENT!
© DOOMSDAY SIGN CO EST. 1875
BOOOO! GO BACK TO ANCIENT GREECE!
WE GO LIVE TO PRETTY ANCHOR LADY DIANE MCLEAN-DELUXE ON THE SCENE.
THANKS, BIP.

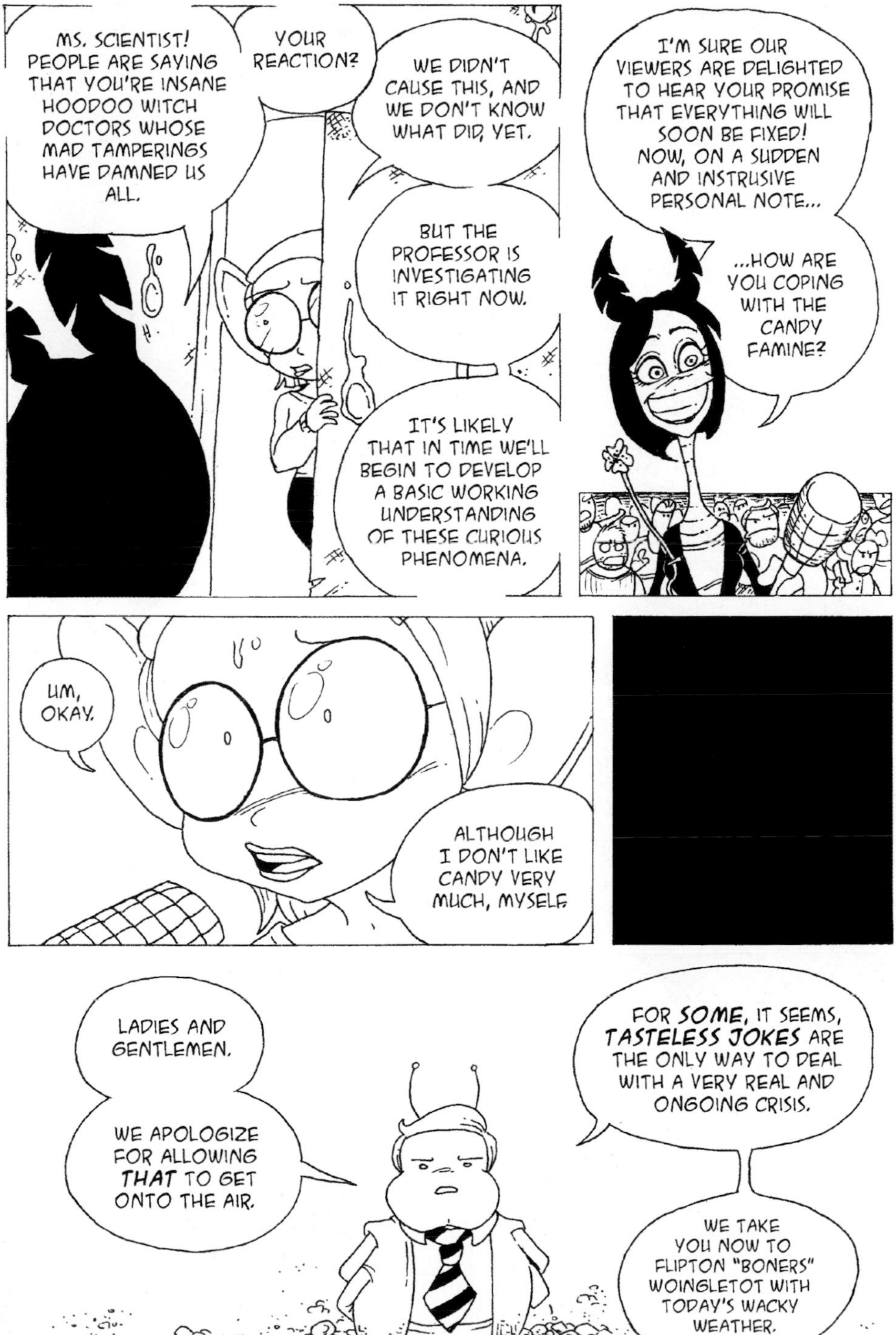

MS. SCIENTIST! PEOPLE ARE SAYING THAT YOU'RE INSANE HOODOO WITCH DOCTORS WHOSE MAD TAMPERINGS HAVE DAMNED US ALL.
YOUR REACTION?
WE DIDN'T CAUSE THIS, AND WE DON'T KNOW WHAT DID, YET.
BUT THE PROFESSOR IS INVESTIGATING IT RIGHT NOW.
IT'S LIKELY THAT IN TIME WE'LL BEGIN TO DEVELOP A BASIC WORKING UNDERSTANDING OF THESE CURIOUS PHENOMENA.
I'M SURE OUR VIEWERS ARE DELIGHTED TO HEAR YOUR PROMISE THAT EVERYTHING WILL SOON BE FIXED! NOW, ON A SUDDEN AND INSTRUSIVE PERSONAL NOTE...
...HOW ARE YOU COPING WITH THE CANDY FAMINE?
UM, OKAY.
ALTHOUGH I DON'T LIKE CANDY VERY MUCH, MYSELF.
LADIES AND GENTLEMEN.
WE APOLOGIZE FOR ALLOWING THAT TO GET ONTO THE AIR.
FOR SOME, IT SEEMS, TASTELESS JOKES ARE THE ONLY WAY TO DEAL WITH A VERY REAL AND ONGOING CRISIS.
WE TAKE YOU NOW TO FLIPTON "BONERS" WOINGLETOT WITH TODAY'S WACKY WEATHER.

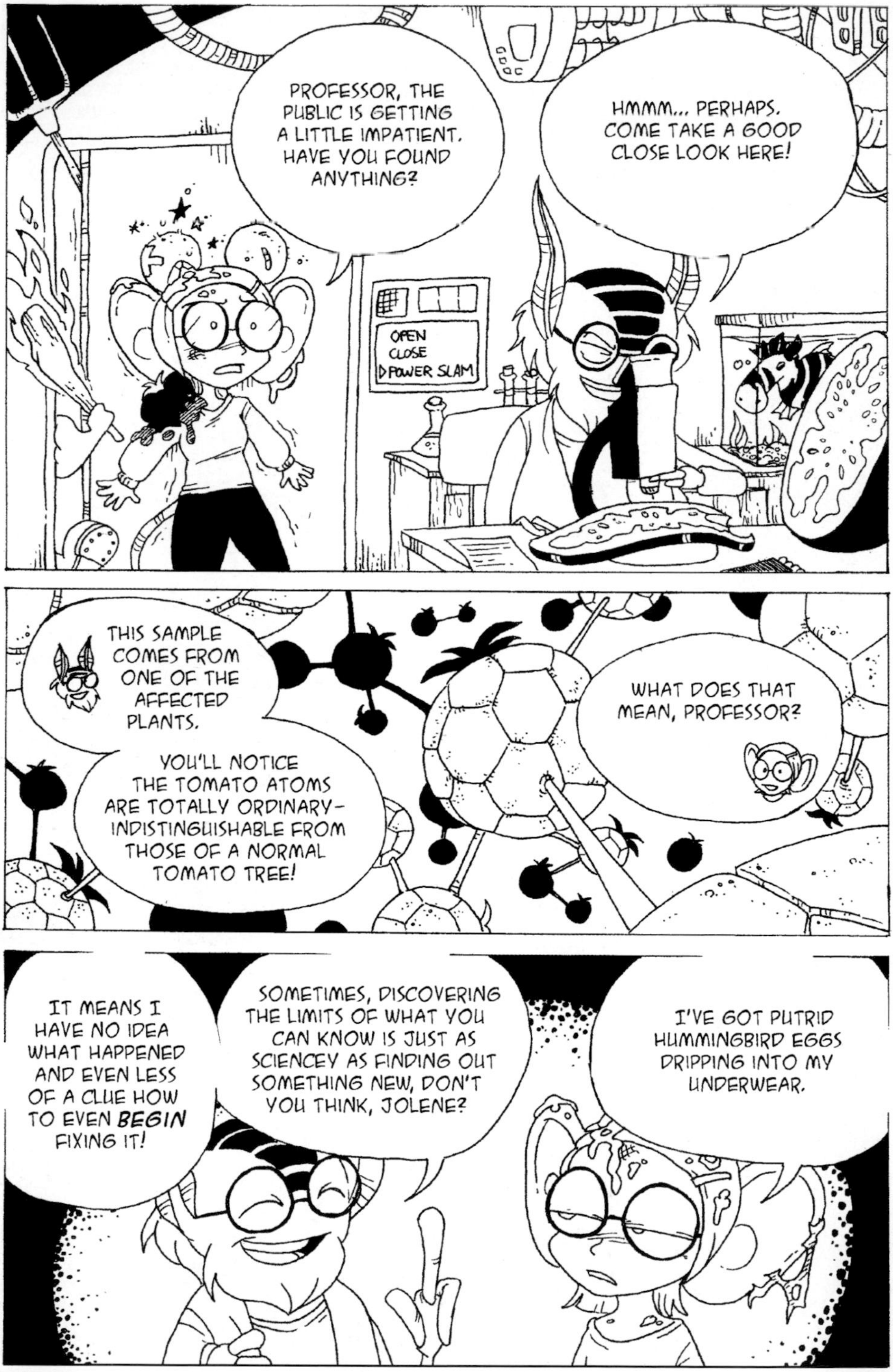
PROFESSOR, THE PUBLIC IS GETTING A LITTLE IMPATIENT. HAVE YOU FOUND ANYTHING?
HMMM... PERHAPS. COME TAKE A GOOD CLOSE LOOK HERE!
OPEN
CLOSE
POWER SLAM
THIS SAMPLE COMES FROM ONE OF THE AFFECTED PLANTS.
YOU'LL NOTICE THE TOMATO ATOMS ARE TOTALLY ORDINARY—INDISTINGUISHABLE FROM THOSE OF A NORMAL TOMATO TREE!
WHAT DOES THAT MEAN, PROFESSOR?
IT MEANS I HAVE NO IDEA WHAT HAPPENED AND EVEN LESS OF A CLUE HOW TO EVEN *BEGIN* FIXING IT!
SOMETIMES, DISCOVERING THE LIMITS OF WHAT YOU CAN KNOW IS JUST AS SCIENCEY AS FINDING OUT SOMETHING NEW, DON'T YOU THINK, JOLENE?
I'VE GOT PUTRID HUMMINGBIRD EGGS DRIPPING INTO MY UNDERWEAR.

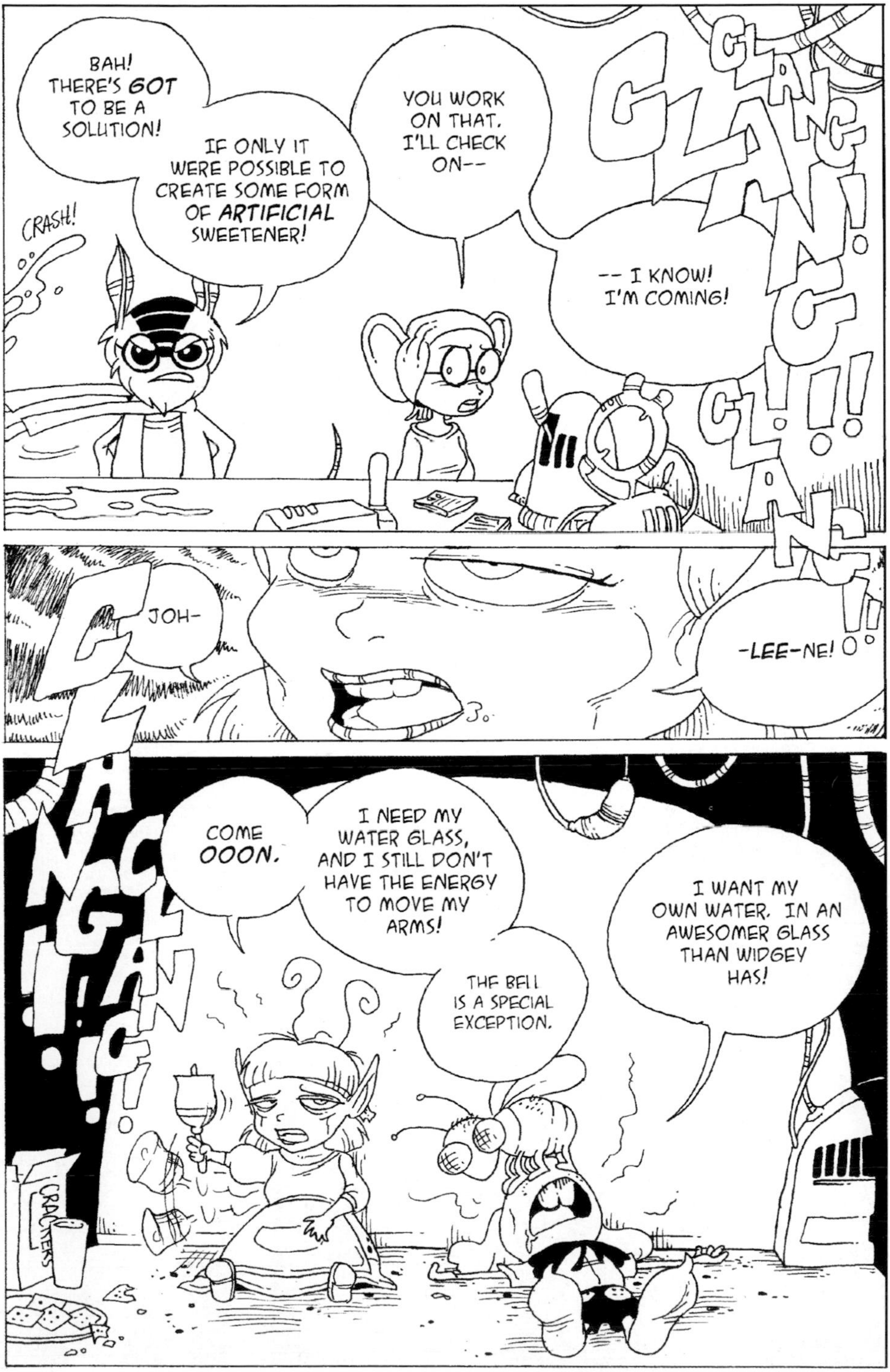
BAH! THERE'S GOT TO BE A SOLUTION!
IF ONLY IT WERE POSSIBLE TO CREATE SOME FORM OF ARTIFICIAL SWEETENER!
CRASH!
YOU WORK ON THAT. I'LL CHECK ON--
CLANG CLANG CLANG! CLANG!!!
-- I KNOW! I'M COMING!
JOH-
-LEE-NE!
CLANG CLANG!!
COME OOON.
I NEED MY WATER GLASS, AND I STILL DON'T HAVE THE ENERGY TO MOVE MY ARMS!
THE BELL IS A SPECIAL EXCEPTION.
I WANT MY OWN WATER. IN AN AWESOMER GLASS THAN WIDGEY HAS!
CRACKERS

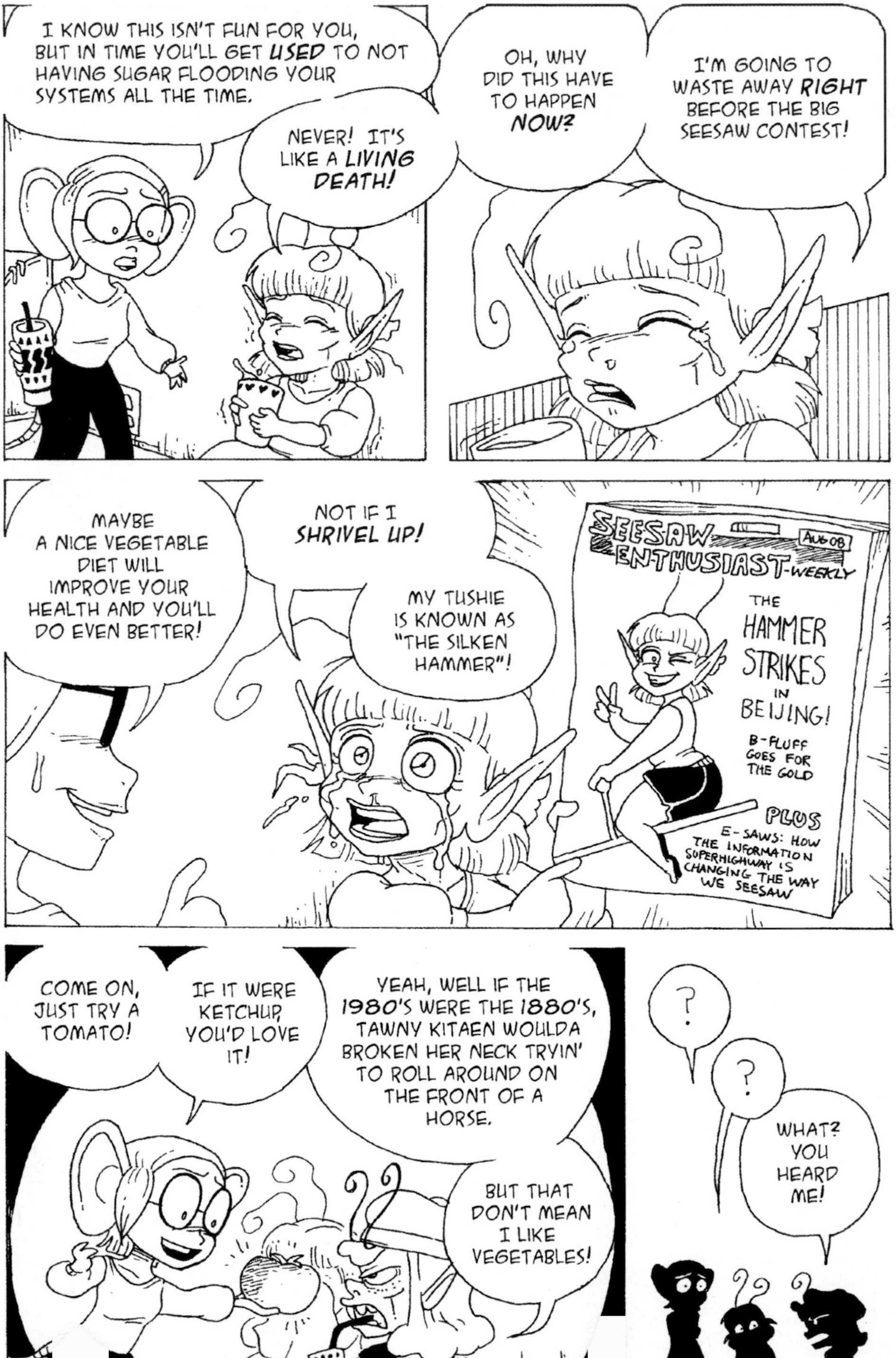
I KNOW THIS ISN'T FUN FOR YOU, BUT IN TIME YOU'LL GET USED TO NOT HAVING SUGAR FLOODING YOUR SYSTEMS ALL THE TIME.
NEVER! IT'S LIKE A LIVING DEATH!
OH, WHY DID THIS HAVE TO HAPPEN NOW?
I'M GOING TO WASTE AWAY RIGHT BEFORE THE BIG SEESAW CONTEST!
MAYBE A NICE VEGETABLE DIET WILL IMPROVE YOUR HEALTH AND YOU'LL DO EVEN BETTER!
NOT IF I SHRIVEL UP!
MY TUSHIE IS KNOWN AS "THE SILKEN HAMMER"!
SEESAW ENTHUSIAST-WEEKLY
AUG 08
THE HAMMER STRIKES IN BEIJING!
B-FLUFF GOES FOR THE GOLD
PLUS
E-SAWS: HOW THE INFORMATION SUPERHIGHWAY IS CHANGING THE WAY WE SEESAW
COME ON, JUST TRY A TOMATO!
IF IT WERE KETCHUP, YOU'D LOVE IT!
YEAH, WELL IF THE 1980'S WERE THE 1880'S, TAWNY KITAEN WOULDA BROKEN HER NECK TRYIN' TO ROLL AROUND ON THE FRONT OF A HORSE.
BUT THAT DON'T MEAN I LIKE VEGETABLES!
?
?
WHAT? YOU HEARD ME!

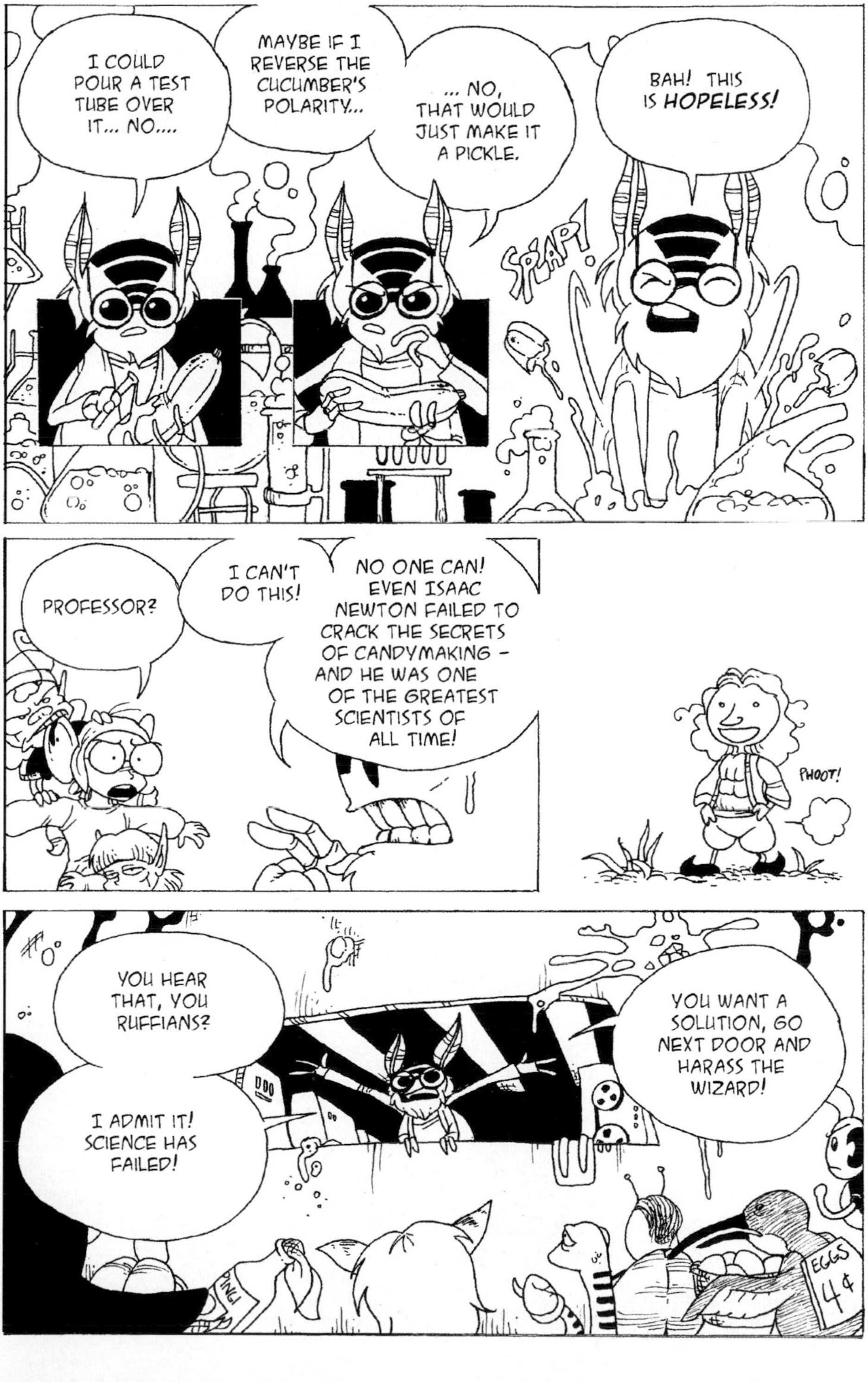
I COULD POUR A TEST TUBE OVER IT... NO....
MAYBE IF I REVERSE THE CUCUMBER'S POLARITY...
... NO, THAT WOULD JUST MAKE IT A PICKLE.
SPLAP!
BAH! THIS IS **HOPELESS!**
PROFESSOR?
I CAN'T DO THIS!
NO ONE CAN! EVEN ISAAC NEWTON FAILED TO CRACK THE SECRETS OF CANDYMAKING - AND HE WAS ONE OF THE GREATEST SCIENTISTS OF ALL TIME!
PHOOT!
YOU HEAR THAT, YOU RUFFIANS?
I ADMIT IT! SCIENCE HAS FAILED!
YOU WANT A SOLUTION, GO NEXT DOOR AND HARASS THE WIZARD!
EGGS 4¢

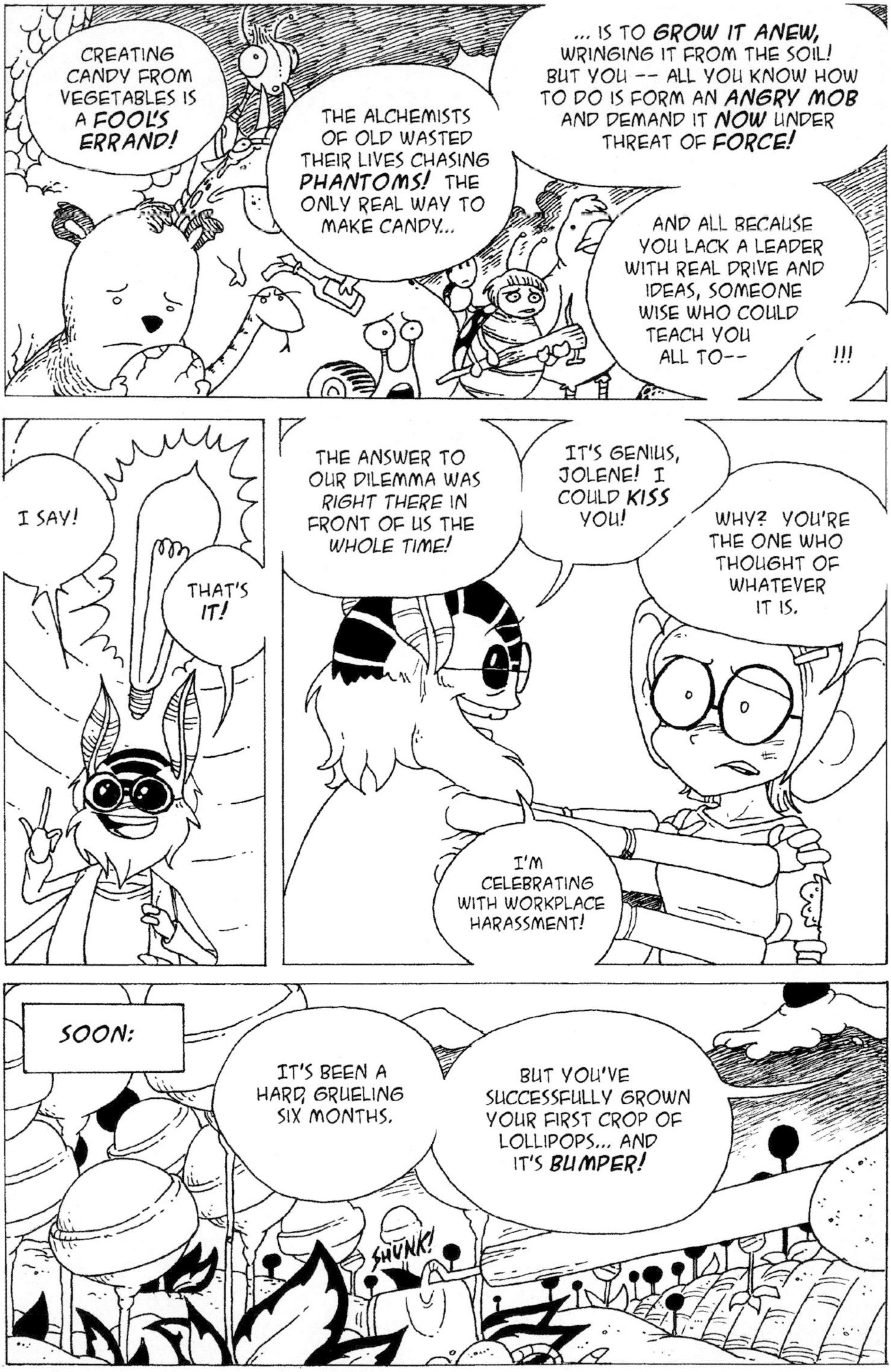
CREATING CANDY FROM VEGETABLES IS A FOOL'S ERRAND!
THE ALCHEMISTS OF OLD WASTED THEIR LIVES CHASING PHANTOMS! THE ONLY REAL WAY TO MAKE CANDY...
... IS TO GROW IT ANEW, WRINGING IT FROM THE SOIL! BUT YOU -- ALL YOU KNOW HOW TO DO IS FORM AN ANGRY MOB AND DEMAND IT NOW UNDER THREAT OF FORCE!
AND ALL BECAUSE YOU LACK A LEADER WITH REAL DRIVE AND IDEAS, SOMEONE WISE WHO COULD TEACH YOU ALL TO--
!!!
I SAY!
THAT'S IT!
THE ANSWER TO OUR DILEMMA WAS RIGHT THERE IN FRONT OF US THE WHOLE TIME!
IT'S GENIUS, JOLENE! I COULD KISS YOU!
WHY? YOU'RE THE ONE WHO THOUGHT OF WHATEVER IT IS.
I'M CELEBRATING WITH WORKPLACE HARASSMENT!
SOON:
IT'S BEEN A HARD, GRUELING SIX MONTHS.
BUT YOU'VE SUCCESSFULLY GROWN YOUR FIRST CROP OF LOLLIPOPS... AND IT'S BUMPER!
SHUNK!

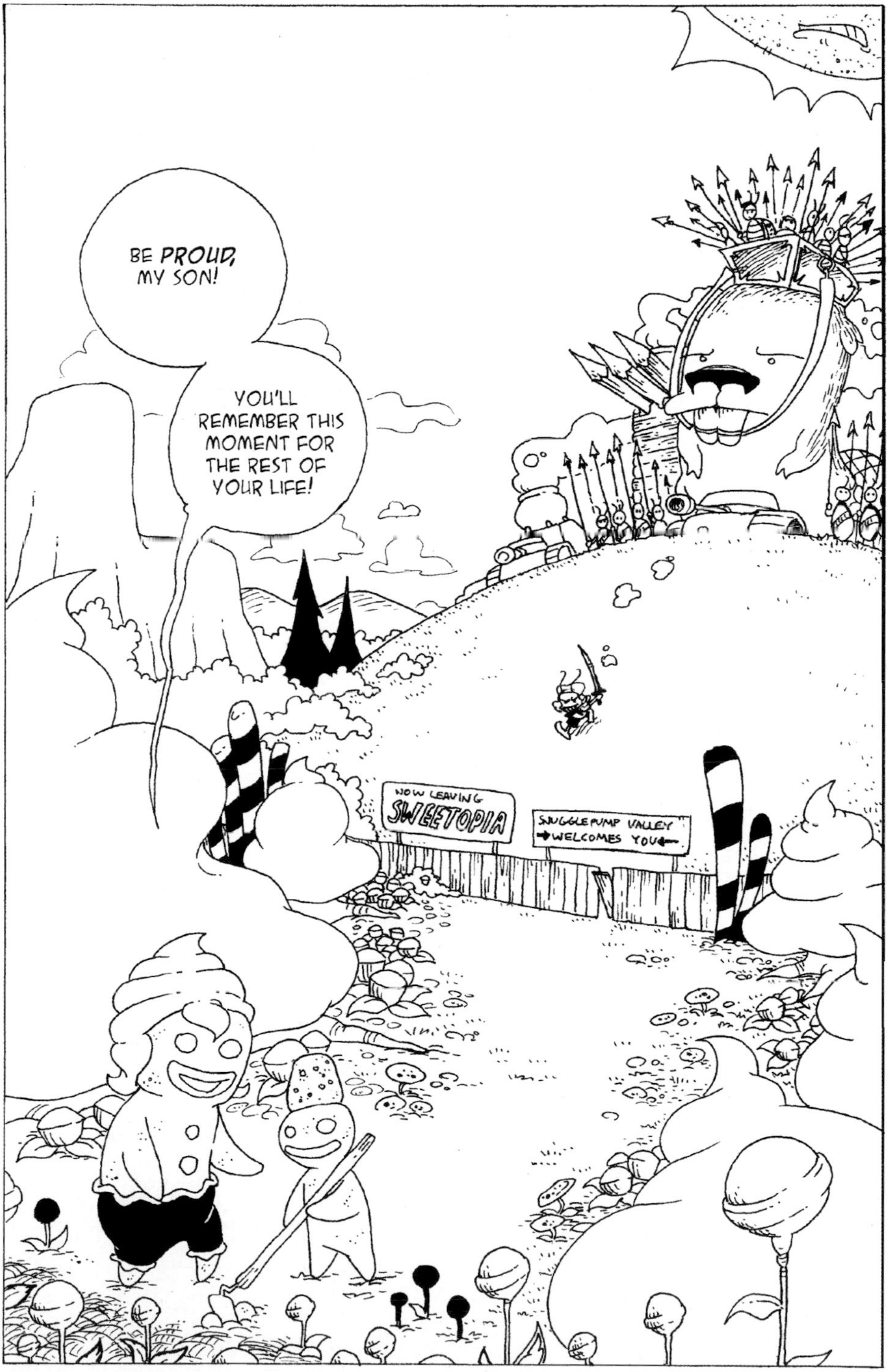
BE *PROUD,* MY SON!
YOU'LL REMEMBER THIS MOMENT FOR THE REST OF YOUR LIFE!
NOW LEAVING SWEETOPIA
SNUGGLEPUMP VALLEY WELCOMES YOU

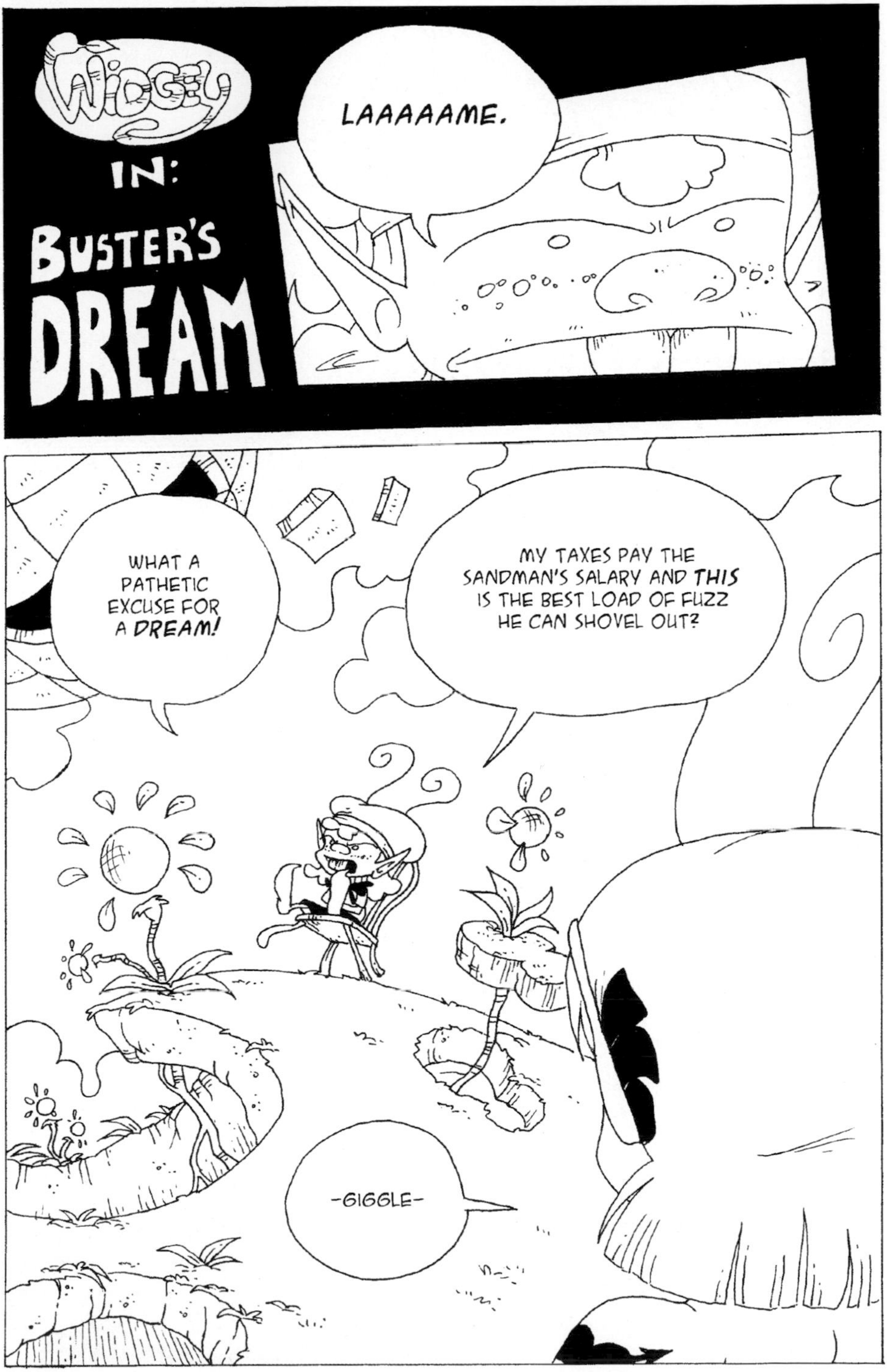
WIDGEY
IN:
BUSTER'S DREAM
LAAAAAME.
WHAT A PATHETIC EXCUSE FOR A DREAM!
MY TAXES PAY THE SANDMAN'S SALARY AND THIS IS THE BEST LOAD OF FUZZ HE CAN SHOVEL OUT?
-GIGGLE-

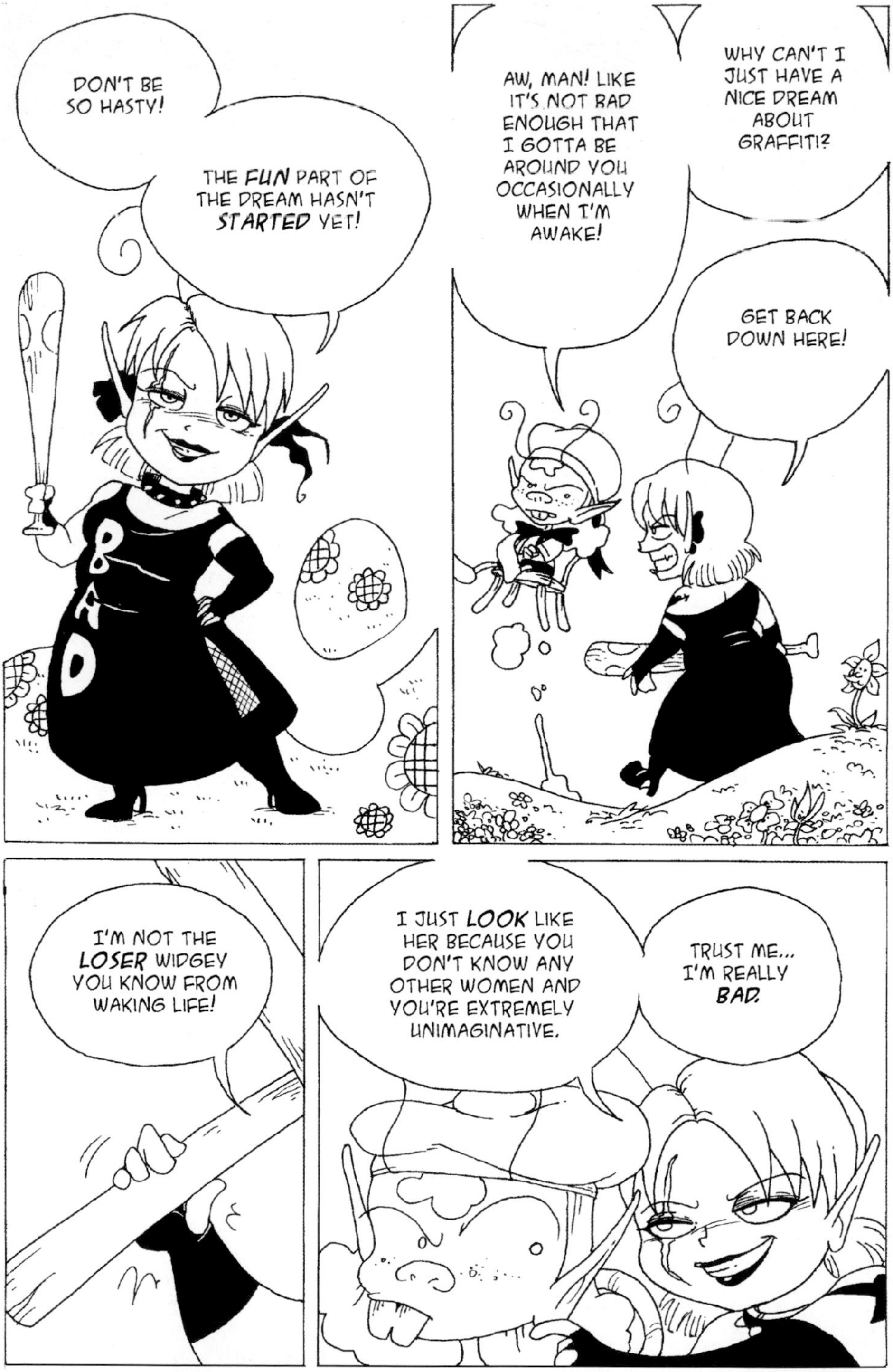
DON'T BE SO HASTY!
THE FUN PART OF THE DREAM HASN'T STARTED YET!
AW, MAN! LIKE IT'S NOT BAD ENOUGH THAT I GOTTA BE AROUND YOU OCCASIONALLY WHEN I'M AWAKE!
WHY CAN'T I JUST HAVE A NICE DREAM ABOUT GRAFFITI?
GET BACK DOWN HERE!
I'M NOT THE LOSER WIDGEY YOU KNOW FROM WAKING LIFE!
I JUST LOOK LIKE HER BECAUSE YOU DON'T KNOW ANY OTHER WOMEN AND YOU'RE EXTREMELY UNIMAGINATIVE.
TRUST ME... I'M REALLY BAD.

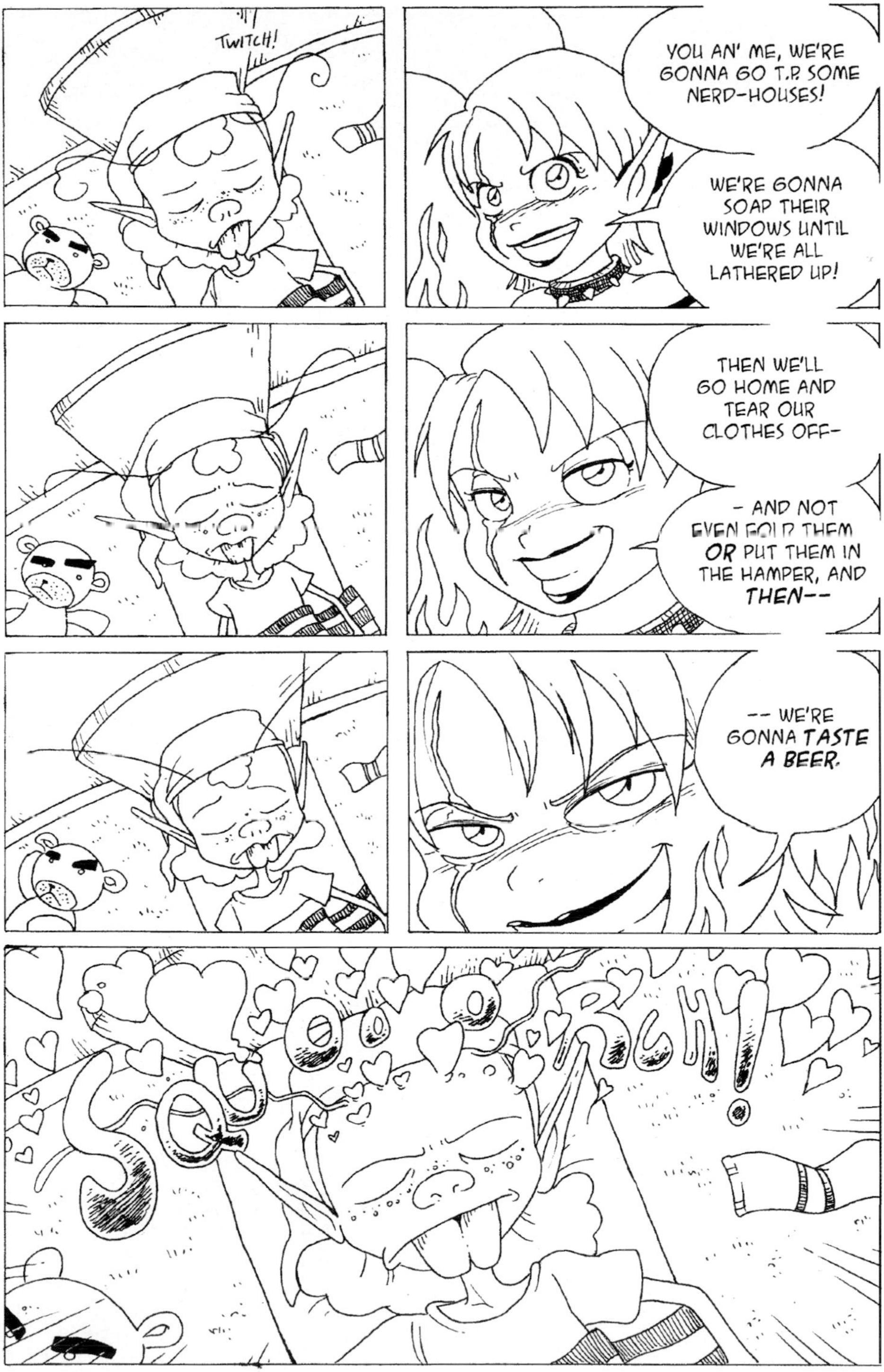
TWITCH!
YOU AN' ME, WE'RE GONNA GO T.P. SOME NERD-HOUSES!
WE'RE GONNA SOAP THEIR WINDOWS UNTIL WE'RE ALL LATHERED UP!
THEN WE'LL GO HOME AND TEAR OUR CLOTHES OFF-
- AND NOT EVEN FOLD THEM ***OR*** PUT THEM IN THE HAMPER, AND ***THEN***--
-- WE'RE GONNA ***TASTE A BEER.***
SQUOOORCH!

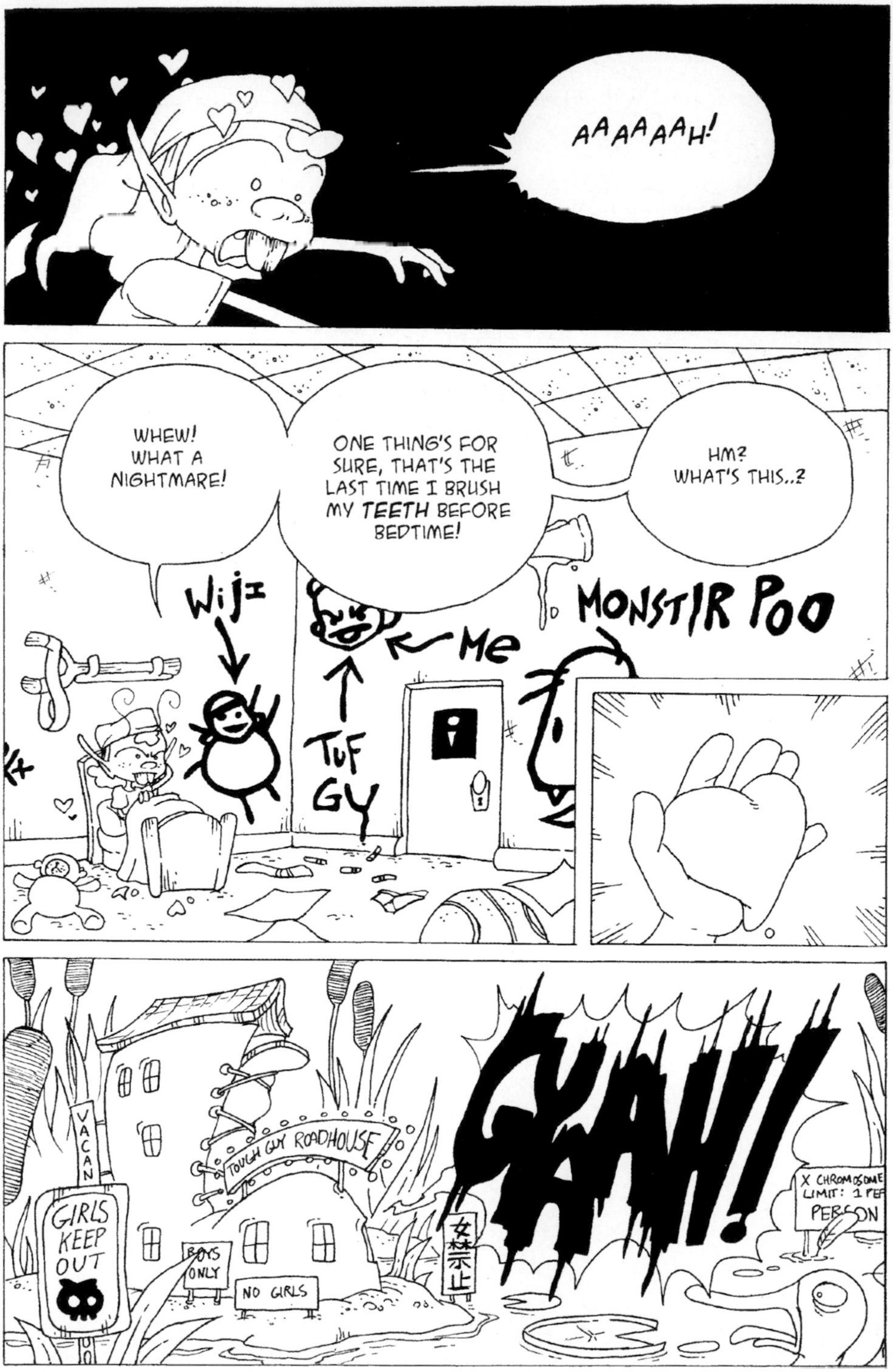
AAAAAAH!
WHEW! WHAT A NIGHTMARE!
ONE THING'S FOR SURE, THAT'S THE LAST TIME I BRUSH MY TEETH BEFORE BEDTIME!
HM? WHAT'S THIS..?
WIJI
ME
TUF GY
MONSTIR POO
TOUGH GUY ROADHOUSE
VACAN
GIRLS KEEP OUT
BOYS ONLY
NO GIRLS
女禁止
GYAAH!
X CHROMOSOME LIMIT: 1 PER PERSON

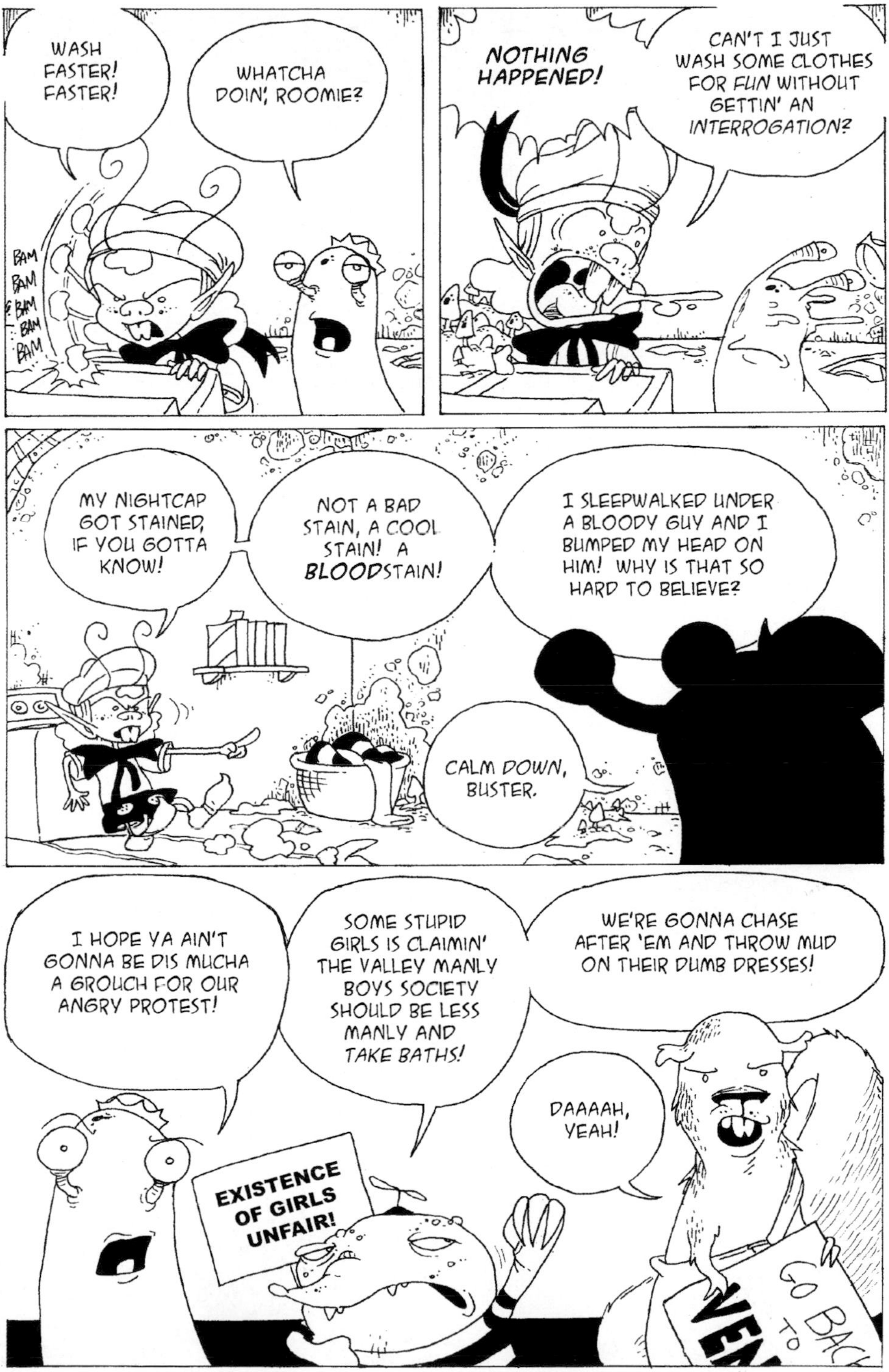
WASH FASTER! FASTER!
BAM BAM BAM BAM BAM
WHATCHA DOIN', ROOMIE?
NOTHING HAPPENED!
CAN'T I JUST WASH SOME CLOTHES FOR FUN WITHOUT GETTIN' AN INTERROGATION?
MY NIGHTCAP GOT STAINED, IF YOU GOTTA KNOW!
NOT A BAD STAIN, A COOL STAIN! A BLOODSTAIN!
I SLEEPWALKED UNDER A BLOODY GUY AND I BUMPED MY HEAD ON HIM! WHY IS THAT SO HARD TO BELIEVE?
CALM DOWN, BUSTER.
I HOPE YA AIN'T GONNA BE DIS MUCHA A GROUCH FOR OUR ANGRY PROTEST!
SOME STUPID GIRLS IS CLAIMIN' THE VALLEY MANLY BOYS SOCIETY SHOULD BE LESS MANLY AND TAKE BATHS!
WE'RE GONNA CHASE AFTER 'EM AND THROW MUD ON THEIR DUMB DRESSES!
DAAAAH, YEAH!
EXISTENCE OF GIRLS UNFAIR!

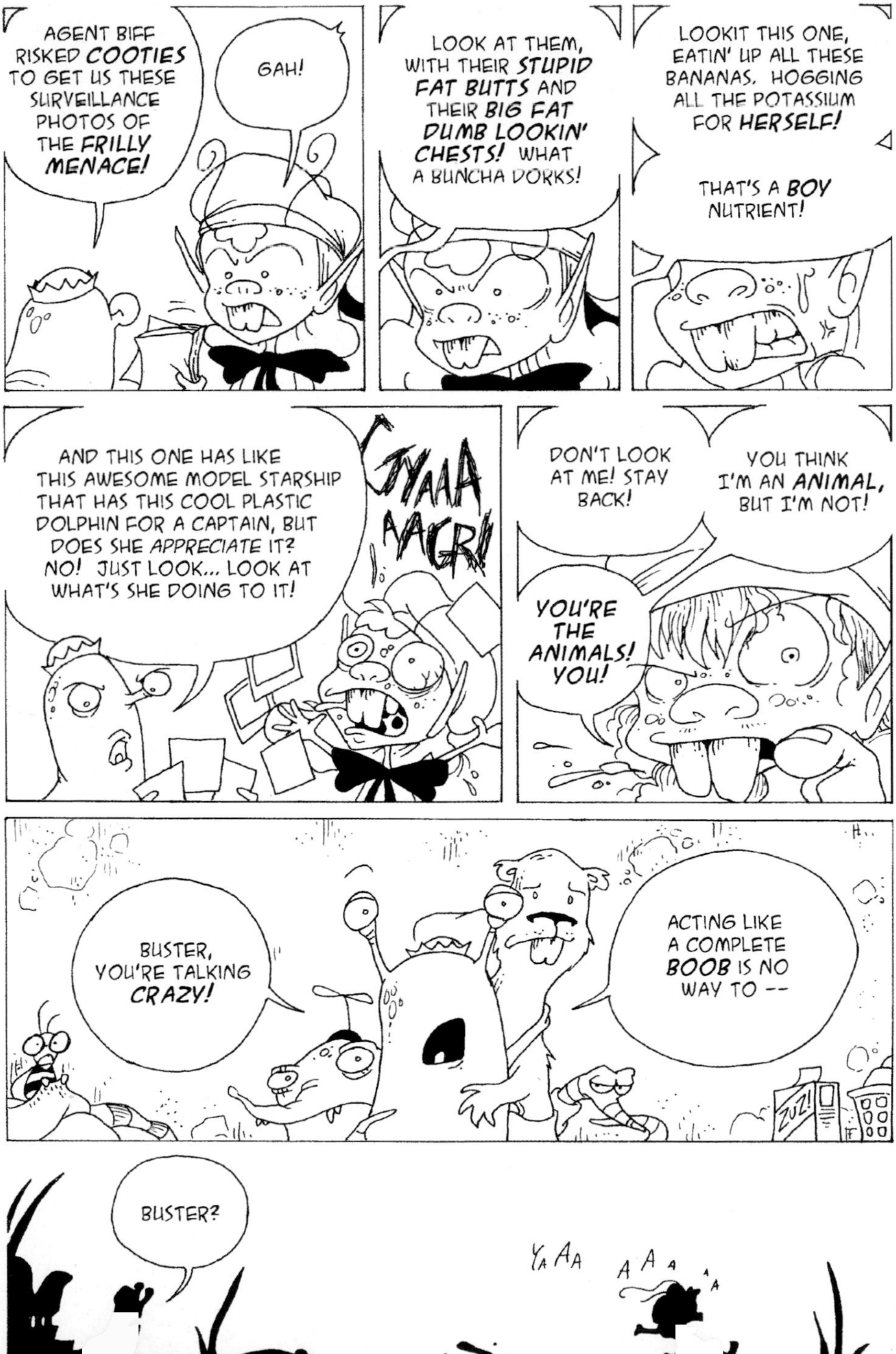
AGENT BIFF RISKED COOTIES TO GET US THESE SURVEILLANCE PHOTOS OF THE FRILLY MENACE!
GAH!
LOOK AT THEM, WITH THEIR STUPID FAT BUTTS AND THEIR BIG FAT DUMB LOOKIN' CHESTS! WHAT A BUNCHA DORKS!
LOOKIT THIS ONE, EATIN' UP ALL THESE BANANAS. HOGGING ALL THE POTASSIUM FOR HERSELF!
THAT'S A BOY NUTRIENT!
AND THIS ONE HAS LIKE THIS AWESOME MODEL STARSHIP THAT HAS THIS COOL PLASTIC DOLPHIN FOR A CAPTAIN, BUT DOES SHE APPRECIATE IT? NO! JUST LOOK... LOOK AT WHAT'S SHE DOING TO IT!
GYAAA AAGR!
DON'T LOOK AT ME! STAY BACK!
YOU THINK I'M AN ANIMAL, BUT I'M NOT!
YOU'RE THE ANIMALS! YOU!
BUSTER, YOU'RE TALKING CRAZY!
ACTING LIKE A COMPLETE BOOB IS NO WAY TO --
ZUZ!
BUSTER?
YAAA AAAAA

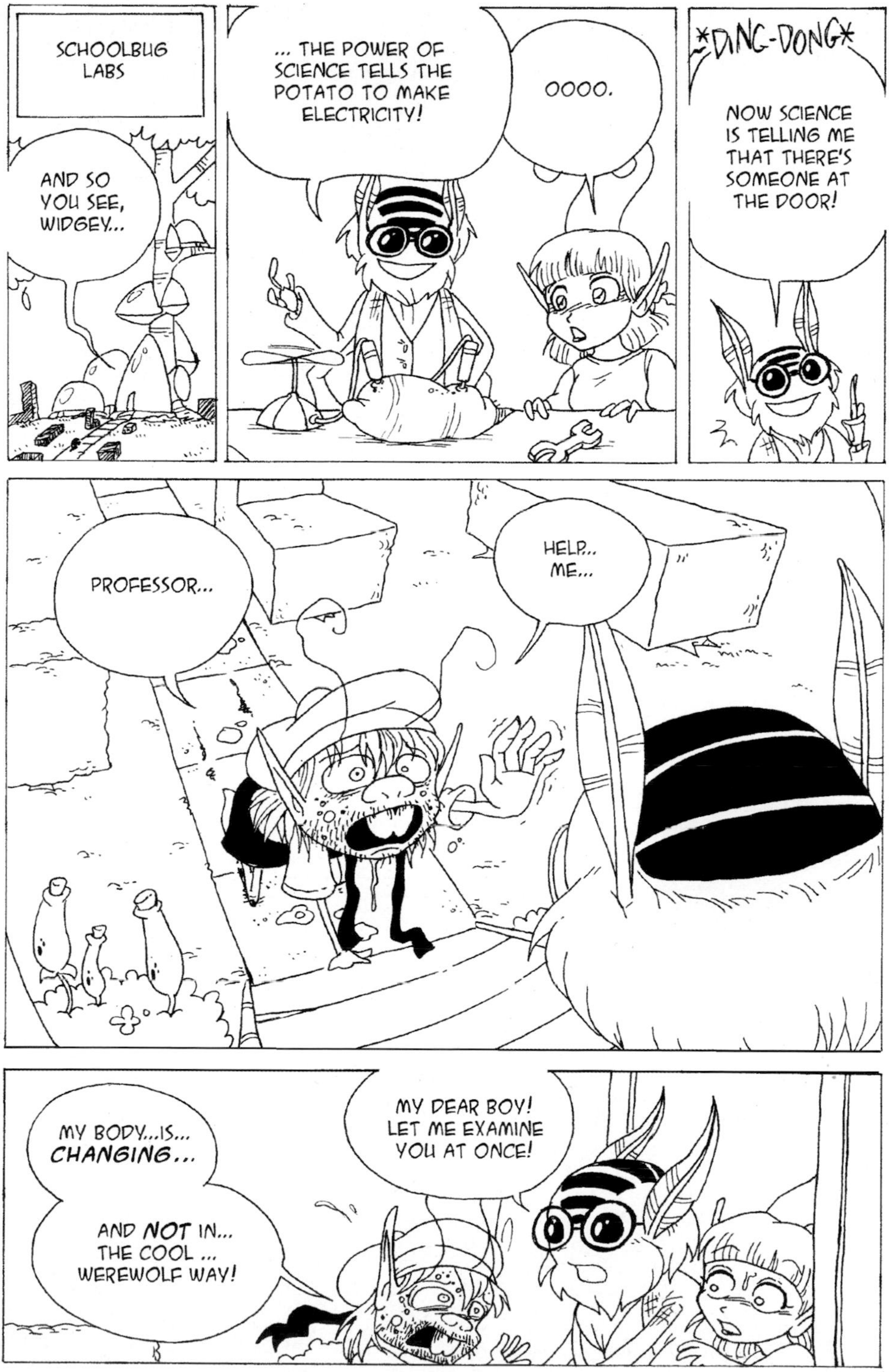
SCHOOLBUG LABS
AND SO YOU SEE, WIDGEY...
... THE POWER OF SCIENCE TELLS THE POTATO TO MAKE ELECTRICITY!
OOOO.
DING-DONG
NOW SCIENCE IS TELLING ME THAT THERE'S SOMEONE AT THE DOOR!
PROFESSOR...
HELP... ME...
MY BODY...IS... **CHANGING...**
AND **NOT** IN... THE COOL ... WEREWOLF WAY!
MY DEAR BOY! LET ME EXAMINE YOU AT ONCE!

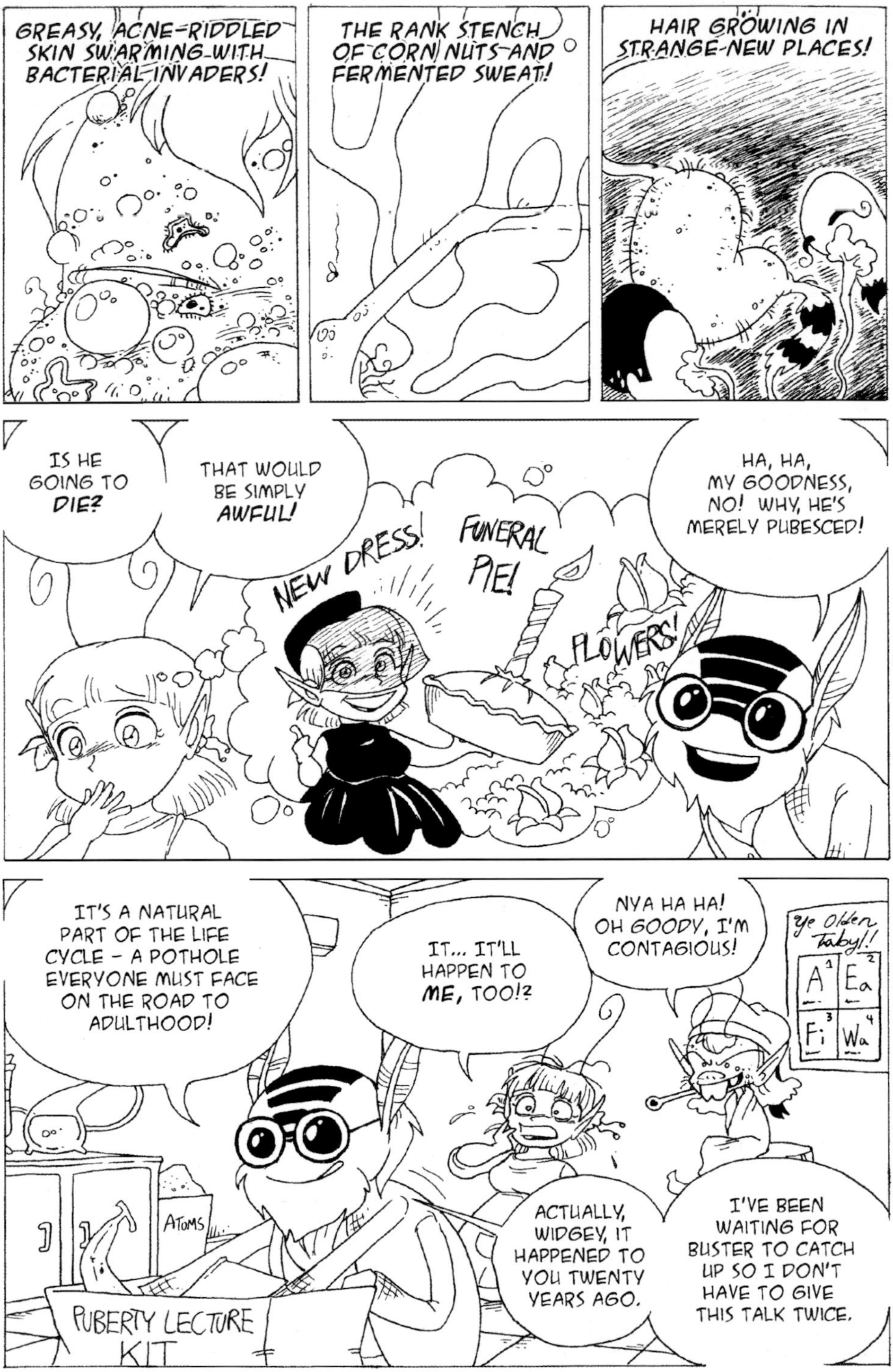
GREASY, ACNE-RIDDLED SKIN SWARMING WITH BACTERIAL INVADERS!
THE RANK STENCH OF CORN NUTS AND FERMENTED SWEAT!
HAIR GROWING IN STRANGE NEW PLACES!
IS HE GOING TO DIE?
THAT WOULD BE SIMPLY AWFUL!
NEW DRESS!
FUNERAL PIE!
FLOWERS!
HA, HA, MY GOODNESS, NO! WHY, HE'S MERELY PUBESCED!
IT'S A NATURAL PART OF THE LIFE CYCLE - A POTHOLE EVERYONE MUST FACE ON THE ROAD TO ADULTHOOD!
IT... IT'LL HAPPEN TO ME, TOO!?
NYA HA HA! OH GOODY, I'M CONTAGIOUS!
Ye Olden Table!!
A 1
Ea 2
Fi 3
Wa 4
ATOMS
PUBERTY LECTURE KIT
ACTUALLY, WIDGEY, IT HAPPENED TO YOU TWENTY YEARS AGO.
I'VE BEEN WAITING FOR BUSTER TO CATCH UP SO I DON'T HAVE TO GIVE THIS TALK TWICE.

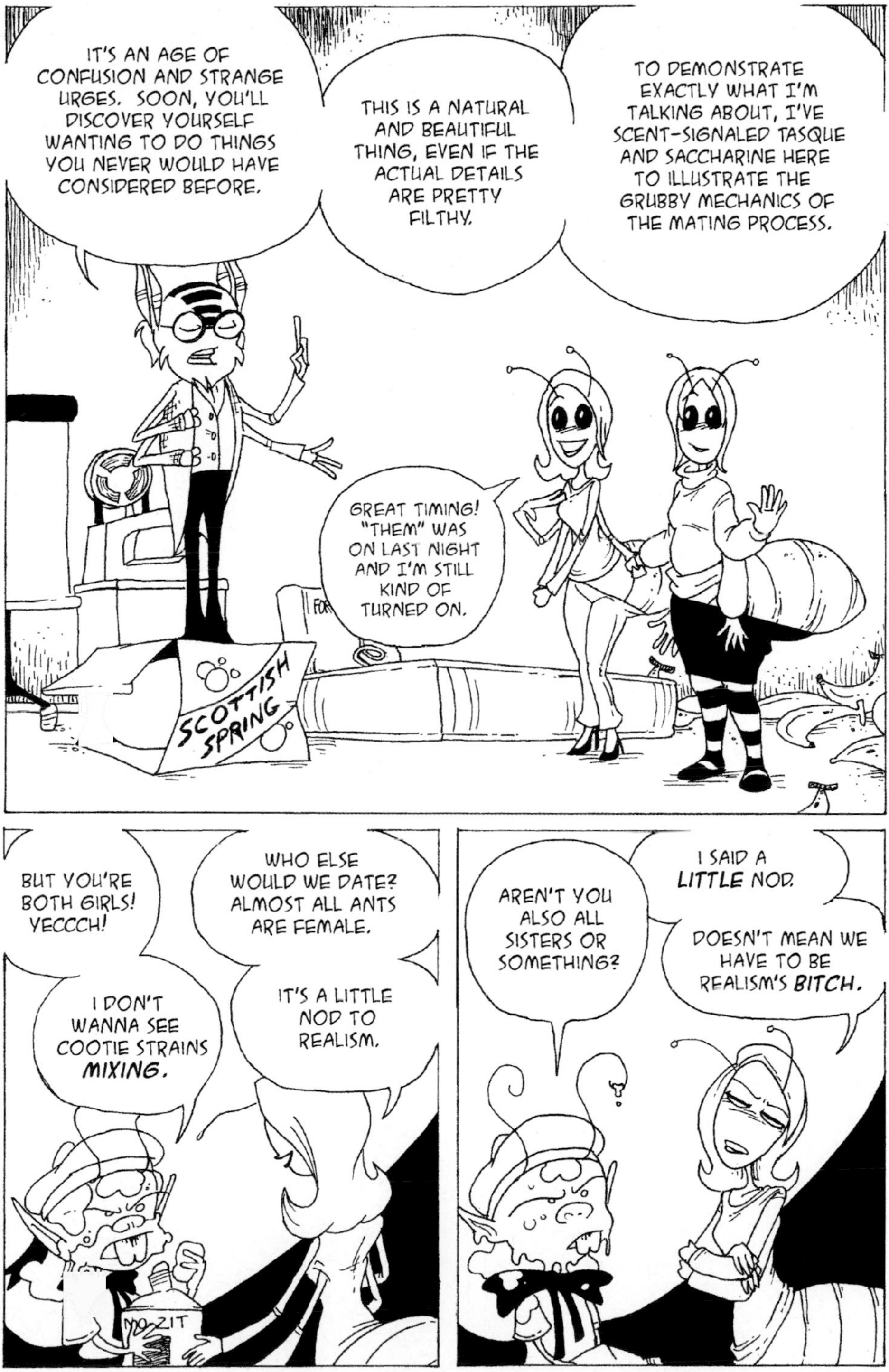
IT'S AN AGE OF CONFUSION AND STRANGE URGES. SOON, YOU'LL DISCOVER YOURSELF WANTING TO DO THINGS YOU NEVER WOULD HAVE CONSIDERED BEFORE.
THIS IS A NATURAL AND BEAUTIFUL THING, EVEN IF THE ACTUAL DETAILS ARE PRETTY FILTHY.
TO DEMONSTRATE EXACTLY WHAT I'M TALKING ABOUT, I'VE SCENT-SIGNALED TASQUE AND SACCHARINE HERE TO ILLUSTRATE THE GRUBBY MECHANICS OF THE MATING PROCESS.
GREAT TIMING! "THEM" WAS ON LAST NIGHT AND I'M STILL KIND OF TURNED ON.
SCOTTISH SPRING
BUT YOU'RE BOTH GIRLS! YECCCH!
I DON'T WANNA SEE COOTIE STRAINS ***MIXING.***
WHO ELSE WOULD WE DATE? ALMOST ALL ANTS ARE FEMALE.
IT'S A LITTLE NOD TO REALISM.
NO-ZIT
AREN'T YOU ALSO ALL SISTERS OR SOMETHING?
I SAID A ***LITTLE*** NOD.
DOESN'T MEAN WE HAVE TO BE REALISM'S ***BITCH.***

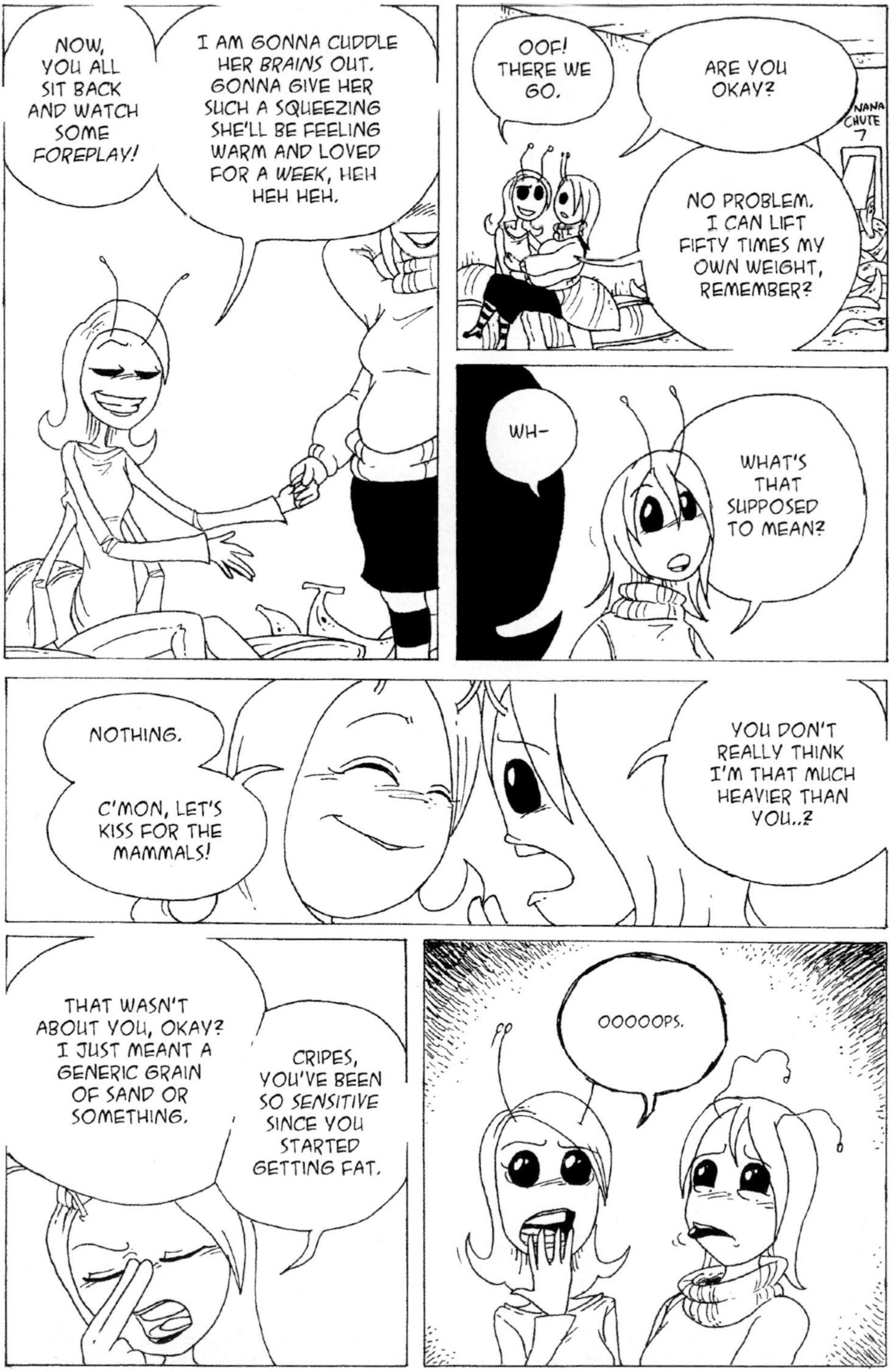
NOW, YOU ALL SIT BACK AND WATCH SOME *FOREPLAY!*
I AM GONNA CUDDLE HER *BRAINS* OUT. GONNA GIVE HER SUCH A SQUEEZING SHE'LL BE FEELING WARM AND LOVED FOR A *WEEK*, HEH HEH HEH.
OOF! THERE WE GO.
ARE YOU OKAY?
NANA CHUTE 7
NO PROBLEM. I CAN LIFT FIFTY TIMES MY OWN WEIGHT, REMEMBER?
WH-
WHAT'S THAT SUPPOSED TO MEAN?
NOTHING.
C'MON, LET'S KISS FOR THE MAMMALS!
YOU DON'T REALLY THINK I'M THAT MUCH HEAVIER THAN YOU..?
THAT WASN'T ABOUT YOU, OKAY? I JUST MEANT A GENERIC GRAIN OF SAND OR SOMETHING.
CRIPES, YOU'VE BEEN SO *SENSITIVE* SINCE YOU STARTED GETTING FAT.
OOOOOPS.

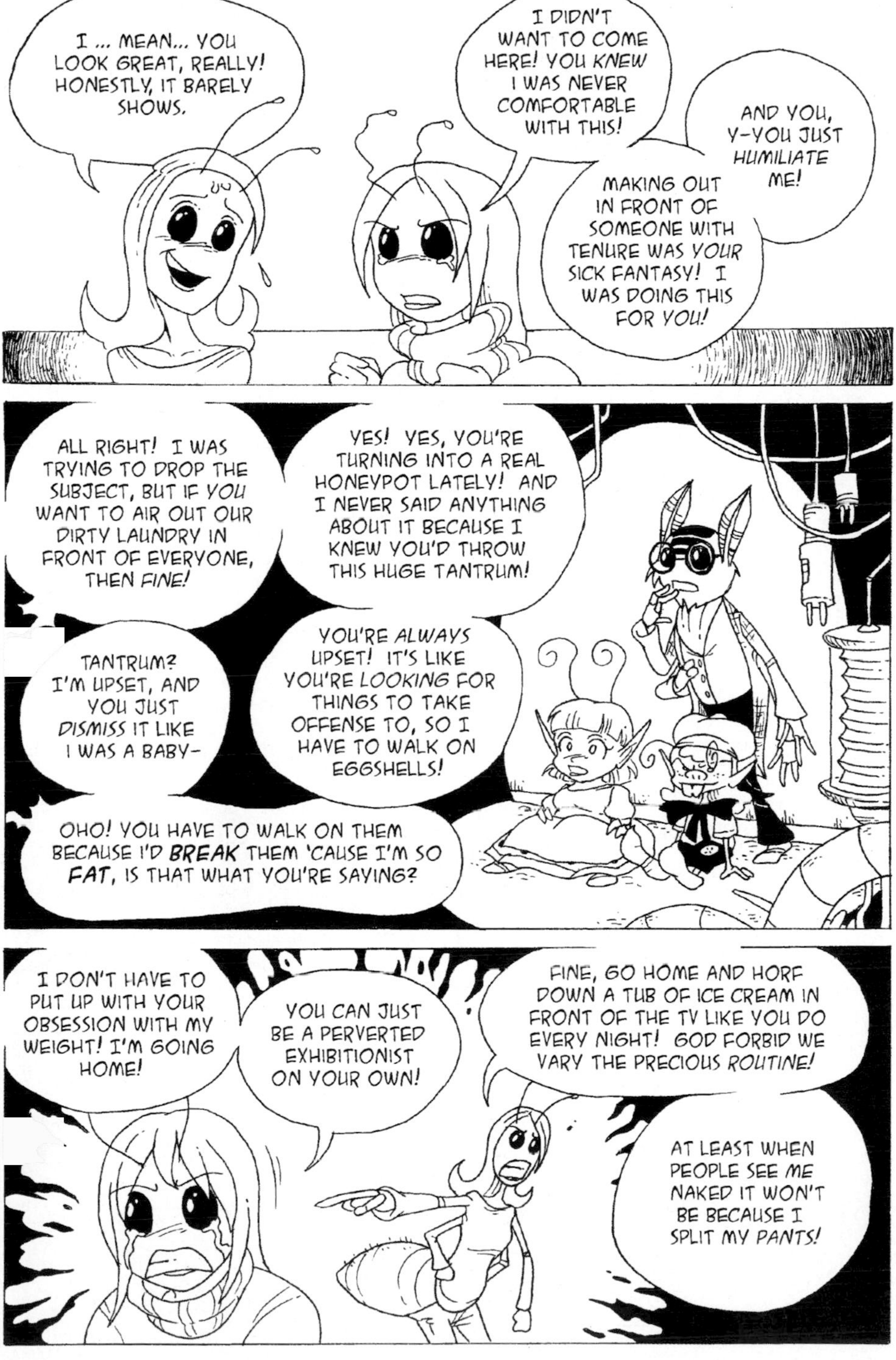
I ... MEAN... YOU LOOK GREAT, REALLY! HONESTLY, IT BARELY SHOWS.
I DIDN'T WANT TO COME HERE! YOU KNEW I WAS NEVER COMFORTABLE WITH THIS!
MAKING OUT IN FRONT OF SOMEONE WITH TENURE WAS YOUR SICK FANTASY! I WAS DOING THIS FOR YOU!
AND YOU, Y-YOU JUST HUMILIATE ME!
ALL RIGHT! I WAS TRYING TO DROP THE SUBJECT, BUT IF YOU WANT TO AIR OUT OUR DIRTY LAUNDRY IN FRONT OF EVERYONE, THEN FINE!
YES! YES, YOU'RE TURNING INTO A REAL HONEYPOT LATELY! AND I NEVER SAID ANYTHING ABOUT IT BECAUSE I KNEW YOU'D THROW THIS HUGE TANTRUM!
TANTRUM? I'M UPSET, AND YOU JUST DISMISS IT LIKE I WAS A BABY-
YOU'RE ALWAYS UPSET! IT'S LIKE YOU'RE LOOKING FOR THINGS TO TAKE OFFENSE TO, SO I HAVE TO WALK ON EGGSHELLS!
OHO! YOU HAVE TO WALK ON THEM BECAUSE I'D BREAK THEM 'CAUSE I'M SO FAT, IS THAT WHAT YOU'RE SAYING?
I DON'T HAVE TO PUT UP WITH YOUR OBSESSION WITH MY WEIGHT! I'M GOING HOME!
YOU CAN JUST BE A PERVERTED EXHIBITIONIST ON YOUR OWN!
FINE, GO HOME AND HORF DOWN A TUB OF ICE CREAM IN FRONT OF THE TV LIKE YOU DO EVERY NIGHT! GOD FORBID WE VARY THE PRECIOUS ROUTINE!
AT LEAST WHEN PEOPLE SEE ME NAKED IT WON'T BE BECAUSE I SPLIT MY PANTS!

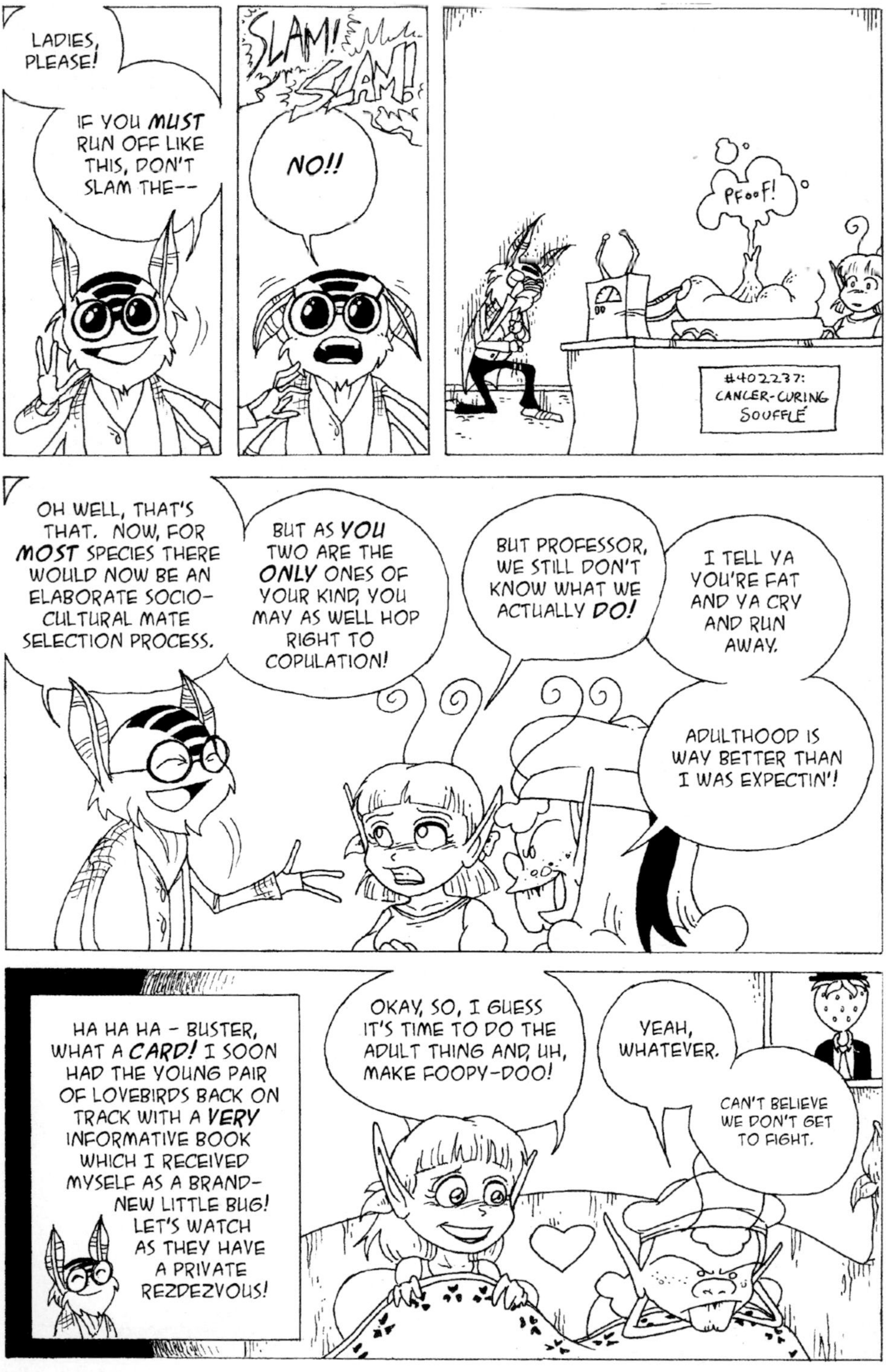
LADIES, PLEASE!
IF YOU MUST RUN OFF LIKE THIS, DON'T SLAM THE--
SLAM! SLAM!
NO!!
PFOOF!
#402237: CANCER-CURING SOUFFLÉ
OH WELL, THAT'S THAT. NOW, FOR MOST SPECIES THERE WOULD NOW BE AN ELABORATE SOCIO-CULTURAL MATE SELECTION PROCESS.
BUT AS YOU TWO ARE THE ONLY ONES OF YOUR KIND, YOU MAY AS WELL HOP RIGHT TO COPULATION!
BUT PROFESSOR, WE STILL DON'T KNOW WHAT WE ACTUALLY DO!
I TELL YA YOU'RE FAT AND YA CRY AND RUN AWAY.
ADULTHOOD IS WAY BETTER THAN I WAS EXPECTIN'!
HA HA HA - BUSTER, WHAT A CARD! I SOON HAD THE YOUNG PAIR OF LOVEBIRDS BACK ON TRACK WITH A VERY INFORMATIVE BOOK WHICH I RECEIVED MYSELF AS A BRAND-NEW LITTLE BUG! LET'S WATCH AS THEY HAVE A PRIVATE REZDEZVOUS!
OKAY, SO, I GUESS IT'S TIME TO DO THE ADULT THING AND, UH, MAKE FOOPY-DOO!
YEAH, WHATEVER.
CAN'T BELIEVE WE DON'T GET TO FIGHT.

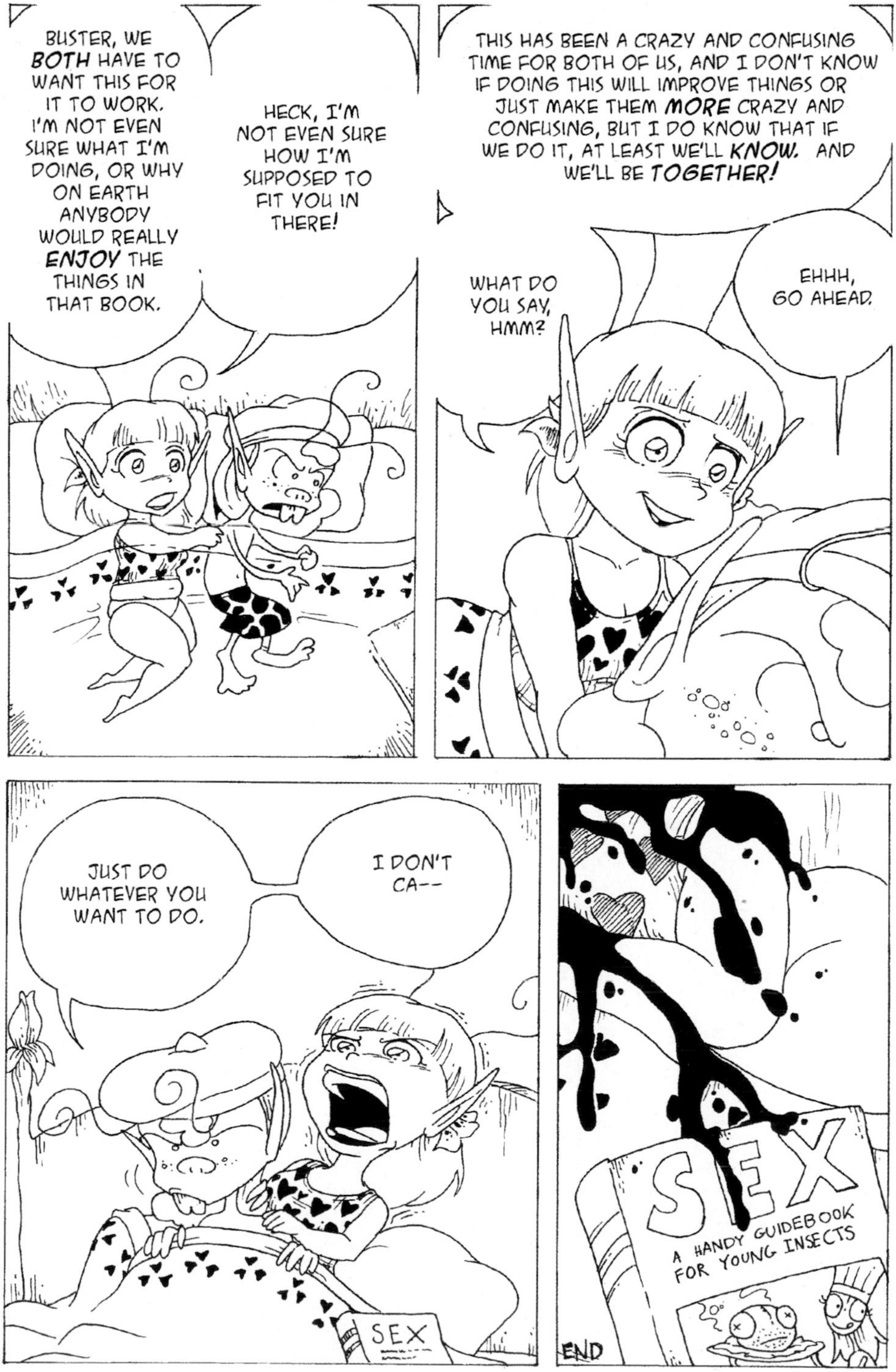
BUSTER, WE BOTH HAVE TO WANT THIS FOR IT TO WORK. I'M NOT EVEN SURE WHAT I'M DOING, OR WHY ON EARTH ANYBODY WOULD REALLY ENJOY THE THINGS IN THAT BOOK.
HECK, I'M NOT EVEN SURE HOW I'M SUPPOSED TO FIT YOU IN THERE!
THIS HAS BEEN A CRAZY AND CONFUSING TIME FOR BOTH OF US, AND I DON'T KNOW IF DOING THIS WILL IMPROVE THINGS OR JUST MAKE THEM MORE CRAZY AND CONFUSING, BUT I DO KNOW THAT IF WE DO IT, AT LEAST WE'LL KNOW. AND WE'LL BE TOGETHER!
WHAT DO YOU SAY, HMM?
EHHH, GO AHEAD.
JUST DO WHATEVER YOU WANT TO DO.
I DON'T CA--
SEX
SEX
A HANDY GUIDEBOOK FOR YOUNG INSECTS
END

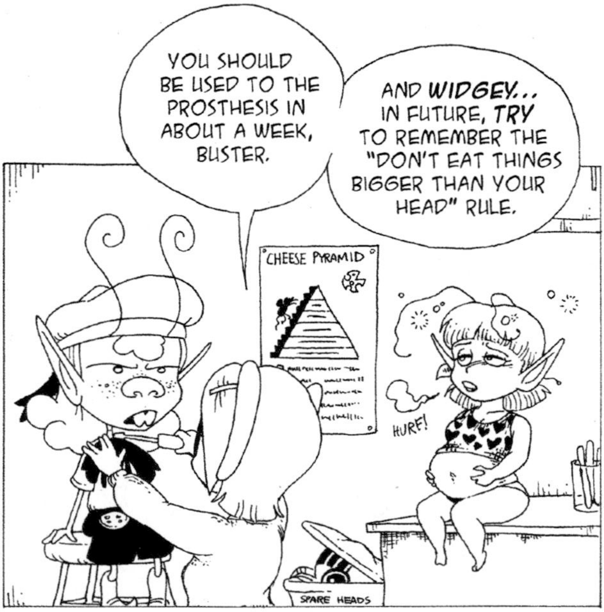
YOU SHOULD BE USED TO THE PROSTHESIS IN ABOUT A WEEK, BUSTER.
AND WIDGEY... IN FUTURE, TRY TO REMEMBER THE "DON'T EAT THINGS BIGGER THAN YOUR HEAD" RULE.
CHEESE PYRAMID
HURF!
SPARE HEADS

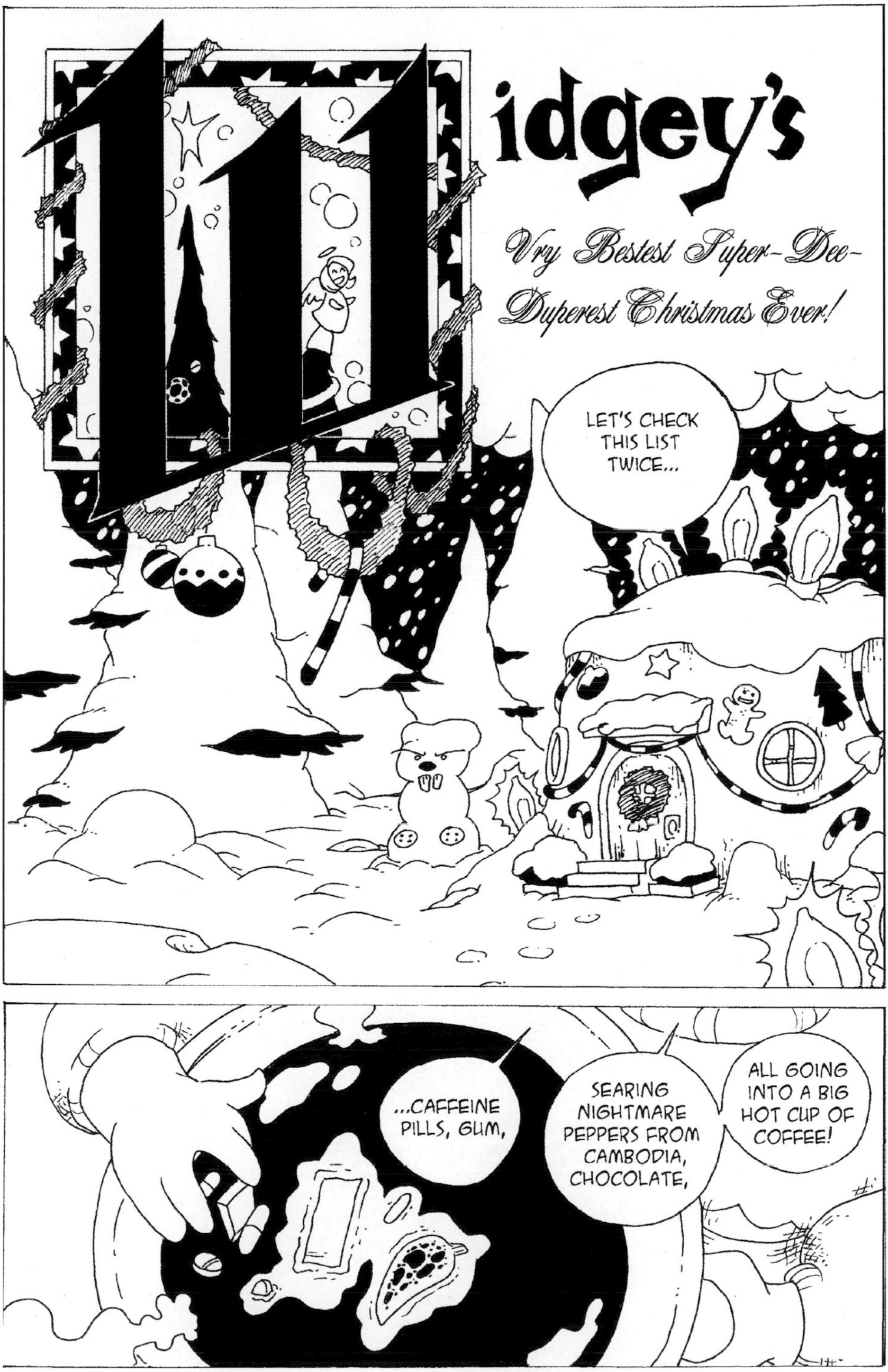
Widgey's
Vry Bestest Super-Dee-Duperest Christmas Ever!
LET'S CHECK THIS LIST TWICE...
...CAFFEINE PILLS, GUM,
SEARING NIGHTMARE PEPPERS FROM CAMBODIA, CHOCOLATE,
ALL GOING INTO A BIG HOT CUP OF COFFEE!

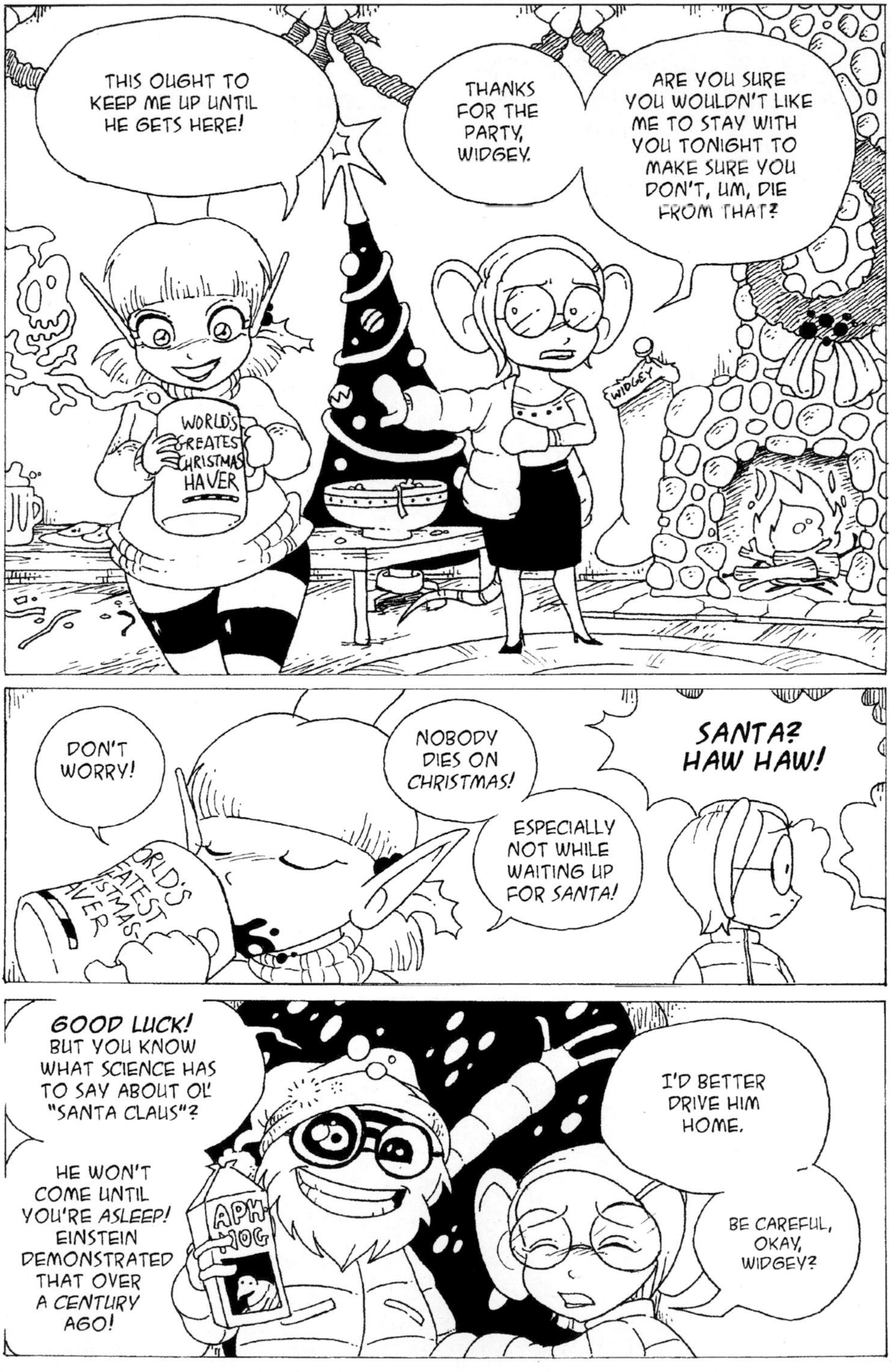
THIS OUGHT TO KEEP ME UP UNTIL HE GETS HERE!
WORLD'S GREATEST CHRISTMAS HAVER
THANKS FOR THE PARTY, WIDGEY.
ARE YOU SURE YOU WOULDN'T LIKE ME TO STAY WITH YOU TONIGHT TO MAKE SURE YOU DON'T, UM, DIE FROM THAT?
WIDGEY
DON'T WORRY!
NOBODY DIES ON CHRISTMAS!
ESPECIALLY NOT WHILE WAITING UP FOR SANTA!
SANTA? HAW HAW!
GOOD LUCK! BUT YOU KNOW WHAT SCIENCE HAS TO SAY ABOUT OL' "SANTA CLAUS"?
HE WON'T COME UNTIL YOU'RE ASLEEP! EINSTEIN DEMONSTRATED THAT OVER A CENTURY AGO!
APH NOG
I'D BETTER DRIVE HIM HOME.
BE CAREFUL, OKAY, WIDGEY?

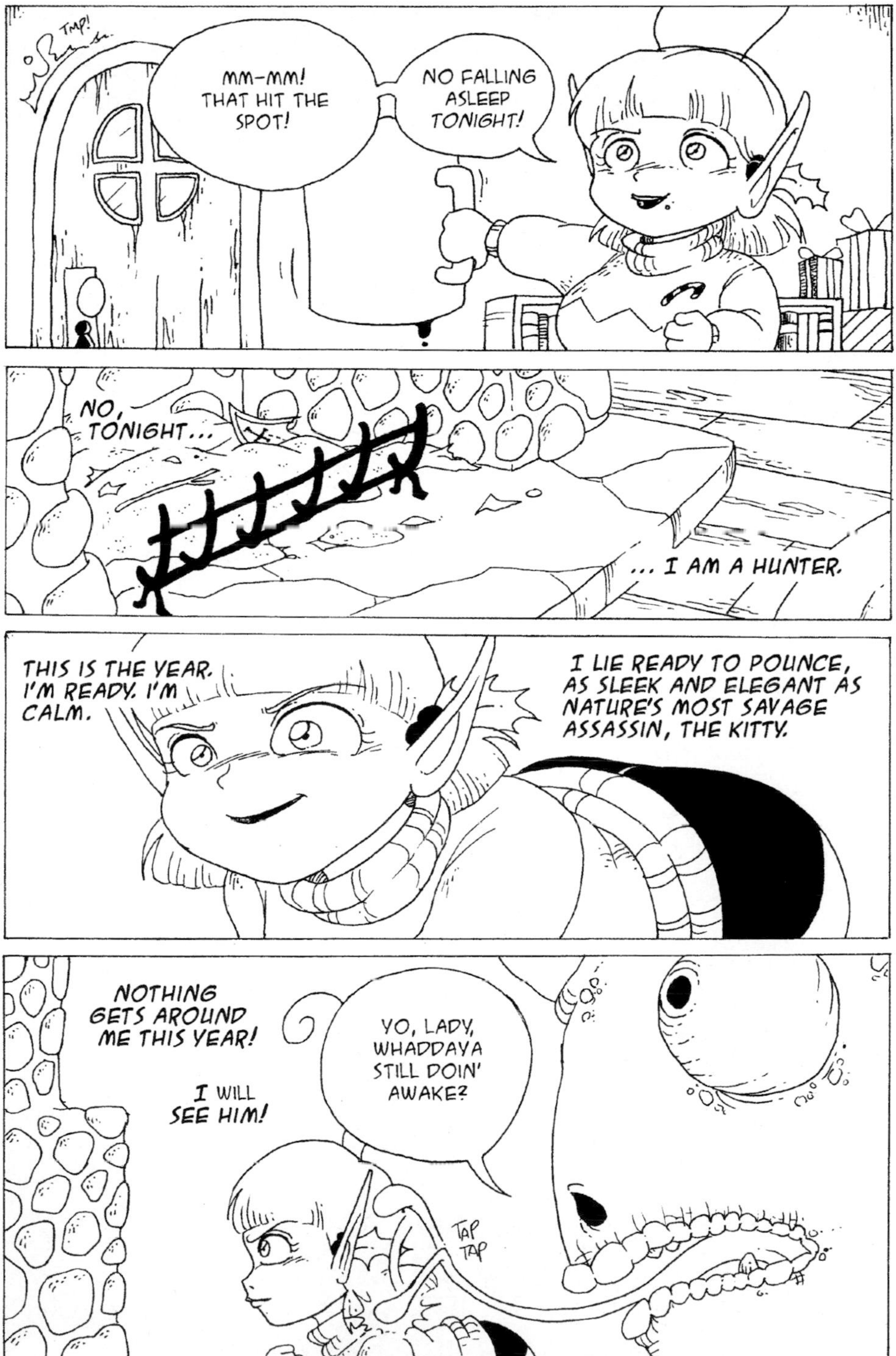
TMP!
MM-MM! THAT HIT THE SPOT!
NO FALLING ASLEEP TONIGHT!
NO, TONIGHT...
... I AM A HUNTER.
THIS IS THE YEAR. I'M READY. I'M CALM.
I LIE READY TO POUNCE, AS SLEEK AND ELEGANT AS NATURE'S MOST SAVAGE ASSASSIN, THE KITTY.
NOTHING GETS AROUND ME THIS YEAR!
I WILL SEE HIM!
YO, LADY, WHADDAYA STILL DOIN' AWAKE?
TAP TAP

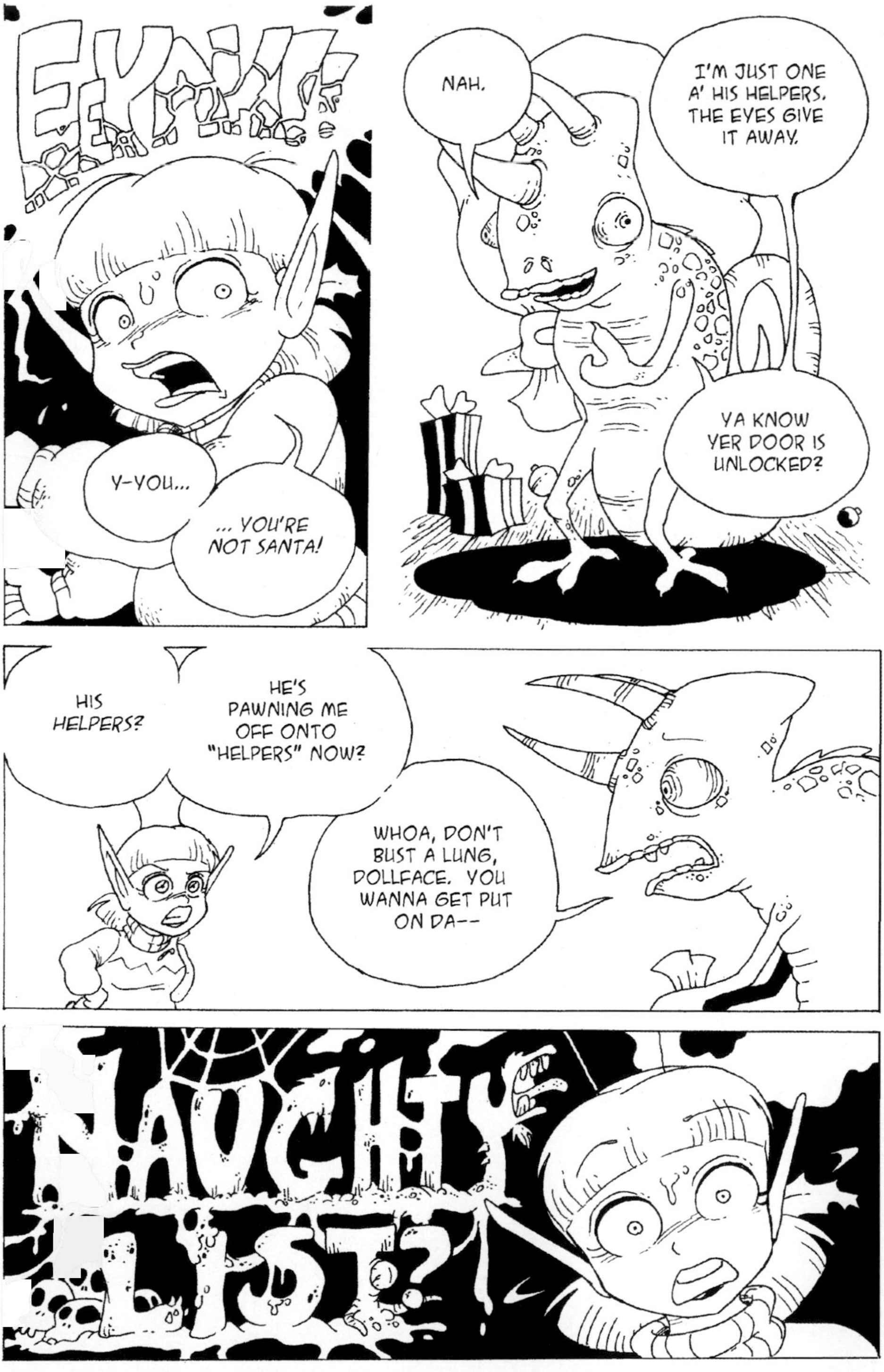
EEYAAAK!
NAH.
I'M JUST ONE A' HIS HELPERS. THE EYES GIVE IT AWAY.
Y-YOU...
... YOU'RE NOT SANTA!
YA KNOW YER DOOR IS UNLOCKED?
HIS HELPERS?
HE'S PAWNING ME OFF ONTO "HELPERS" NOW?
WHOA, DON'T BUST A LUNG, DOLLFACE. YOU WANNA GET PUT ON DA--
NAUGHTY LIST?!

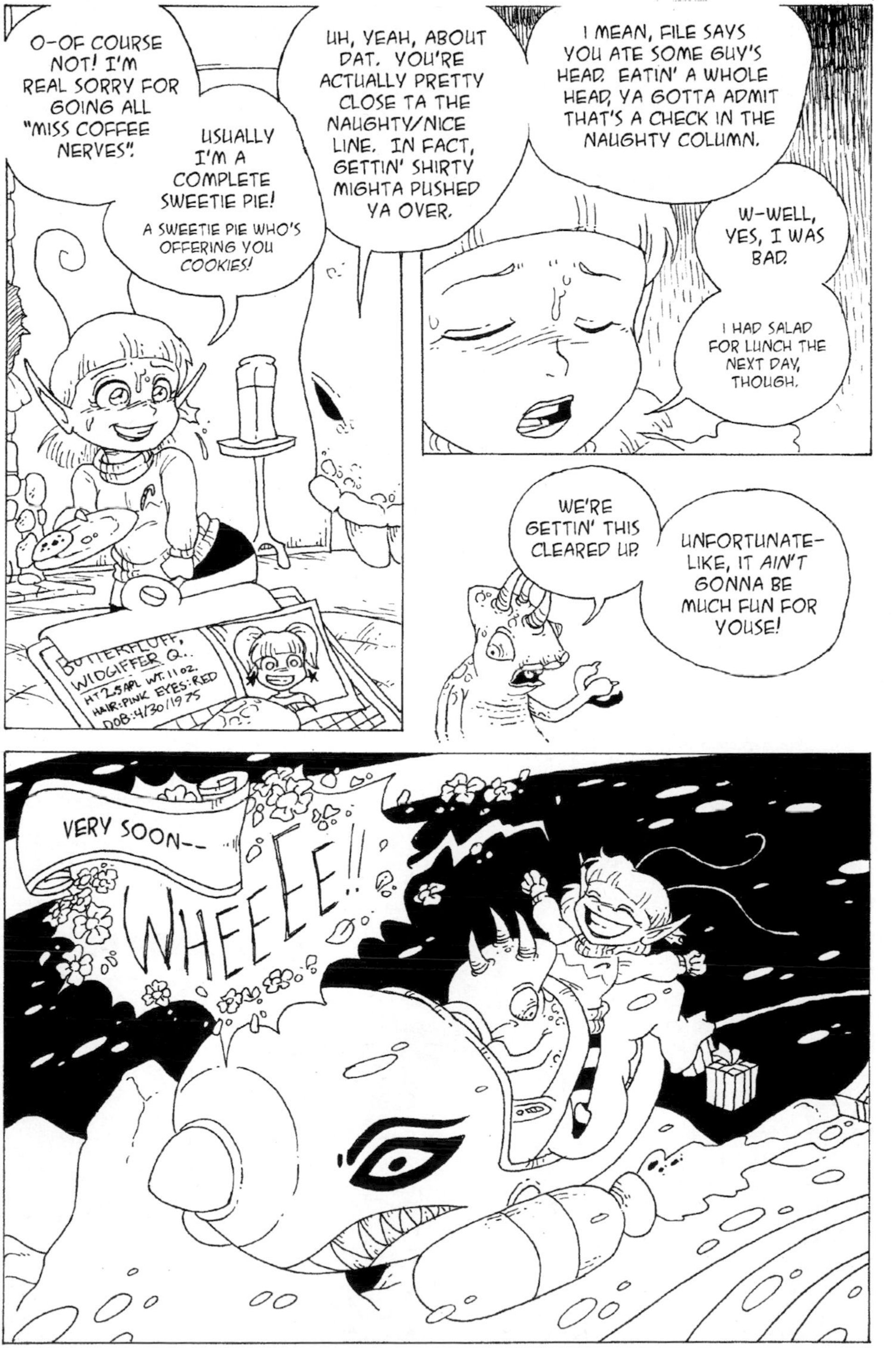
O-OF COURSE NOT! I'M REAL SORRY FOR GOING ALL "MISS COFFEE NERVES".
USUALLY I'M A COMPLETE SWEETIE PIE!
A SWEETIE PIE WHO'S OFFERING YOU COOKIES!
UH, YEAH, ABOUT DAT. YOU'RE ACTUALLY PRETTY CLOSE TA THE NAUGHTY/NICE LINE. IN FACT, GETTIN' SHIRTY MIGHTA PUSHED YA OVER.
BUTTERFLUFF, WIDGIFFER Q.
HT 2.5APL WT. 11 OZ.
HAIR: PINK EYES: RED
DOB: 4/30/1975
I MEAN, FILE SAYS YOU ATE SOME GUY'S HEAD. EATIN' A WHOLE HEAD, YA GOTTA ADMIT THAT'S A CHECK IN THE NAUGHTY COLUMN.
W-WELL, YES, I WAS BAD.
I HAD SALAD FOR LUNCH THE NEXT DAY, THOUGH.
WE'RE GETTIN' THIS CLEARED UP.
UNFORTUNATE-LIKE, IT AIN'T GONNA BE MUCH FUN FOR YOUSE!
VERY SOON--
WHEEEE!!

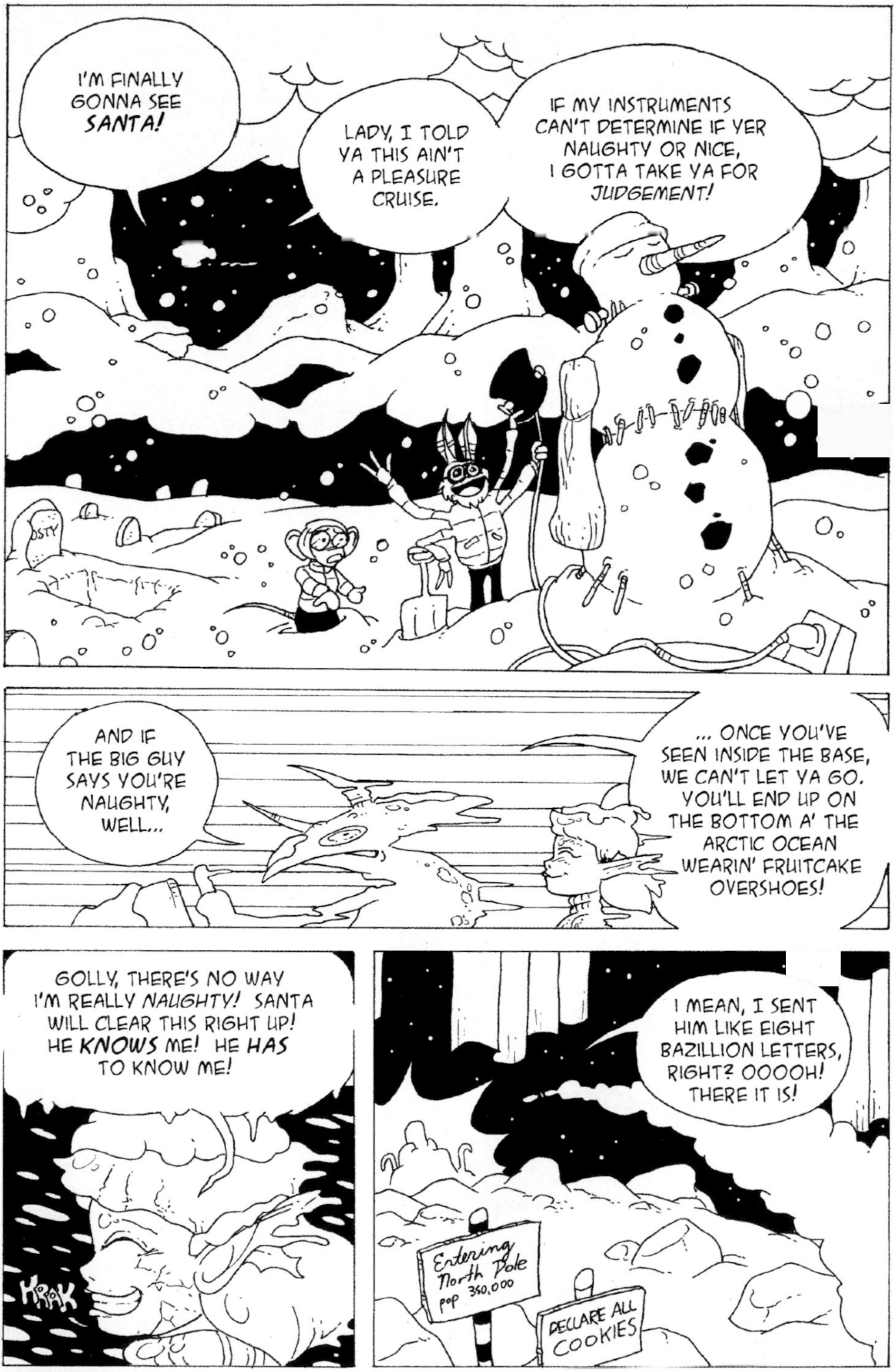
I'M FINALLY GONNA SEE SANTA!
LADY, I TOLD YA THIS AIN'T A PLEASURE CRUISE.
IF MY INSTRUMENTS CAN'T DETERMINE IF YER NAUGHTY OR NICE, I GOTTA TAKE YA FOR JUDGEMENT!
AND IF THE BIG GUY SAYS YOU'RE NAUGHTY, WELL...
... ONCE YOU'VE SEEN INSIDE THE BASE, WE CAN'T LET YA GO. YOU'LL END UP ON THE BOTTOM A' THE ARCTIC OCEAN WEARIN' FRUITCAKE OVERSHOES!
GOLLY, THERE'S NO WAY I'M REALLY NAUGHTY! SANTA WILL CLEAR THIS RIGHT UP! HE KNOWS ME! HE HAS TO KNOW ME!
KRRAK
I MEAN, I SENT HIM LIKE EIGHT BAZILLION LETTERS, RIGHT? OOOOH! THERE IT IS!
Entering North Pole pop 350,000
DECLARE ALL COOKIES

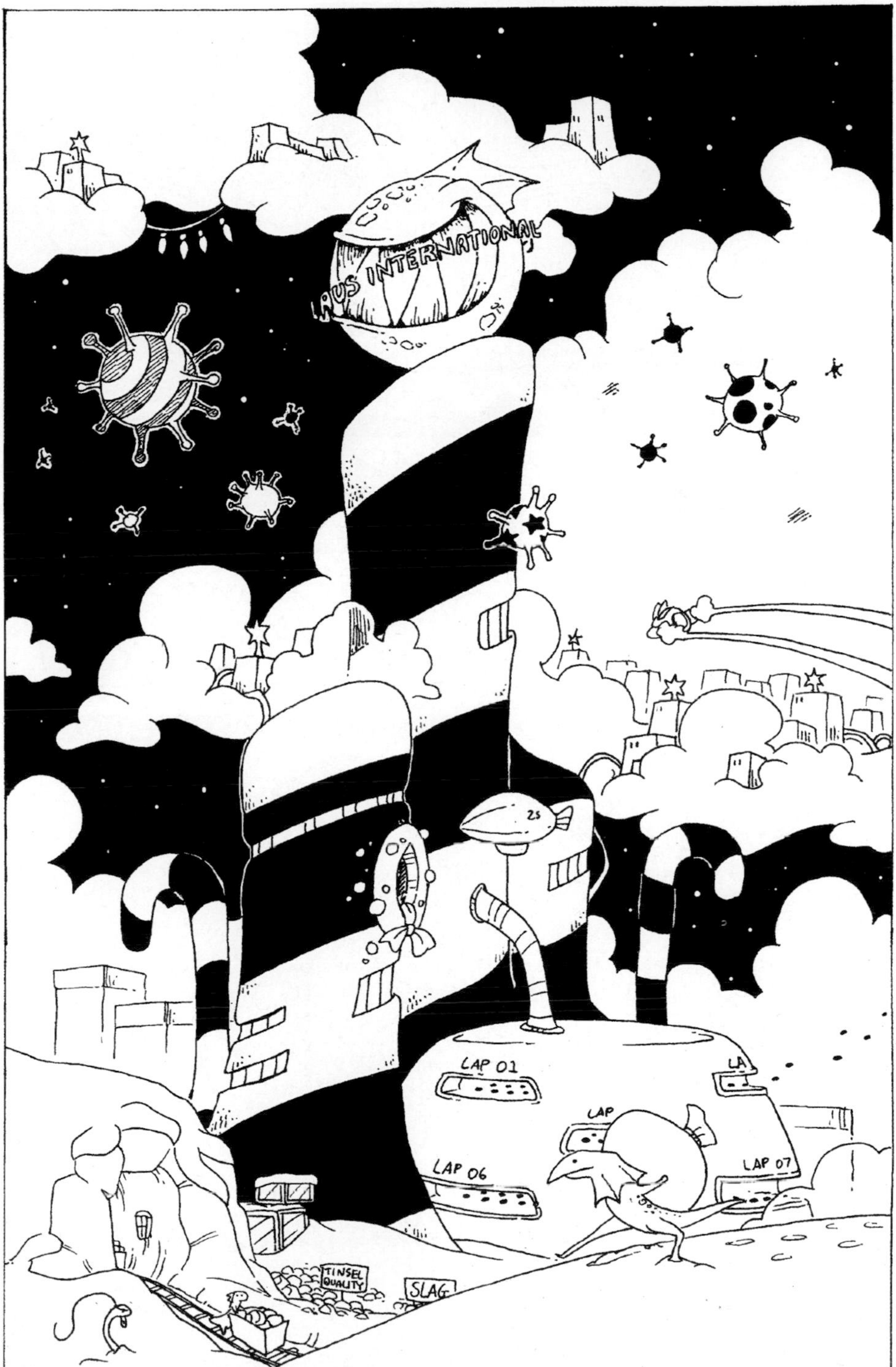
LAUS INTERNATIONAL
25
LAP 01
LA
LAP
LAP 06
LAP 07
TINSEL QUALITY
SLAG

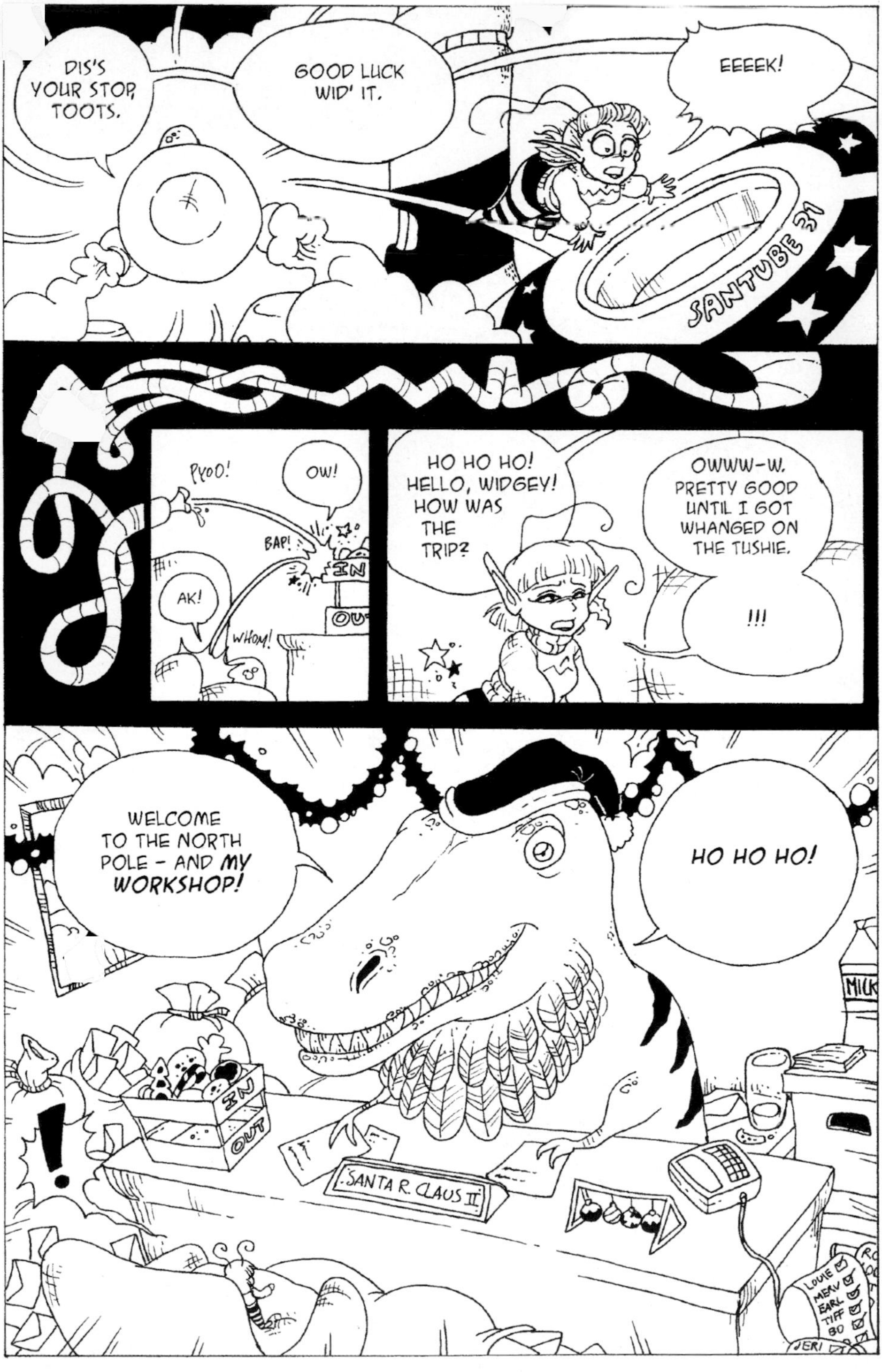
DIS'S YOUR STOP, TOOTS.
GOOD LUCK WID' IT.
EEEEK!
SANTUBE 31
PYOO!
OW!
BAP!
IN
OUT
AK!
WHOM!
HO HO HO! HELLO, WIDGEY! HOW WAS THE TRIP?
OWWW-W. PRETTY GOOD UNTIL I GOT WHANGED ON THE TUSHIE.
!!!
WELCOME TO THE NORTH POLE - AND *MY* *WORKSHOP!*
HO HO HO!
!
IN
OUT
SANTA R. CLAUS II
LOUIE
MERV
EARL
TIFF
BO
JERI

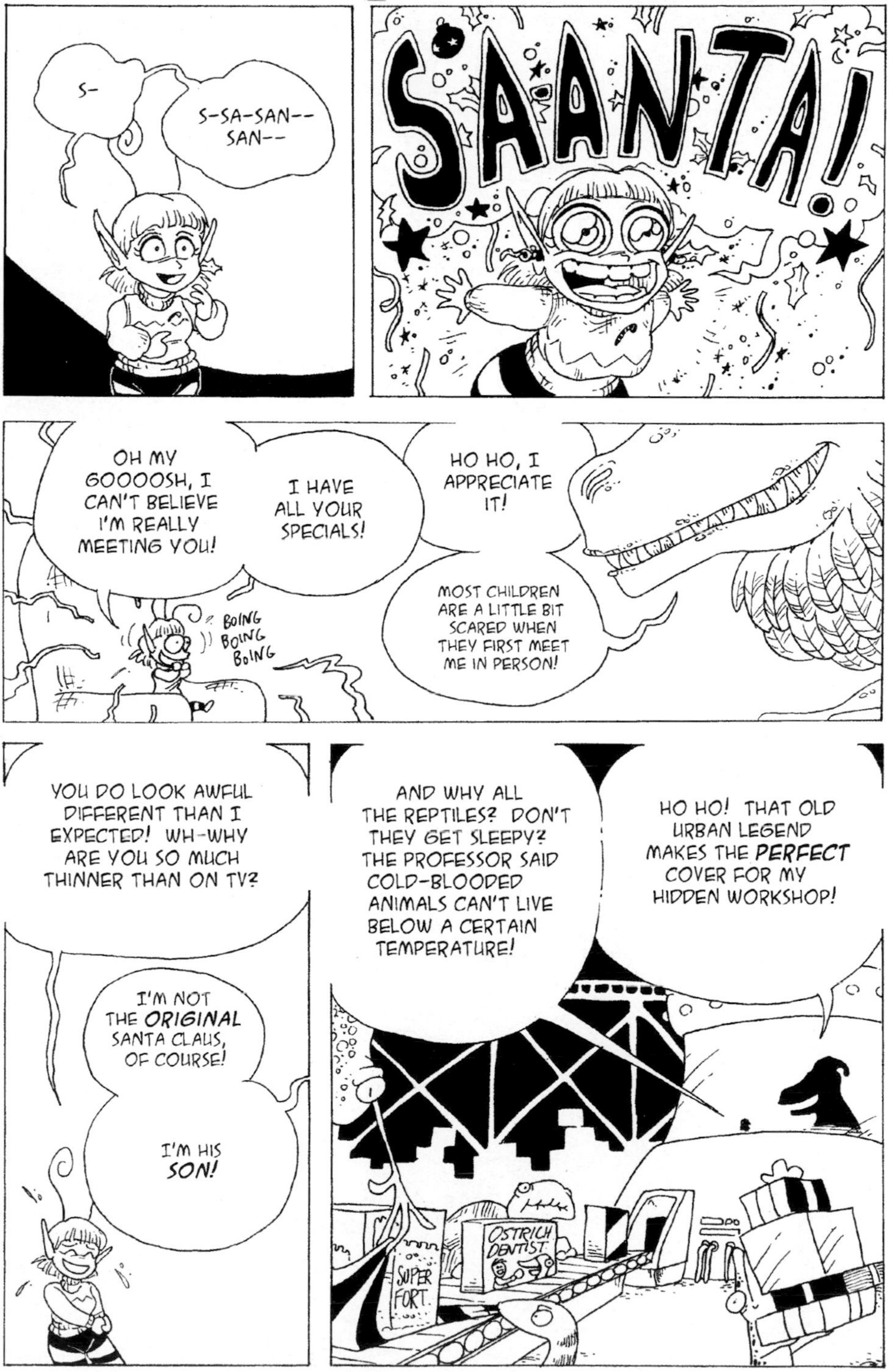

S-
S-SA-SAN--
SAN--
SAANTA!
OH MY GOOOOSH, I CAN'T BELIEVE I'M REALLY MEETING YOU!
I HAVE ALL YOUR SPECIALS!
BOING BOING BOING
HO HO, I APPRECIATE IT!
MOST CHILDREN ARE A LITTLE BIT SCARED WHEN THEY FIRST MEET ME IN PERSON!
YOU DO LOOK AWFUL DIFFERENT THAN I EXPECTED! WH-WHY ARE YOU SO MUCH THINNER THAN ON TV?
I'M NOT THE ORIGINAL SANTA CLAUS, OF COURSE!
I'M HIS SON!
AND WHY ALL THE REPTILES? DON'T THEY GET SLEEPY? THE PROFESSOR SAID COLD-BLOODED ANIMALS CAN'T LIVE BELOW A CERTAIN TEMPERATURE!
HO HO! THAT OLD URBAN LEGEND MAKES THE PERFECT COVER FOR MY HIDDEN WORKSHOP!
OSTRICH DENTIST
SUPER FORT

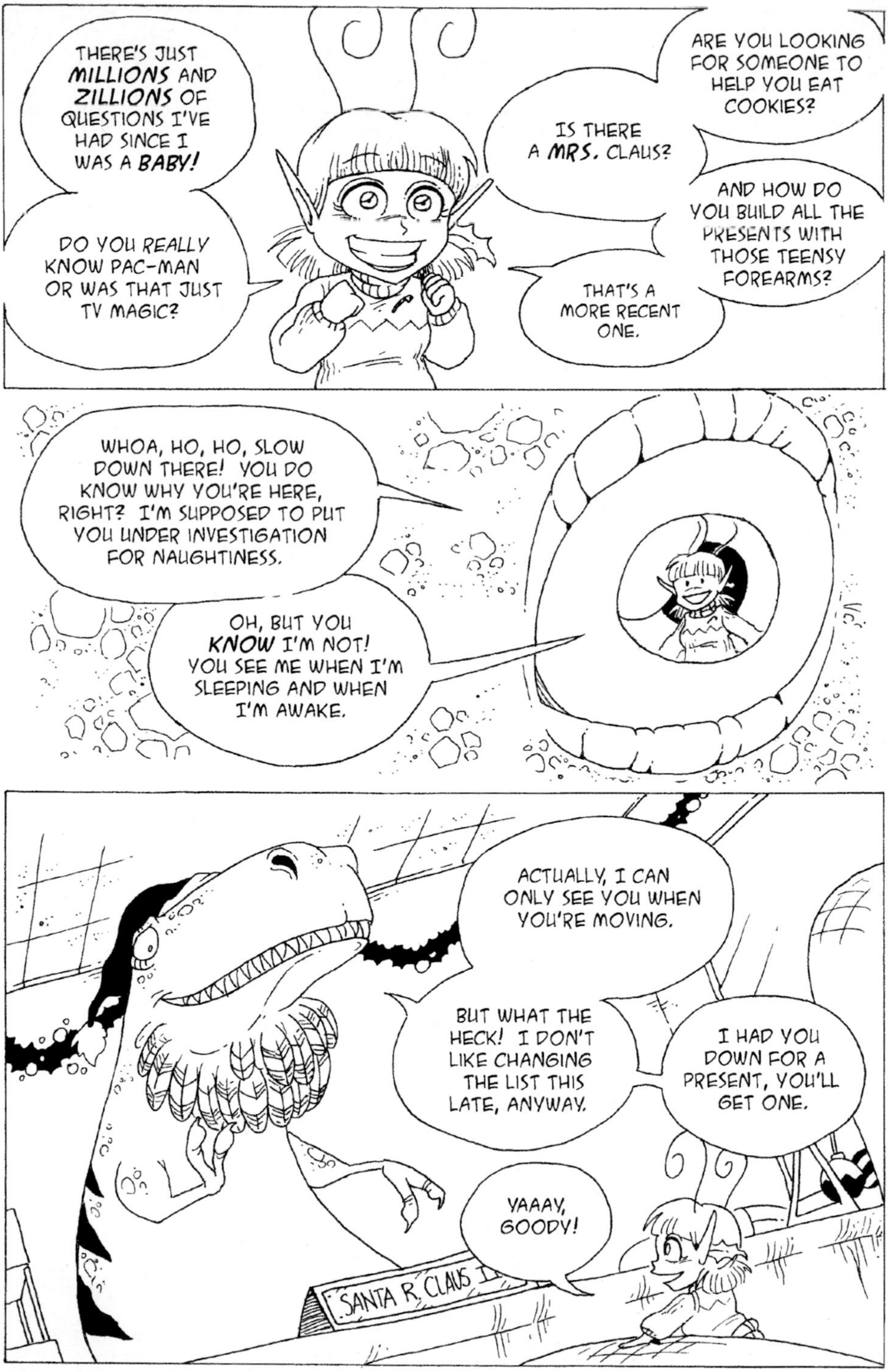
THERE'S JUST MILLIONS AND ZILLIONS OF QUESTIONS I'VE HAD SINCE I WAS A BABY!
DO YOU REALLY KNOW PAC-MAN OR WAS THAT JUST TV MAGIC?
IS THERE A MRS. CLAUS?
ARE YOU LOOKING FOR SOMEONE TO HELP YOU EAT COOKIES?
AND HOW DO YOU BUILD ALL THE PRESENTS WITH THOSE TEENSY FOREARMS?
THAT'S A MORE RECENT ONE.
WHOA, HO, HO, SLOW DOWN THERE! YOU DO KNOW WHY YOU'RE HERE, RIGHT? I'M SUPPOSED TO PUT YOU UNDER INVESTIGATION FOR NAUGHTINESS.
OH, BUT YOU KNOW I'M NOT! YOU SEE ME WHEN I'M SLEEPING AND WHEN I'M AWAKE.
ACTUALLY, I CAN ONLY SEE YOU WHEN YOU'RE MOVING.
BUT WHAT THE HECK! I DON'T LIKE CHANGING THE LIST THIS LATE, ANYWAY.
I HAD YOU DOWN FOR A PRESENT, YOU'LL GET ONE.
YAAAY, GOODY!
SANTA R. CLAUS

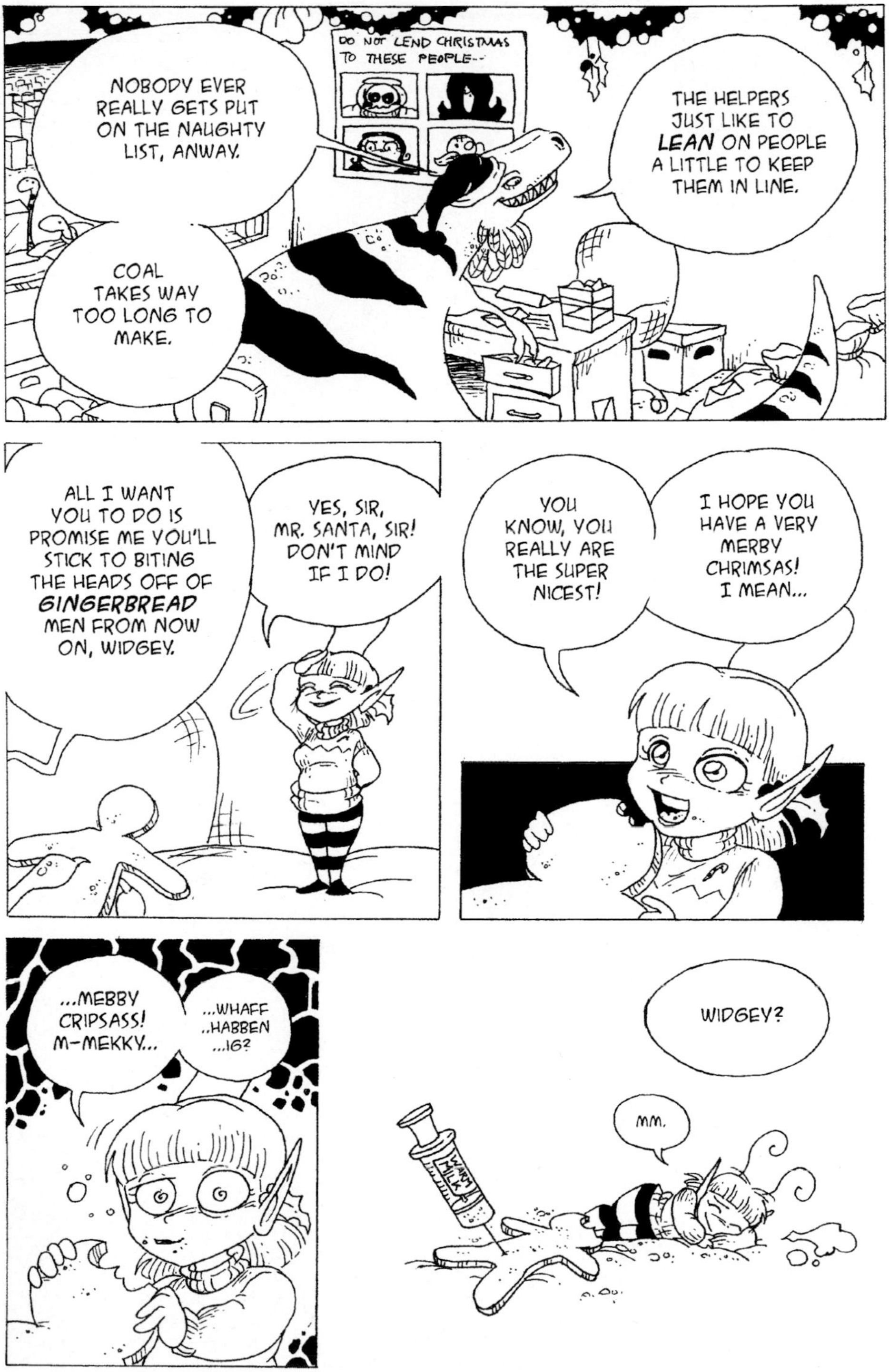
DO NOT LEND CHRISTMAS TO THESE PEOPLE--
NOBODY EVER REALLY GETS PUT ON THE NAUGHTY LIST, ANWAY.
COAL TAKES WAY TOO LONG TO MAKE.
THE HELPERS JUST LIKE TO LEAN ON PEOPLE A LITTLE TO KEEP THEM IN LINE.
ALL I WANT YOU TO DO IS PROMISE ME YOU'LL STICK TO BITING THE HEADS OFF OF GINGERBREAD MEN FROM NOW ON, WIDGEY.
YES, SIR, MR. SANTA, SIR! DON'T MIND IF I DO!
YOU KNOW, YOU REALLY ARE THE SUPER NICEST!
I HOPE YOU HAVE A VERY MERBY CHRIMSAS! I MEAN...
...MEBBY CRIPSASS! M-MEKKY...
...WHAFF ..HABBEN ...16?
WIDGEY?
MM.
WARM MILK

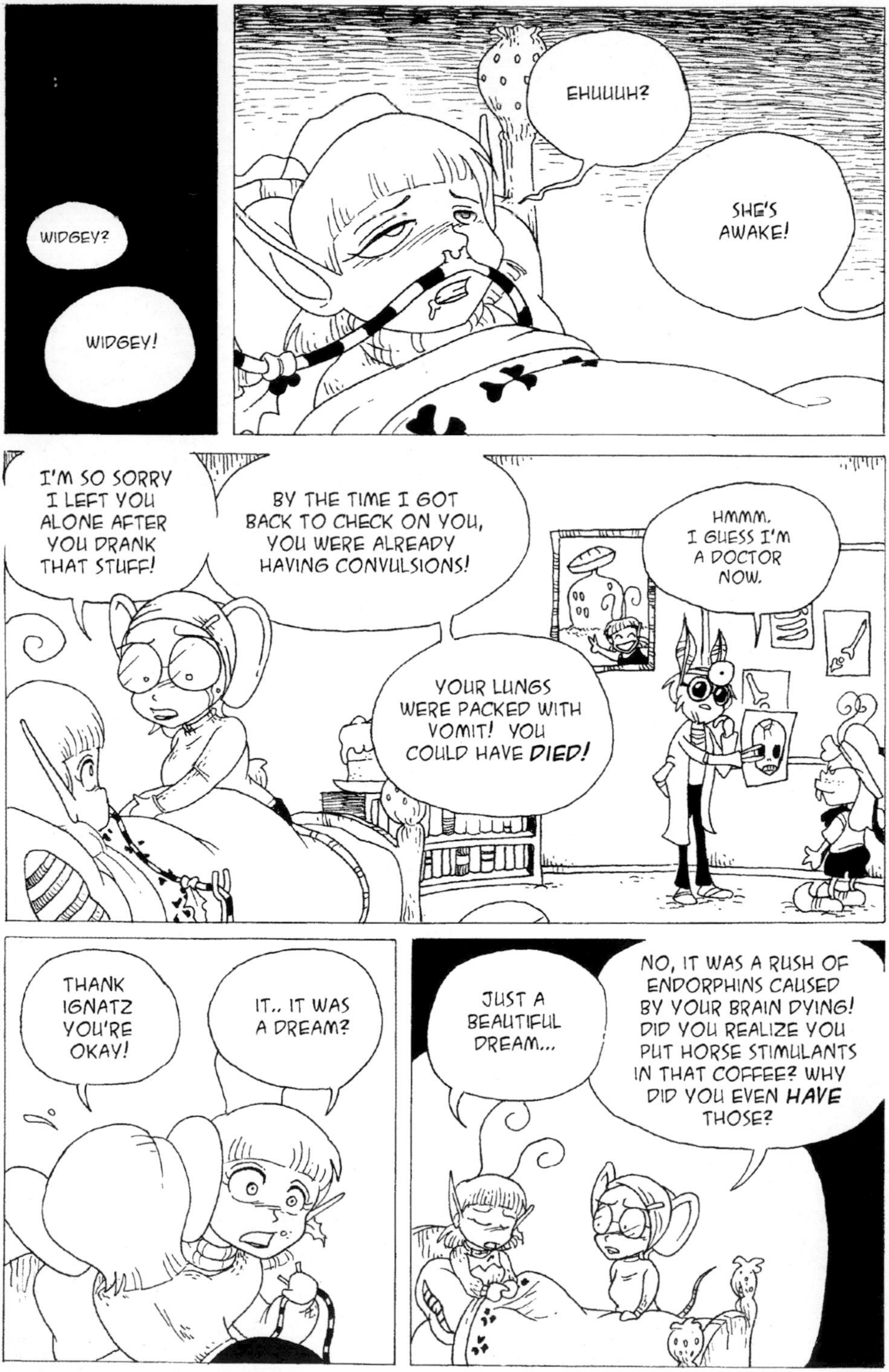
WIDGEY?
WIDGEY!
EHUUUH?
SHE'S AWAKE!
I'M SO SORRY I LEFT YOU ALONE AFTER YOU DRANK THAT STUFF!
BY THE TIME I GOT BACK TO CHECK ON YOU, YOU WERE ALREADY HAVING CONVULSIONS!
YOUR LUNGS WERE PACKED WITH VOMIT! YOU COULD HAVE **DIED!**
HMMM. I GUESS I'M A DOCTOR NOW.
THANK IGNATZ YOU'RE OKAY!
IT.. IT WAS A DREAM?
JUST A BEAUTIFUL DREAM...
NO, IT WAS A RUSH OF ENDORPHINS CAUSED BY YOUR BRAIN DYING! DID YOU REALIZE YOU PUT HORSE STIMULANTS IN THAT COFFEE? WHY DID YOU EVEN **HAVE** THOSE?

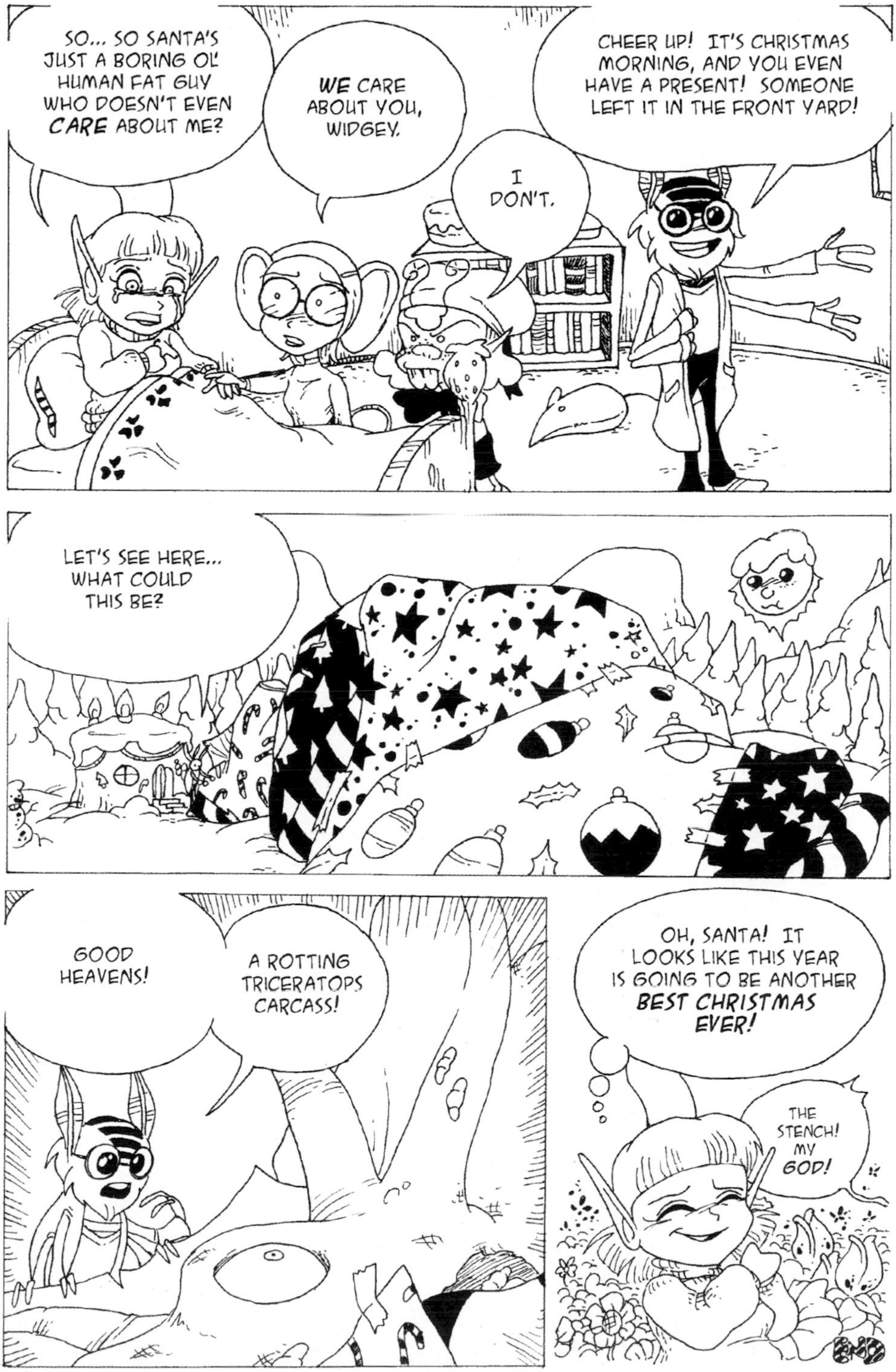
SO... SO SANTA'S JUST A BORING OL' HUMAN FAT GUY WHO DOESN'T EVEN CARE ABOUT ME?
WE CARE ABOUT YOU, WIDGEY.
I DON'T.
CHEER UP! IT'S CHRISTMAS MORNING, AND YOU EVEN HAVE A PRESENT! SOMEONE LEFT IT IN THE FRONT YARD!
LET'S SEE HERE... WHAT COULD THIS BE?
GOOD HEAVENS!
A ROTTING TRICERATOPS CARCASS!
OH, SANTA! IT LOOKS LIKE THIS YEAR IS GOING TO BE ANOTHER BEST CHRISTMAS EVER!
THE STENCH! MY GOD!

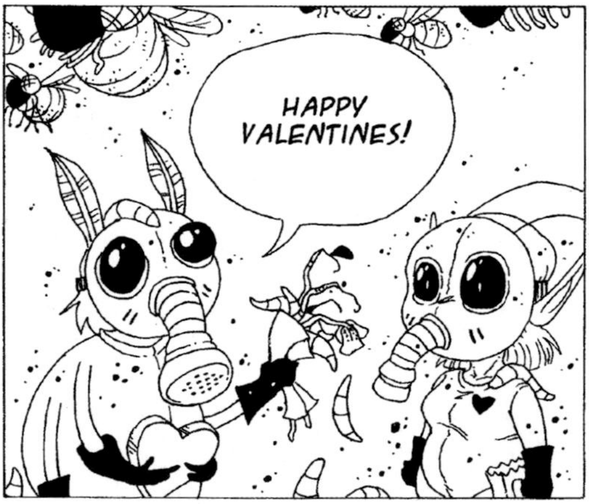
HAPPY VALENTINES!

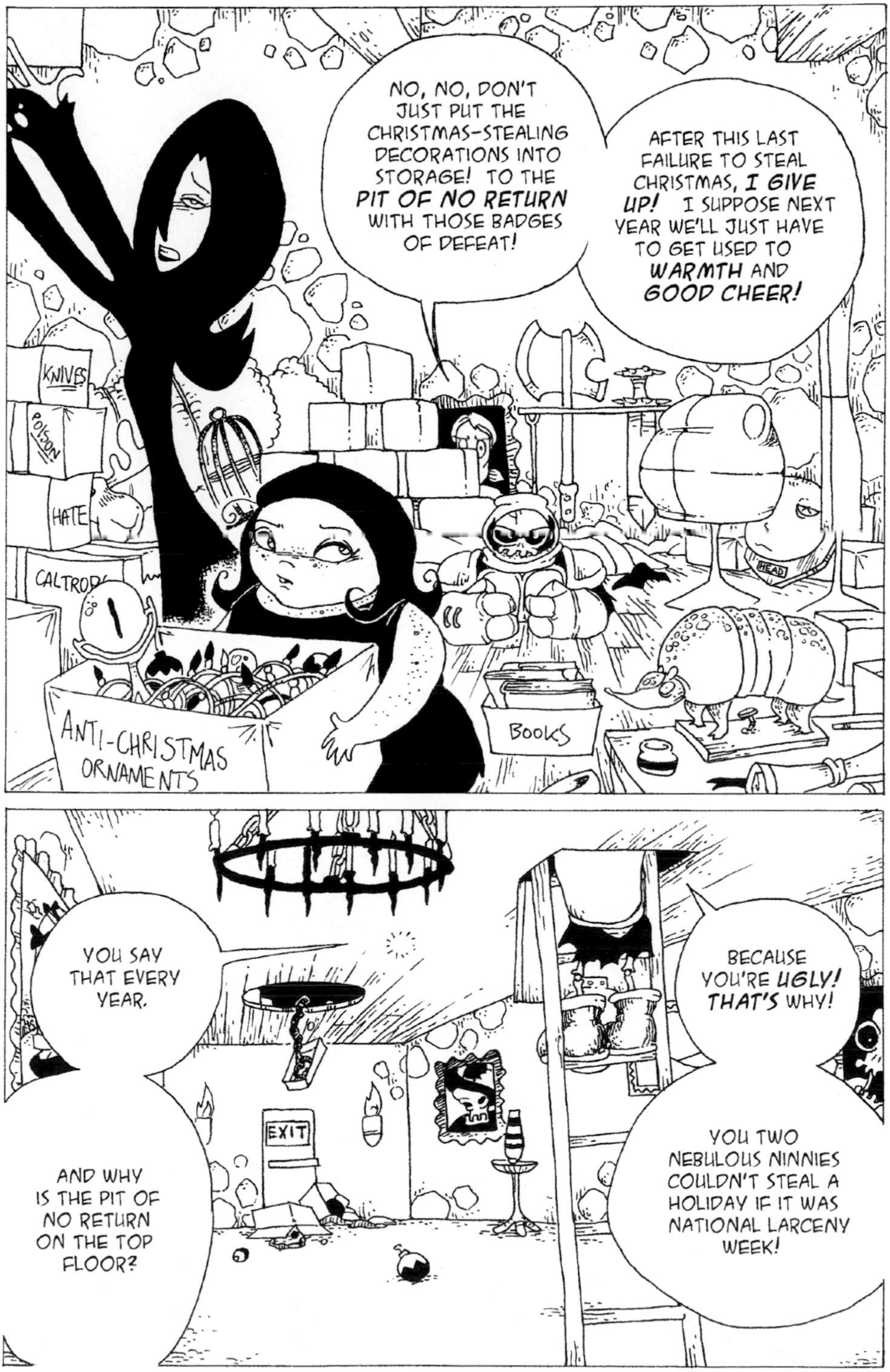
NO, NO, DON'T JUST PUT THE CHRISTMAS-STEALING DECORATIONS INTO STORAGE! TO THE PIT OF NO RETURN WITH THOSE BADGES OF DEFEAT!
AFTER THIS LAST FAILURE TO STEAL CHRISTMAS, I GIVE UP! I SUPPOSE NEXT YEAR WE'LL JUST HAVE TO GET USED TO WARMTH AND GOOD CHEER!
KNIVES
POISON
HATE
ANTI-CHRISTMAS ORNAMENTS
BOOKS
HEAD
YOU SAY THAT EVERY YEAR.
AND WHY IS THE PIT OF NO RETURN ON THE TOP FLOOR?
BECAUSE YOU'RE UGLY! THAT'S WHY!
YOU TWO NEBULOUS NINNIES COULDN'T STEAL A HOLIDAY IF IT WAS NATIONAL LARCENY WEEK!
EXIT

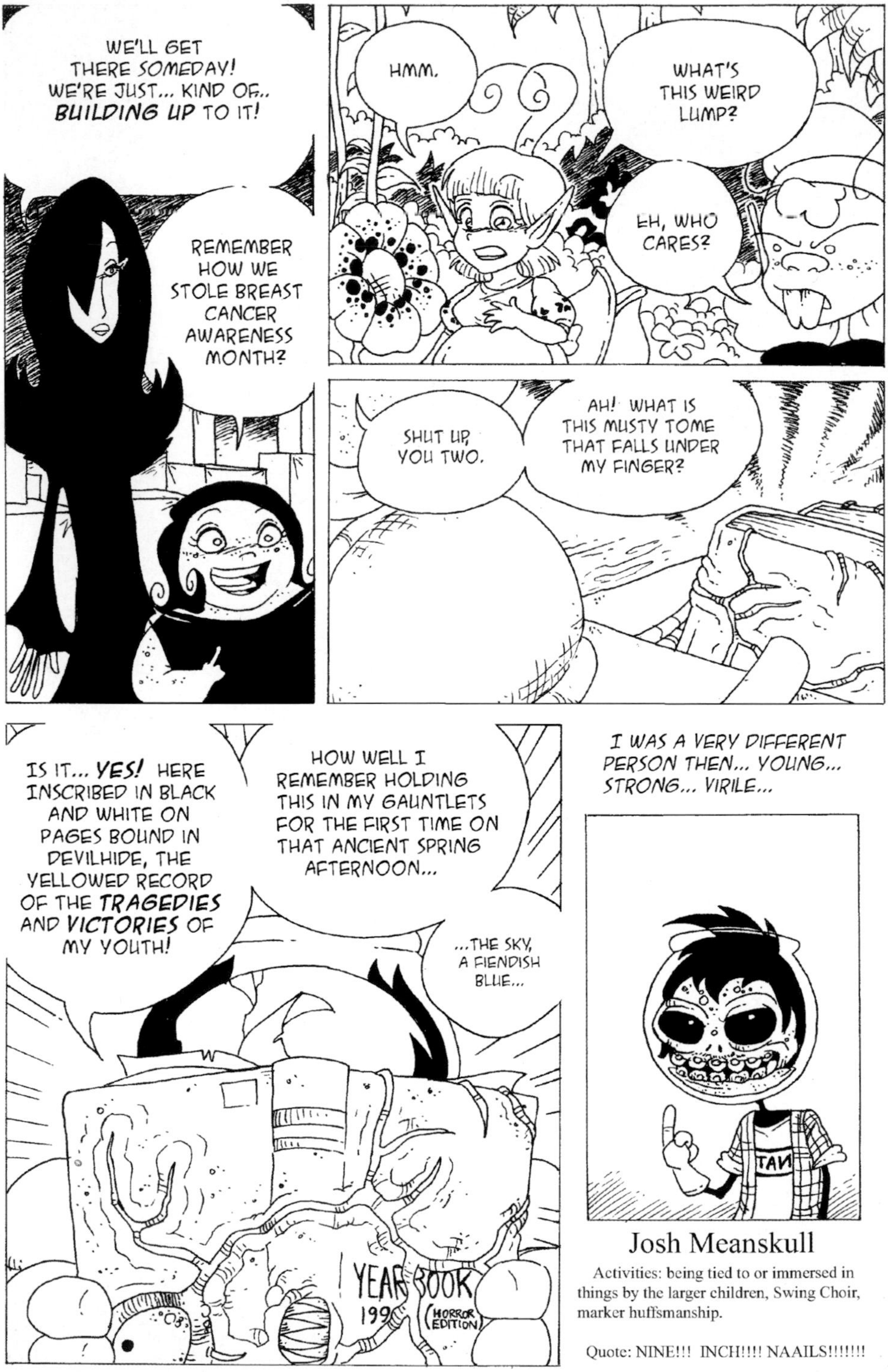
WE'LL GET THERE SOMEDAY! WE'RE JUST... KIND OF.. BUILDING UP TO IT!
REMEMBER HOW WE STOLE BREAST CANCER AWARENESS MONTH?
HMM.
WHAT'S THIS WEIRD LUMP?
EH, WHO CARES?
SHUT UP, YOU TWO.
AH! WHAT IS THIS MUSTY TOME THAT FALLS UNDER MY FINGER?
IS IT... YES! HERE INSCRIBED IN BLACK AND WHITE ON PAGES BOUND IN DEVILHIDE, THE YELLOWED RECORD OF THE TRAGEDIES AND VICTORIES OF MY YOUTH!
HOW WELL I REMEMBER HOLDING THIS IN MY GAUNTLETS FOR THE FIRST TIME ON THAT ANCIENT SPRING AFTERNOON...
...THE SKY, A FIENDISH BLUE...
YEARBOOK
199
(HORROR EDITION)
I WAS A VERY DIFFERENT PERSON THEN... YOUNG... STRONG... VIRILE...
TAN
Josh Meanskull
Activities: being tied to or immersed in things by the larger children, Swing Choir, marker huffsmanship.
Quote: NINE!!! INCH!!!! NAAILS!!!!!!!

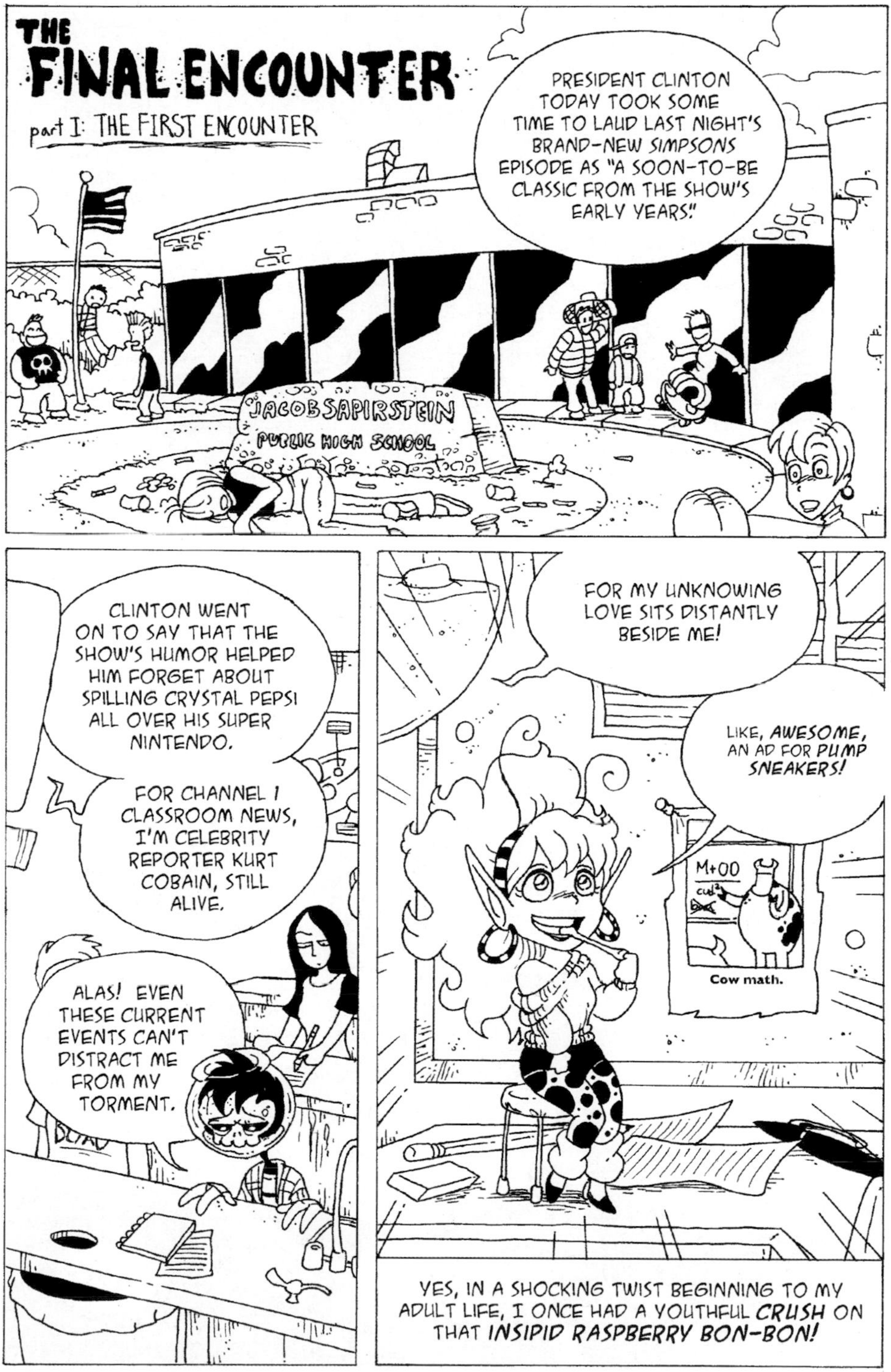
THE FINAL ENCOUNTER
part I: THE FIRST ENCOUNTER
PRESIDENT CLINTON TODAY TOOK SOME TIME TO LAUD LAST NIGHT'S BRAND-NEW SIMPSONS EPISODE AS "A SOON-TO-BE CLASSIC FROM THE SHOW'S EARLY YEARS!"
JACOB SAPIRSTEIN PUBLIC HIGH SCHOOL
CLINTON WENT ON TO SAY THAT THE SHOW'S HUMOR HELPED HIM FORGET ABOUT SPILLING CRYSTAL PEPSI ALL OVER HIS SUPER NINTENDO.
FOR CHANNEL 1 CLASSROOM NEWS, I'M CELEBRITY REPORTER KURT COBAIN, STILL ALIVE.
ALAS! EVEN THESE CURRENT EVENTS CAN'T DISTRACT ME FROM MY TORMENT.
FOR MY UNKNOWING LOVE SITS DISTANTLY BESIDE ME!
LIKE, AWESOME, AN AD FOR PUMP SNEAKERS!
M+OO
Cow math.
YES, IN A SHOCKING TWIST BEGINNING TO MY ADULT LIFE, I ONCE HAD A YOUTHFUL CRUSH ON THAT INSIPID RASPBERRY BON-BON!

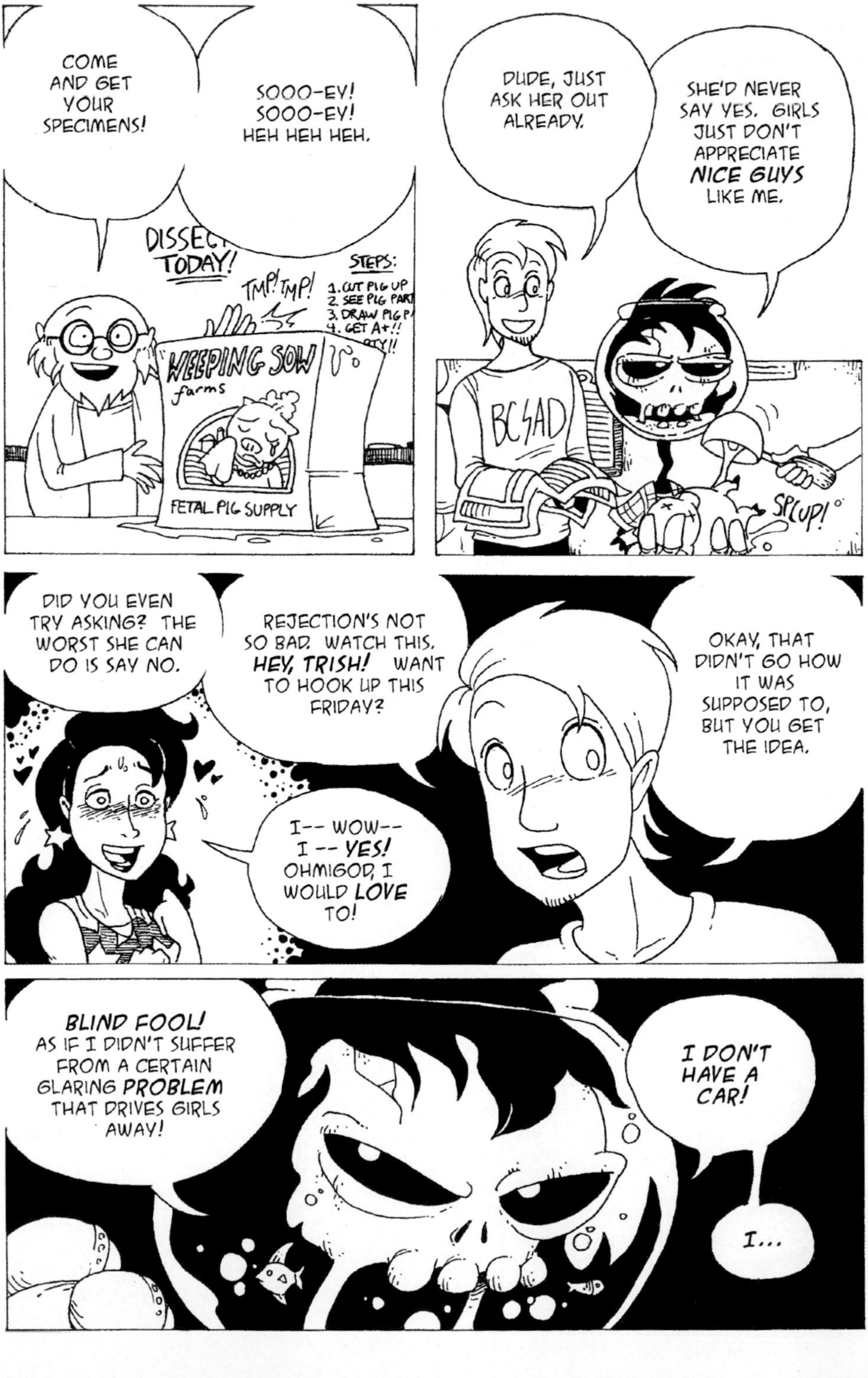
COME AND GET YOUR SPECIMENS!
SOOO-EY! SOOO-EY! HEH HEH HEH.
DISSECT TODAY!
STEPS:
1. CUT PIG UP
2. SEE PIG PART
3. DRAW PIG P
4. GET A+!!
TMP! TMP!
WEEPING SOW farms
FETAL PIG SUPPLY
DUDE, JUST ASK HER OUT ALREADY.
SHE'D NEVER SAY YES. GIRLS JUST DON'T APPRECIATE NICE GUYS LIKE ME.
BCSAD
SPLUP!
DID YOU EVEN TRY ASKING? THE WORST SHE CAN DO IS SAY NO.
REJECTION'S NOT SO BAD. WATCH THIS. HEY, TRISH! WANT TO HOOK UP THIS FRIDAY?
I-- WOW-- I -- YES! OHMIGOD, I WOULD LOVE TO!
OKAY, THAT DIDN'T GO HOW IT WAS SUPPOSED TO, BUT YOU GET THE IDEA.
BLIND FOOL! AS IF I DIDN'T SUFFER FROM A CERTAIN GLARING PROBLEM THAT DRIVES GIRLS AWAY!
I...
I DON'T HAVE A CAR!

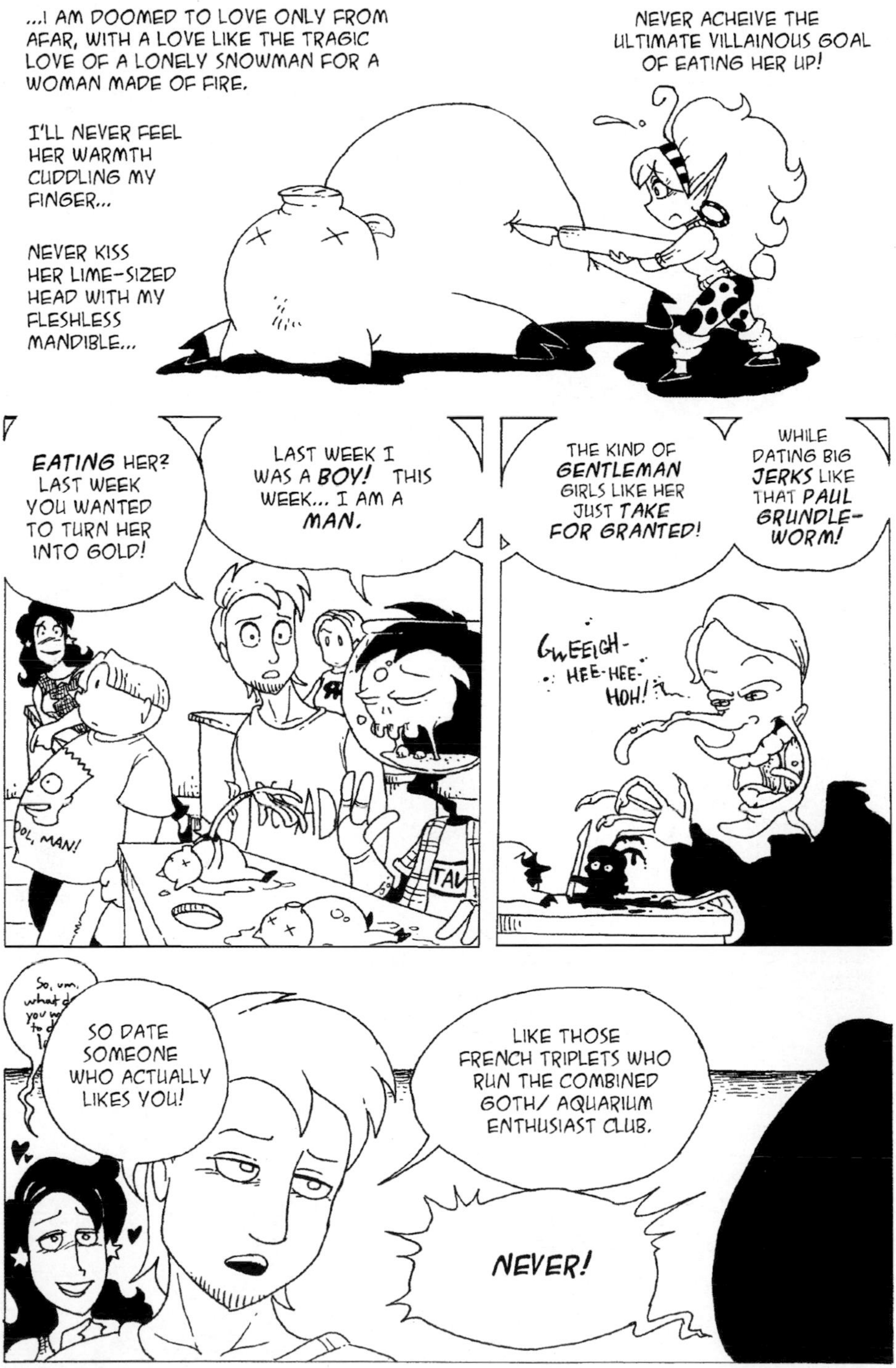
...I AM DOOMED TO LOVE ONLY FROM AFAR, WITH A LOVE LIKE THE TRAGIC LOVE OF A LONELY SNOWMAN FOR A WOMAN MADE OF FIRE.
I'LL NEVER FEEL HER WARMTH CUDDLING MY FINGER...
NEVER KISS HER LIME-SIZED HEAD WITH MY FLESHLESS MANDIBLE...
NEVER ACHEIVE THE ULTIMATE VILLAINOUS GOAL OF EATING HER UP!
EATING HER? LAST WEEK YOU WANTED TO TURN HER INTO GOLD!
LAST WEEK I WAS A BOY! THIS WEEK... I AM A MAN.
DOL, MAN!
THE KIND OF GENTLEMAN GIRLS LIKE HER JUST TAKE FOR GRANTED!
WHILE DATING BIG JERKS LIKE THAT PAUL GRUNDLEWORM!
GWEEIGH-HEE-HEE-HOH!
So, um,
SO DATE SOMEONE WHO ACTUALLY LIKES YOU!
LIKE THOSE FRENCH TRIPLETS WHO RUN THE COMBINED GOTH/ AQUARIUM ENTHUSIAST CLUB.
NEVER!

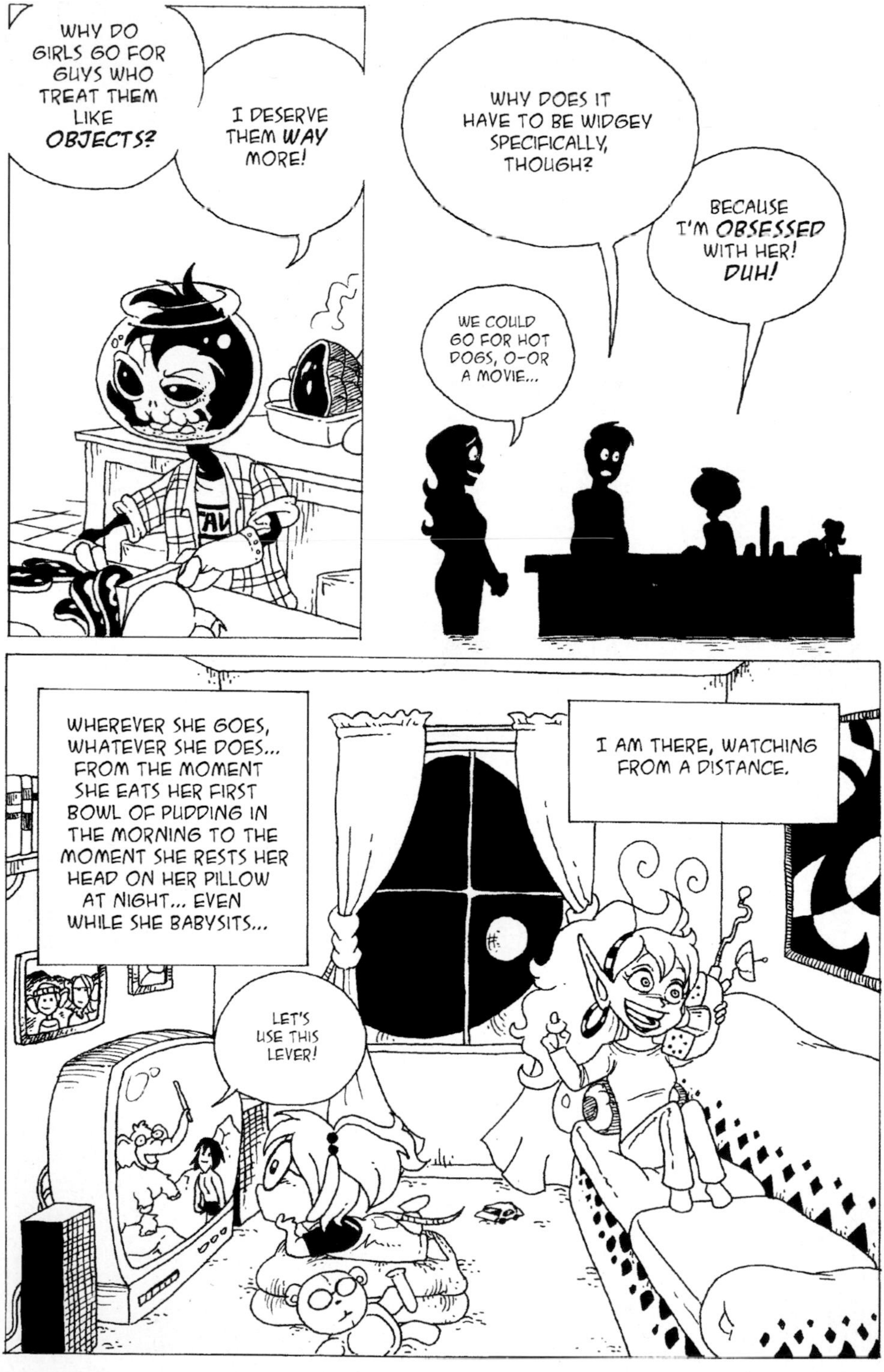
WHY DO GIRLS GO FOR GUYS WHO TREAT THEM LIKE OBJECTS?
I DESERVE THEM WAY MORE!
WHY DOES IT HAVE TO BE WIDGEY SPECIFICALLY, THOUGH?
BECAUSE I'M OBSESSED WITH HER! DUH!
WE COULD GO FOR HOT DOGS, O-OR A MOVIE...
WHEREVER SHE GOES, WHATEVER SHE DOES... FROM THE MOMENT SHE EATS HER FIRST BOWL OF PUDDING IN THE MORNING TO THE MOMENT SHE RESTS HER HEAD ON HER PILLOW AT NIGHT... EVEN WHILE SHE BABYSITS...
I AM THERE, WATCHING FROM A DISTANCE.
LET'S USE THIS LEVER!

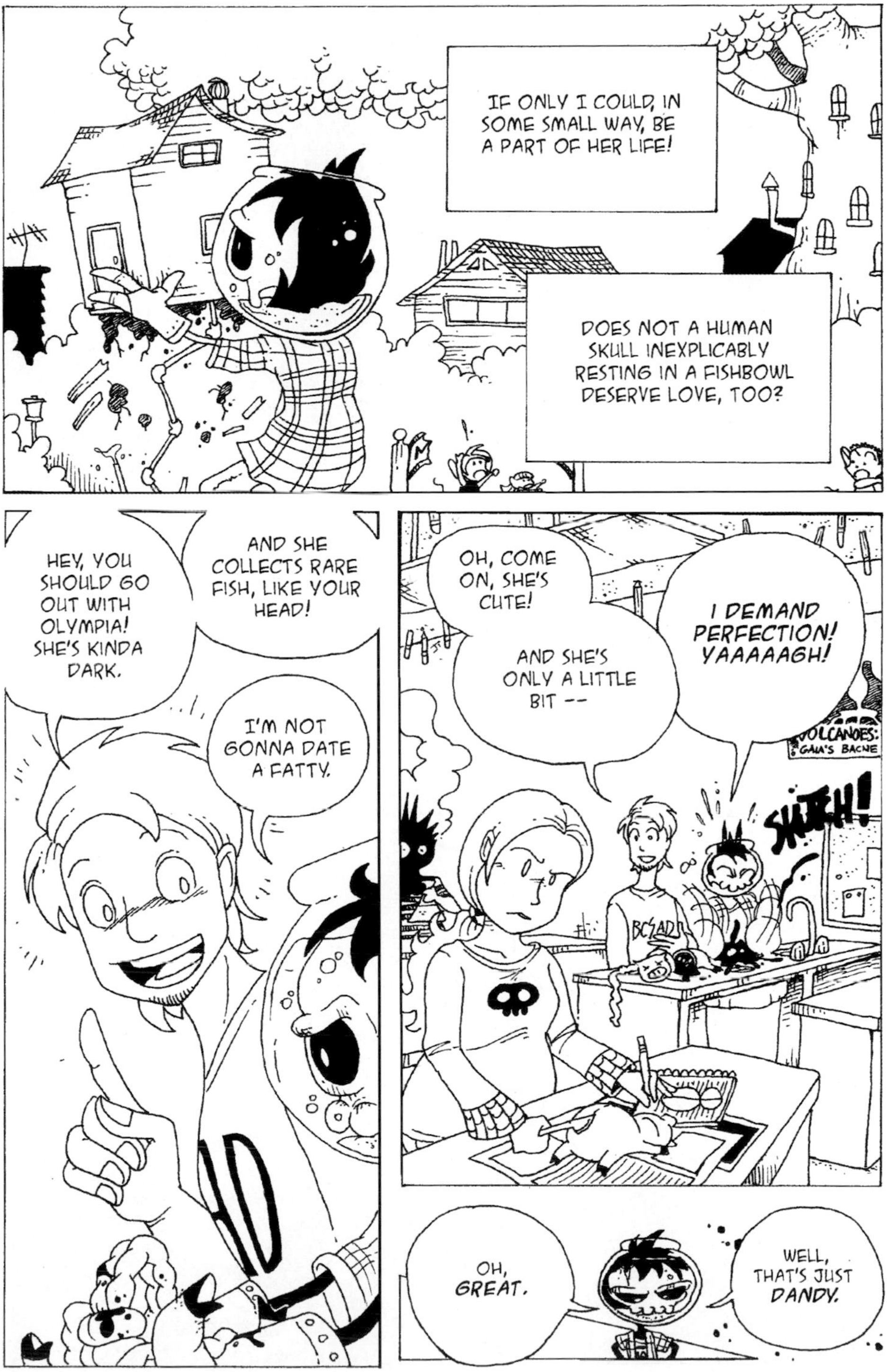
IF ONLY I COULD, IN SOME SMALL WAY, BE A PART OF HER LIFE!
DOES NOT A HUMAN SKULL INEXPLICABLY RESTING IN A FISHBOWL DESERVE LOVE, TOO?
HEY, YOU SHOULD GO OUT WITH OLYMPIA! SHE'S KINDA DARK.
AND SHE COLLECTS RARE FISH, LIKE YOUR HEAD!
I'M NOT GONNA DATE A FATTY.
OH, COME ON, SHE'S CUTE!
AND SHE'S ONLY A LITTLE BIT --
I DEMAND PERFECTION! YAAAAAGH!
VOLCANOES: GAIA'S BACNE
SKLITCH!
OH, GREAT.
WELL, THAT'S JUST DANDY.

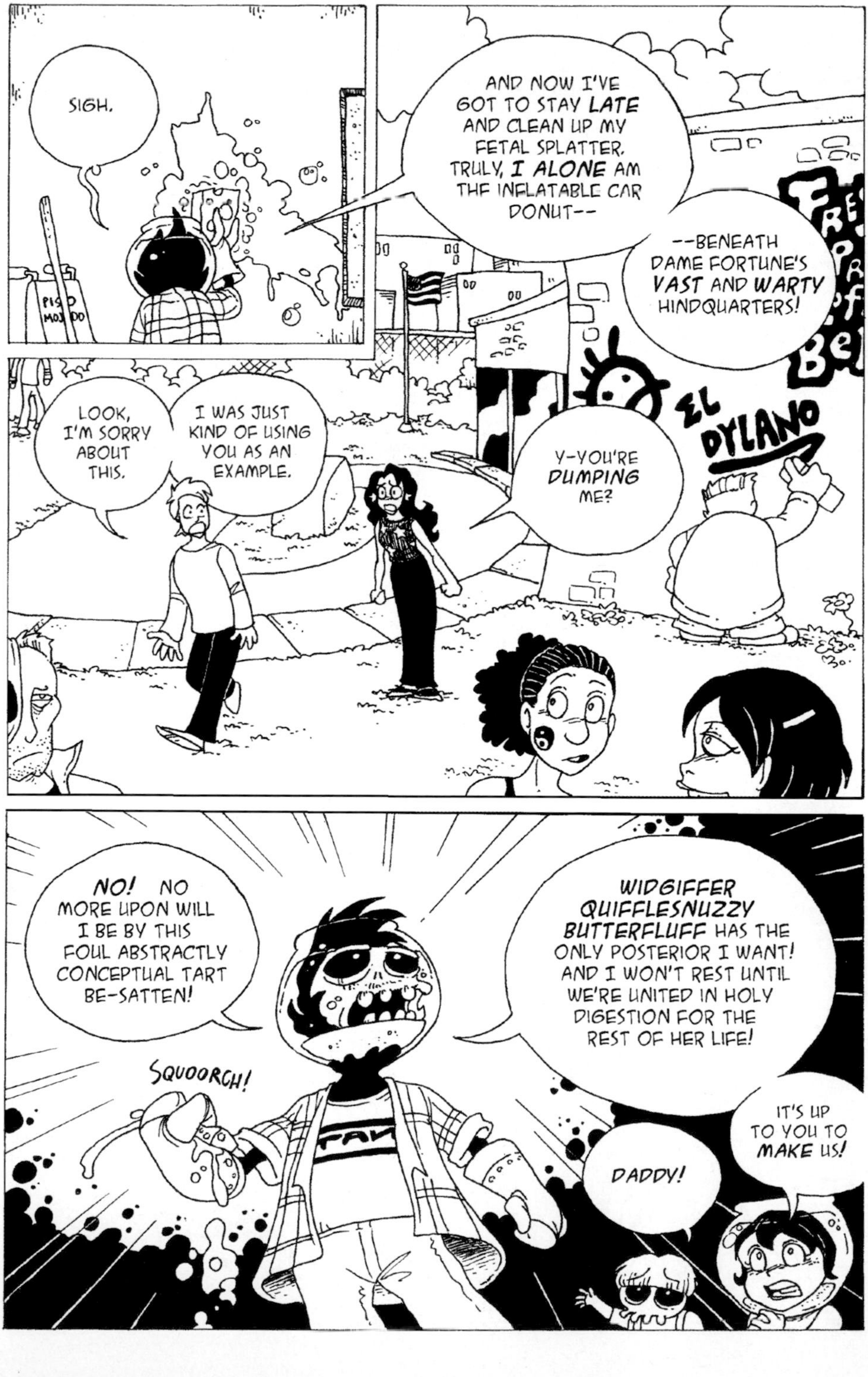
SIGH.
AND NOW I'VE GOT TO STAY LATE AND CLEAN UP MY FETAL SPLATTER. TRULY, I ALONE AM THE INFLATABLE CAR DONUT--
--BENEATH DAME FORTUNE'S VAST AND WARTY HINDQUARTERS!
LOOK, I'M SORRY ABOUT THIS.
I WAS JUST KIND OF USING YOU AS AN EXAMPLE.
Y-YOU'RE DUMPING ME?
EL DYLANO
NO! NO MORE UPON WILL I BE BY THIS FOUL ABSTRACTLY CONCEPTUAL TART BE-SATTEN!
WIDGIFFER QUIFFLESNUZZY BUTTERFLUFF HAS THE ONLY POSTERIOR I WANT! AND I WON'T REST UNTIL WE'RE UNITED IN HOLY DIGESTION FOR THE REST OF HER LIFE!
SQUOORCH!
DADDY!
IT'S UP TO YOU TO MAKE US!

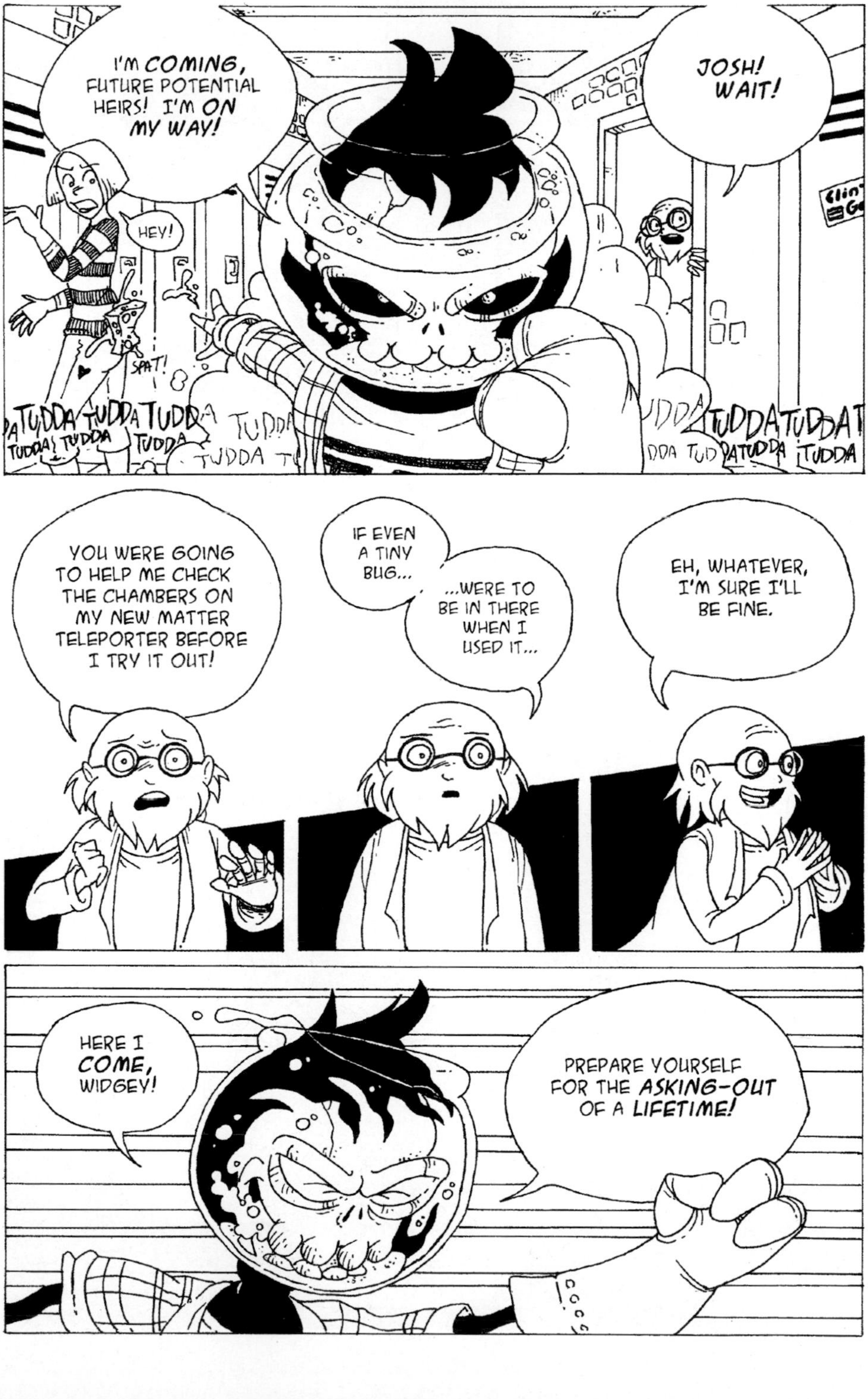
I'M COMING, FUTURE POTENTIAL HEIRS! I'M ON MY WAY!
JOSH! WAIT!
HEY!
SPAT!
TUDDA TUDDA TUDDA TUDDA TUDDA TUDDA TUDDA TUDDA TUDDA
YOU WERE GOING TO HELP ME CHECK THE CHAMBERS ON MY NEW MATTER TELEPORTER BEFORE I TRY IT OUT!
IF EVEN A TINY BUG...
...WERE TO BE IN THERE WHEN I USED IT...
EH, WHATEVER, I'M SURE I'LL BE FINE.
HERE I COME, WIDGEY!
PREPARE YOURSELF FOR THE ASKING-OUT OF A LIFETIME!

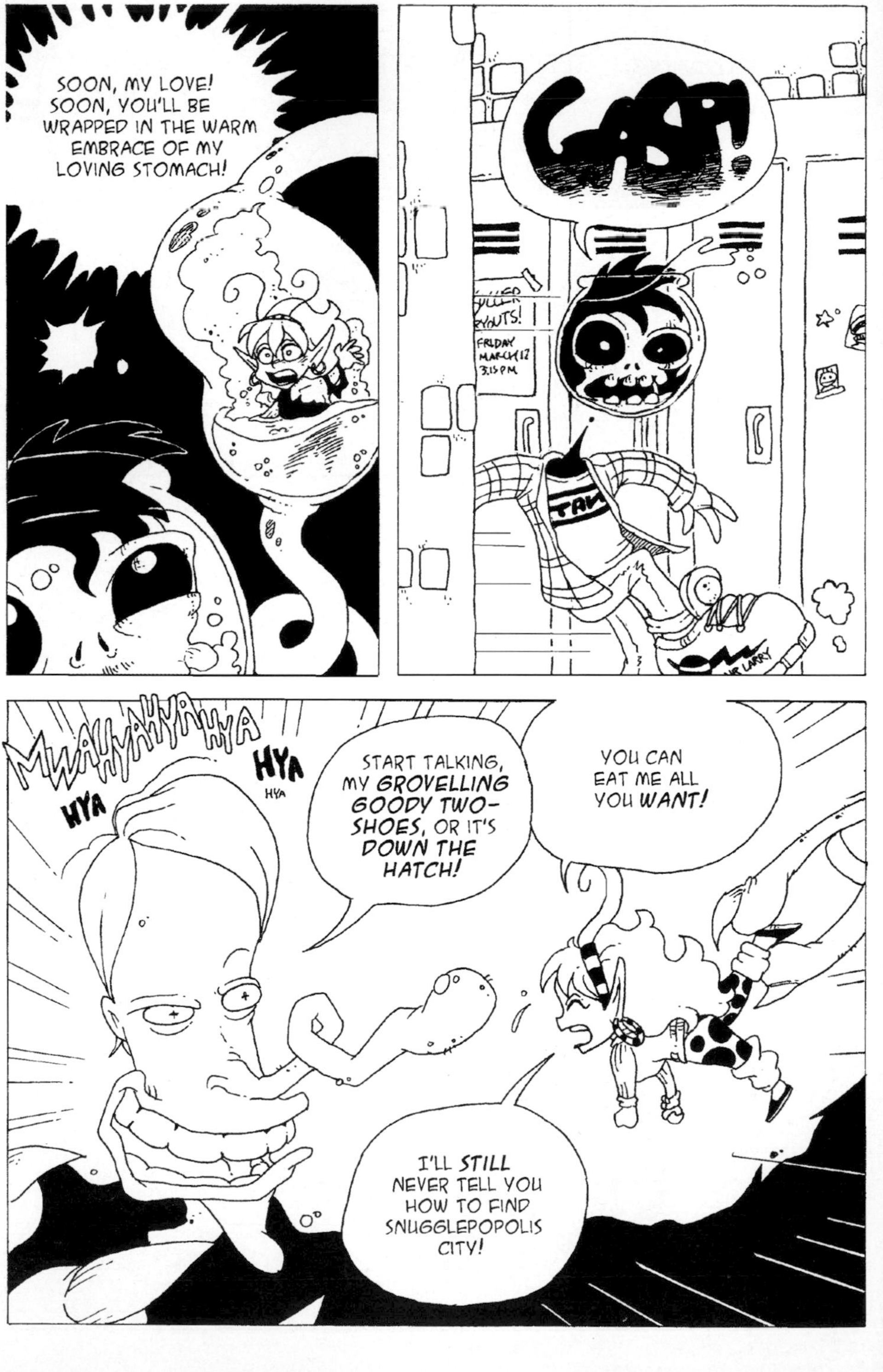
SOON, MY LOVE! SOON, YOU'LL BE WRAPPED IN THE WARM EMBRACE OF MY LOVING STOMACH!
GASP!
MWAHYAHYAHYA
HYA
HYA
HYA
START TALKING, MY *GROVELLING GOODY TWO-SHOES*, OR IT'S *DOWN THE HATCH!*
YOU CAN EAT ME ALL YOU *WANT!*
I'LL *STILL* NEVER TELL YOU HOW TO FIND SNUGGLEPOPOLIS CITY!

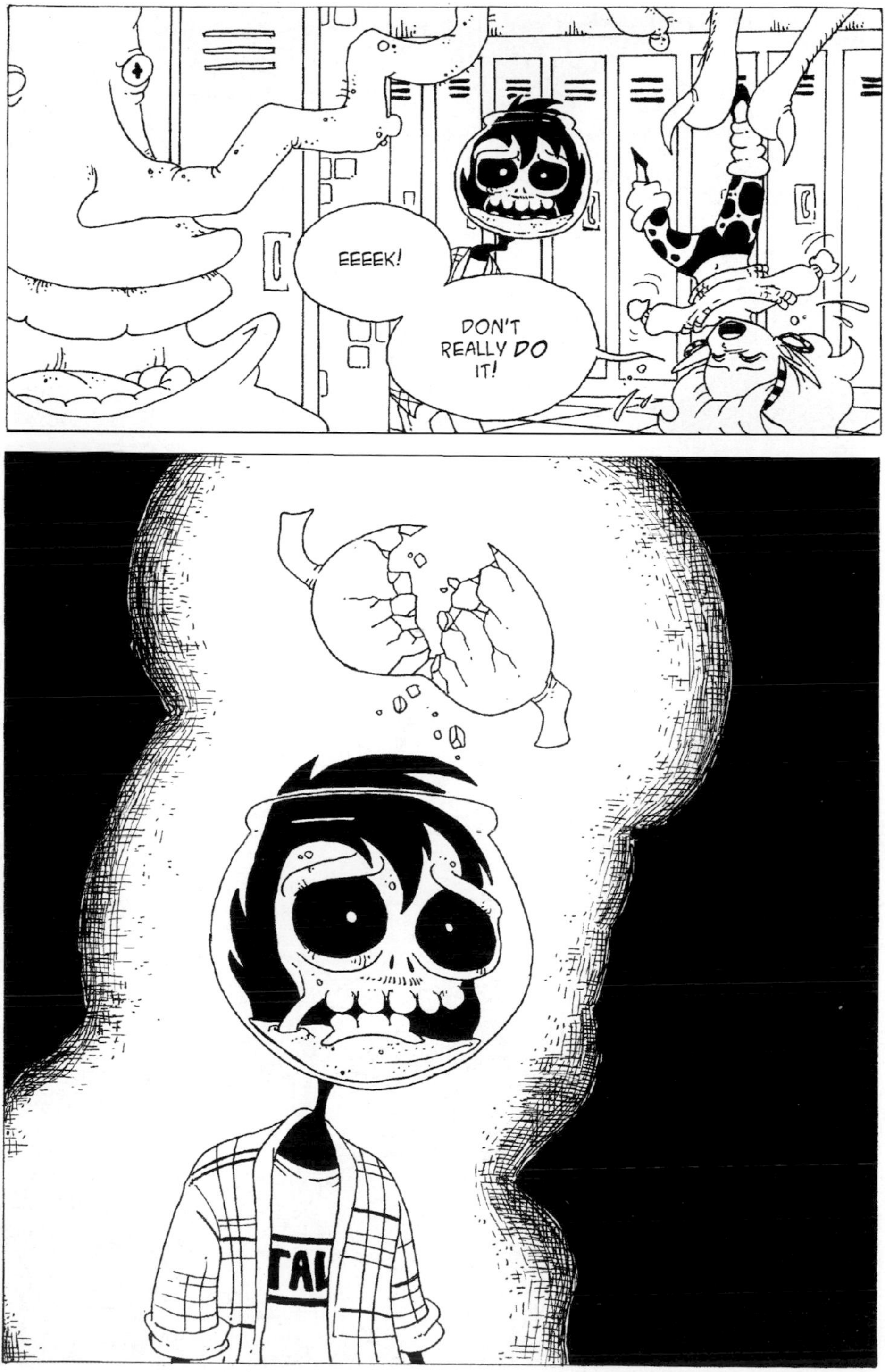
EEEEK!
DON'T REALLY DO IT!
TAL

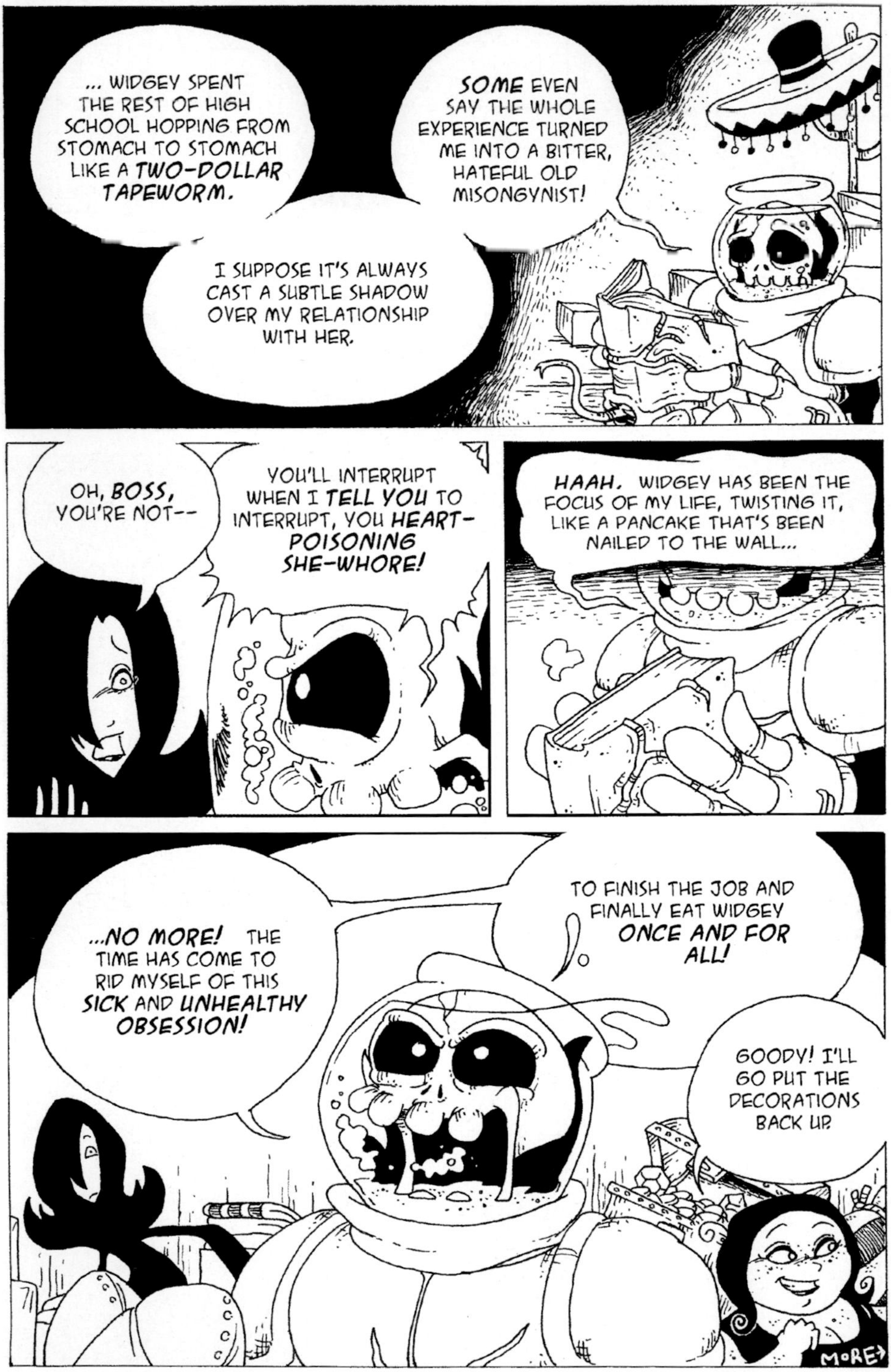
... WIDGEY SPENT THE REST OF HIGH SCHOOL HOPPING FROM STOMACH TO STOMACH LIKE A TWO-DOLLAR TAPEWORM.
SOME EVEN SAY THE WHOLE EXPERIENCE TURNED ME INTO A BITTER, HATEFUL OLD MISONGYNIST!
I SUPPOSE IT'S ALWAYS CAST A SUBTLE SHADOW OVER MY RELATIONSHIP WITH HER.
OH, BOSS, YOU'RE NOT--
YOU'LL INTERRUPT WHEN I TELL YOU TO INTERRUPT, YOU HEART-POISONING SHE-WHORE!
HAAH. WIDGEY HAS BEEN THE FOCUS OF MY LIFE, TWISTING IT, LIKE A PANCAKE THAT'S BEEN NAILED TO THE WALL...
...NO MORE! THE TIME HAS COME TO RID MYSELF OF THIS SICK AND UNHEALTHY OBSESSION!
TO FINISH THE JOB AND FINALLY EAT WIDGEY ONCE AND FOR ALL!
GOODY! I'LL GO PUT THE DECORATIONS BACK UP.
MORE→

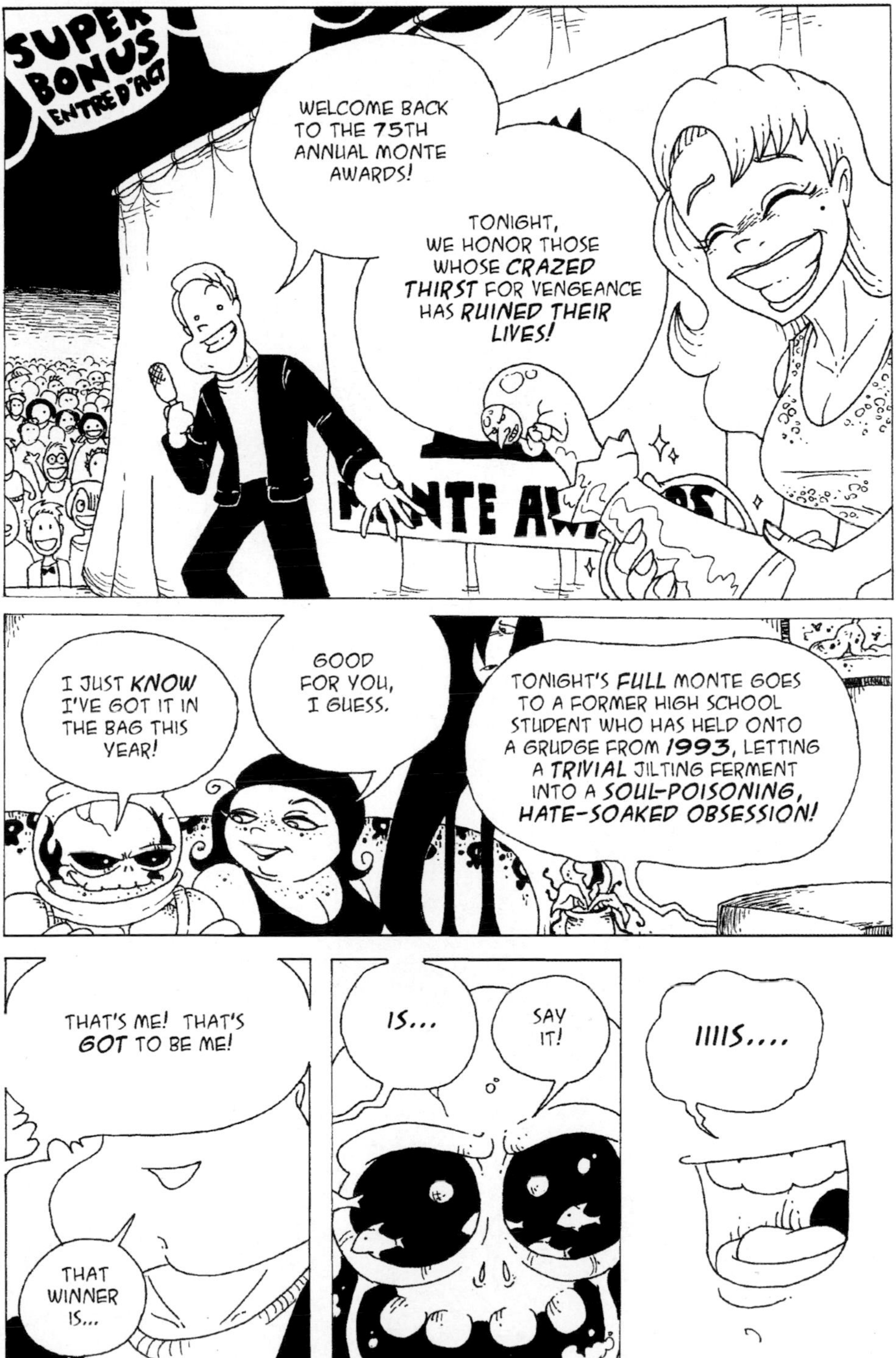
SUPER BONUS ENTRE D'ACT
WELCOME BACK TO THE 75TH ANNUAL MONTE AWARDS!
TONIGHT, WE HONOR THOSE WHOSE CRAZED THIRST FOR VENGEANCE HAS RUINED THEIR LIVES!
I JUST KNOW I'VE GOT IT IN THE BAG THIS YEAR!
GOOD FOR YOU, I GUESS.
TONIGHT'S FULL MONTE GOES TO A FORMER HIGH SCHOOL STUDENT WHO HAS HELD ONTO A GRUDGE FROM 1993, LETTING A TRIVIAL JILTING FERMENT INTO A SOUL-POISONING, HATE-SOAKED OBSESSION!
THAT'S ME! THAT'S GOT TO BE ME!
THAT WINNER IS...
IS...
SAY IT!
IIIIS....

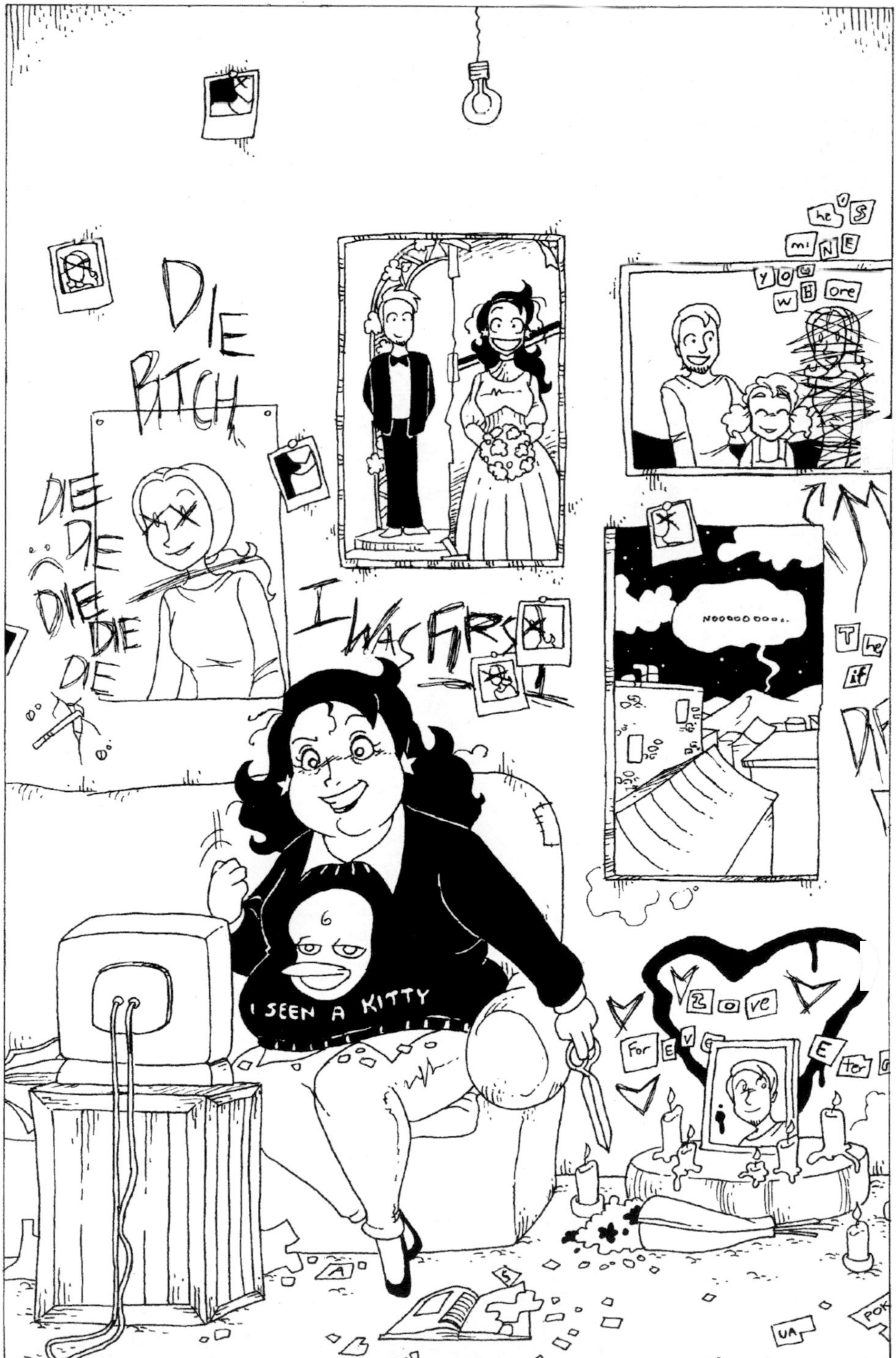
DIE
BITCH
DIE
DIE
DIE
DIE
DIE
I WAS FIRST
he's mINE you whore
Nooooooooo...
I SEEN A KITTY
Love ForEver

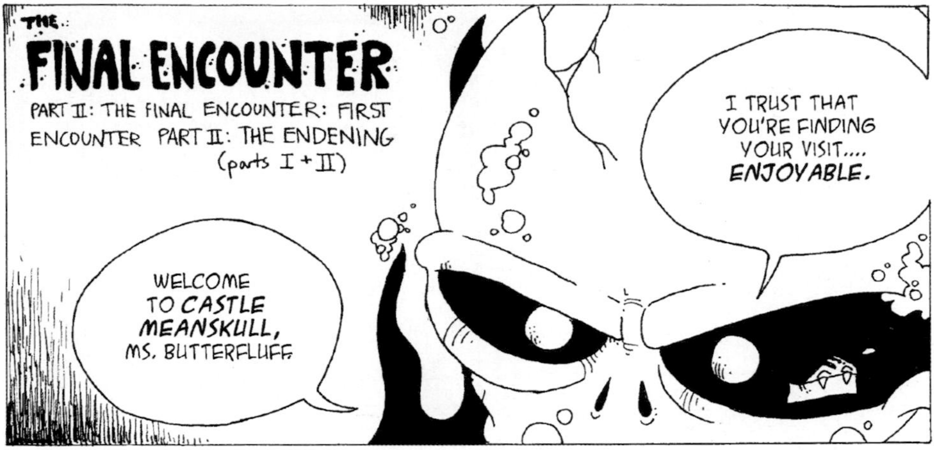
THE FINAL ENCOUNTER
PART II: THE FINAL ENCOUNTER: FIRST ENCOUNTER PART II: THE ENDENING
(parts I + II)
WELCOME TO CASTLE MEANSKULL, MS. BUTTERFLUFF.
I TRUST THAT YOU'RE FINDING YOUR VISIT.... ENJOYABLE.

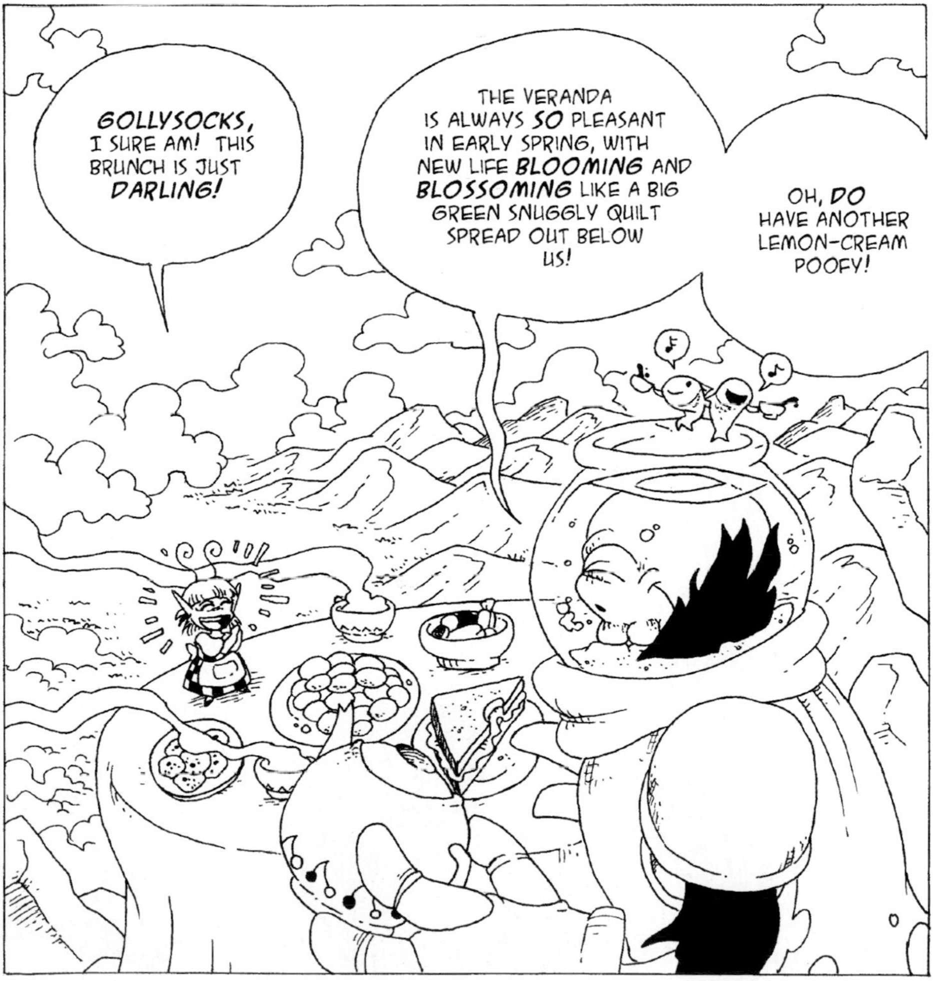
GOLLYSOCKS, I SURE AM! THIS BRUNCH IS JUST DARLING!
THE VERANDA IS ALWAYS SO PLEASANT IN EARLY SPRING, WITH NEW LIFE BLOOMING AND BLOSSOMING LIKE A BIG GREEN SNUGGLY QUILT SPREAD OUT BELOW US!
OH, DO HAVE ANOTHER LEMON-CREAM POOFY!

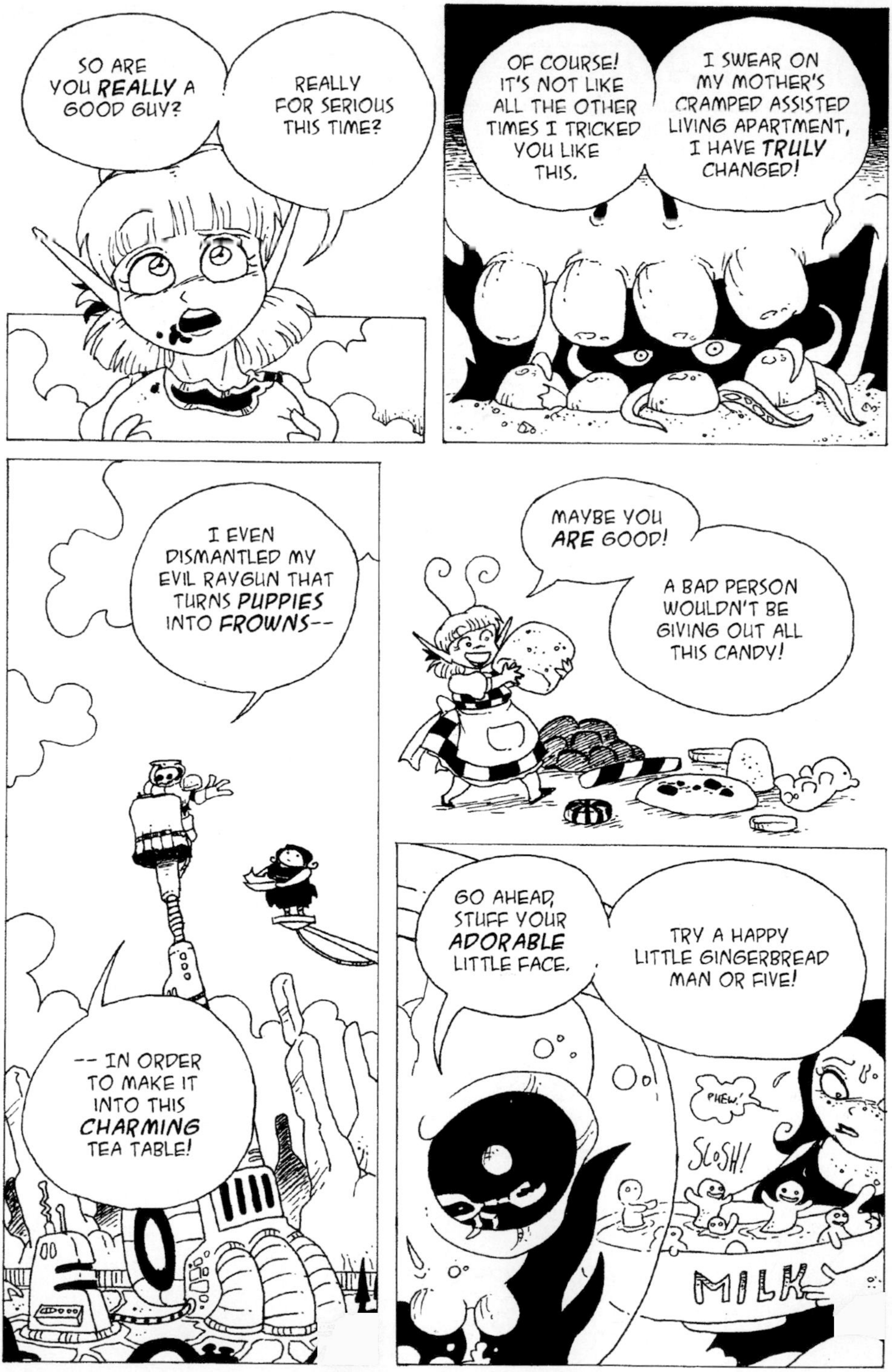
SO ARE YOU **REALLY** A GOOD GUY?
REALLY FOR SERIOUS THIS TIME?
OF COURSE! IT'S NOT LIKE ALL THE OTHER TIMES I TRICKED YOU LIKE THIS.
I SWEAR ON MY MOTHER'S CRAMPED ASSISTED LIVING APARTMENT, I HAVE **TRULY** CHANGED!
I EVEN DISMANTLED MY EVIL RAYGUN THAT TURNS **PUPPIES** INTO **FROWNS**--
-- IN ORDER TO MAKE IT INTO THIS **CHARMING** TEA TABLE!
MAYBE YOU **ARE** GOOD!
A BAD PERSON WOULDN'T BE GIVING OUT ALL THIS CANDY!
GO AHEAD, STUFF YOUR **ADORABLE** LITTLE FACE.
TRY A HAPPY LITTLE GINGERBREAD MAN OR FIVE!
PHEW!
SLOSH!
MILK

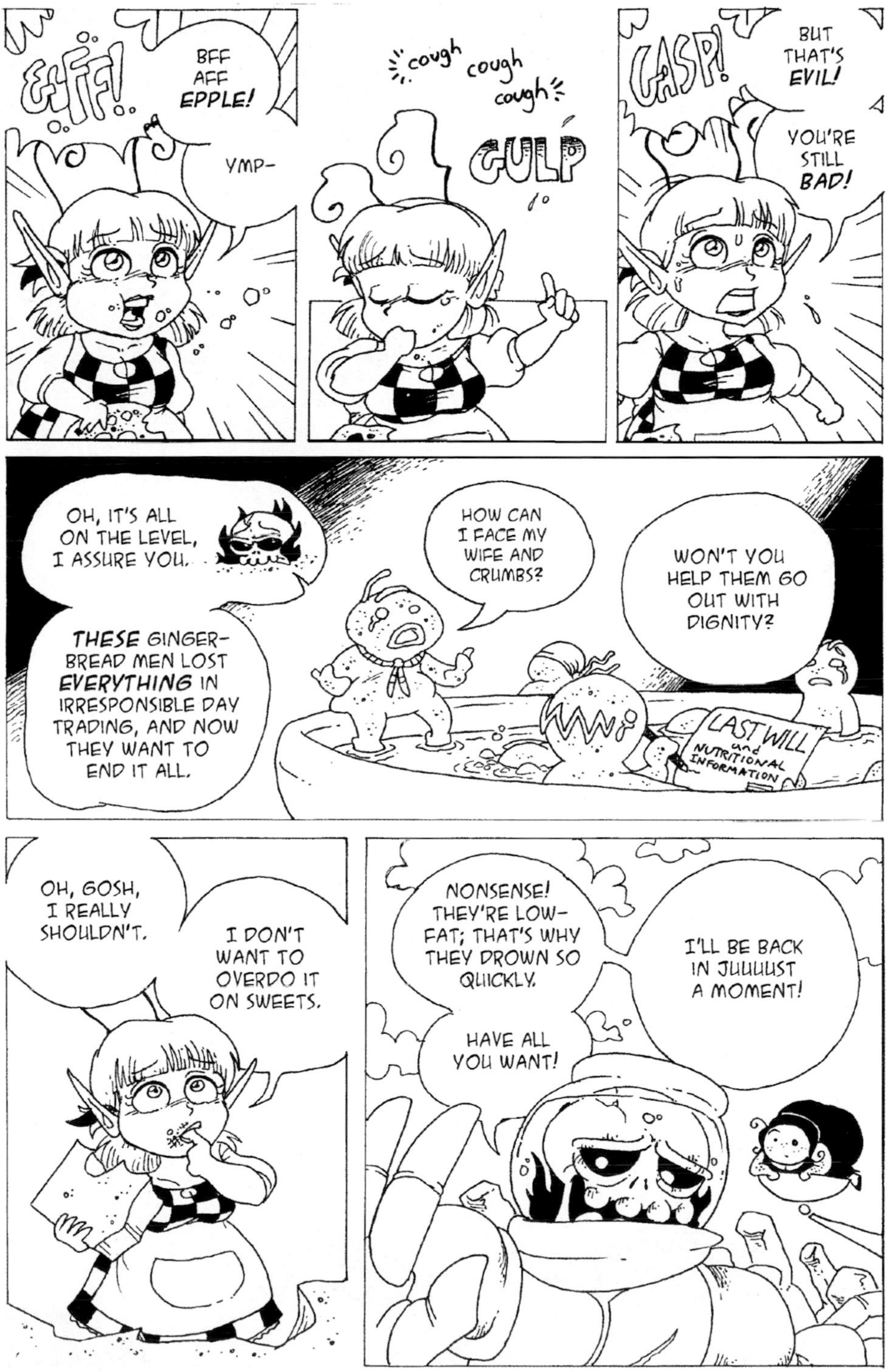

EFFF!
BFF AFF EPPLE!
YMP-
cough cough cough
GULP
GASP!
BUT THAT'S EVIL!
YOU'RE STILL BAD!
OH, IT'S ALL ON THE LEVEL, I ASSURE YOU.
THESE GINGER-BREAD MEN LOST EVERYTHING IN IRRESPONSIBLE DAY TRADING, AND NOW THEY WANT TO END IT ALL.
HOW CAN I FACE MY WIFE AND CRUMBS?
WON'T YOU HELP THEM GO OUT WITH DIGNITY?
LAST WILL and NUTRITIONAL INFORMATION
OH, GOSH, I REALLY SHOULDN'T.
I DON'T WANT TO OVERDO IT ON SWEETS.
NONSENSE! THEY'RE LOW-FAT; THAT'S WHY THEY DROWN SO QUICKLY.
HAVE ALL YOU WANT!
I'LL BE BACK IN JUUUUST A MOMENT!

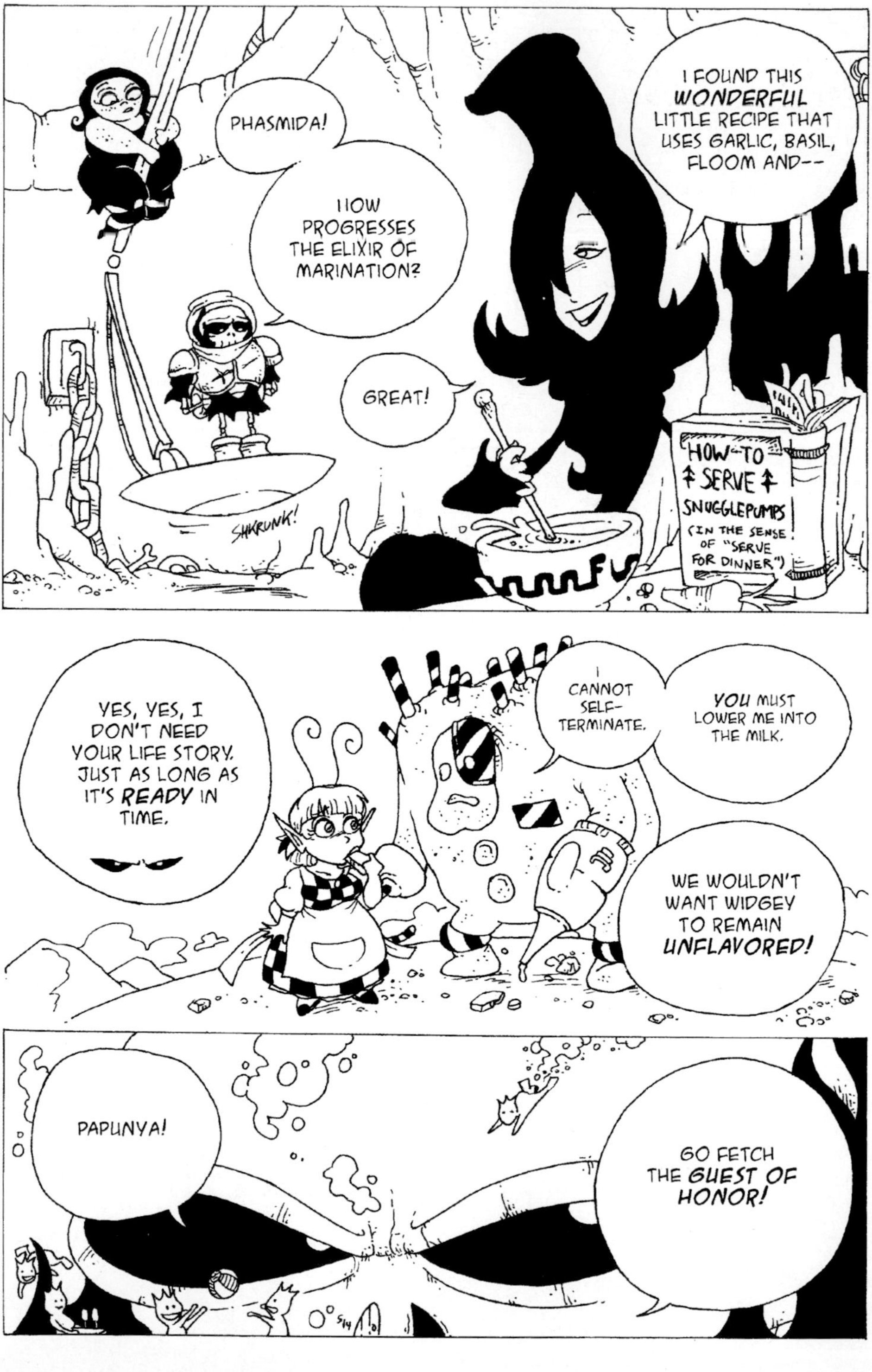
PHASMIDA!
HOW PROGRESSES THE ELIXIR OF MARINATION?
I FOUND THIS **WONDERFUL** LITTLE RECIPE THAT USES GARLIC, BASIL, FLOOM AND--
GREAT!
SHKRUNK!
HOW-TO SERVE SNUGGLEPUMPS (IN THE SENSE OF "SERVE FOR DINNER")
YES, YES, I DON'T NEED YOUR LIFE STORY. JUST AS LONG AS IT'S **READY** IN TIME.
I CANNOT SELF-TERMINATE.
YOU MUST LOWER ME INTO THE MILK.
WE WOULDN'T WANT WIDGEY TO REMAIN **UNFLAVORED!**
PAPUNYA!
GO FETCH THE **GUEST OF HONOR!**

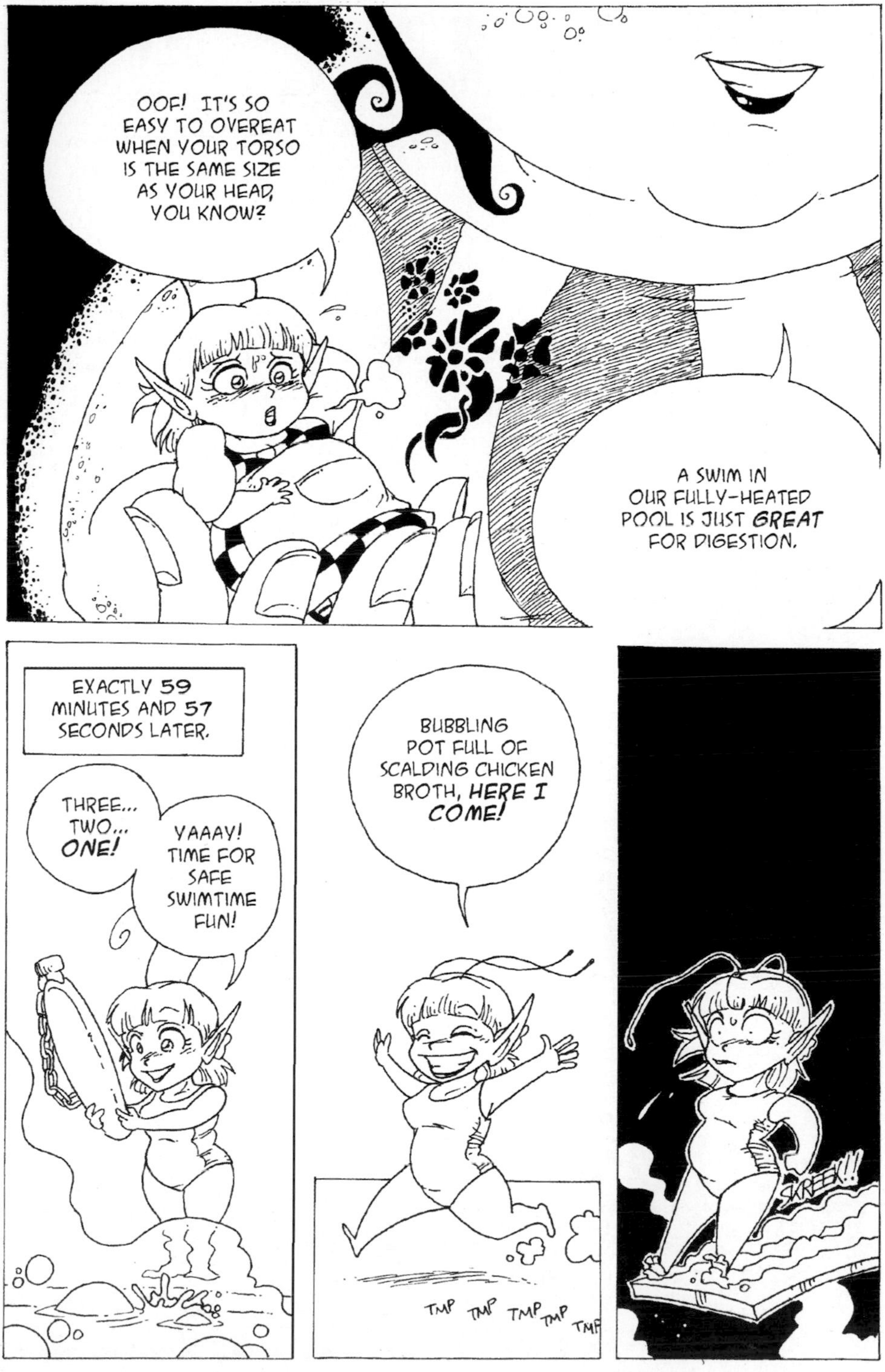
OOF! IT'S SO EASY TO OVEREAT WHEN YOUR TORSO IS THE SAME SIZE AS YOUR HEAD, YOU KNOW?
A SWIM IN OUR FULLY-HEATED POOL IS JUST GREAT FOR DIGESTION.
EXACTLY 59 MINUTES AND 57 SECONDS LATER.
THREE... TWO... ONE!
YAAAY! TIME FOR SAFE SWIMTIME FUN!
BUBBLING POT FULL OF SCALDING CHICKEN BROTH, HERE I COME!
TMP TMP TMP TMP TMP
SKREEK!!

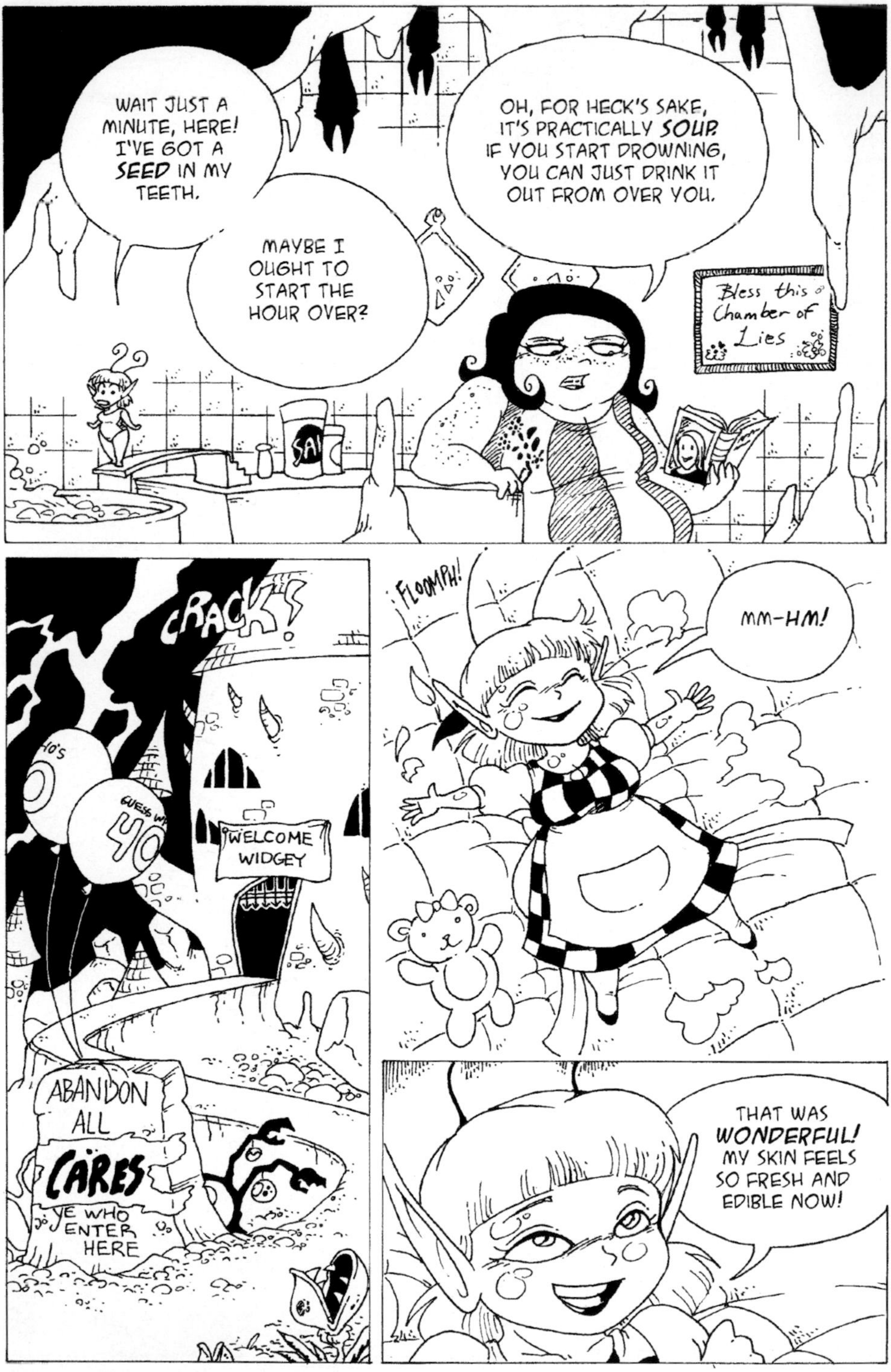
WAIT JUST A MINUTE, HERE! I'VE GOT A SEED IN MY TEETH.
MAYBE I OUGHT TO START THE HOUR OVER?
OH, FOR HECK'S SAKE, IT'S PRACTICALLY SOUP. IF YOU START DROWNING, YOU CAN JUST DRINK IT OUT FROM OVER YOU.
Bless this Chamber of Lies
CRACK!
WELCOME WIDGEY
ABANDON ALL CARES YE WHO ENTER HERE
FLOOMPH!
MM-HM!
THAT WAS WONDERFUL! MY SKIN FEELS SO FRESH AND EDIBLE NOW!

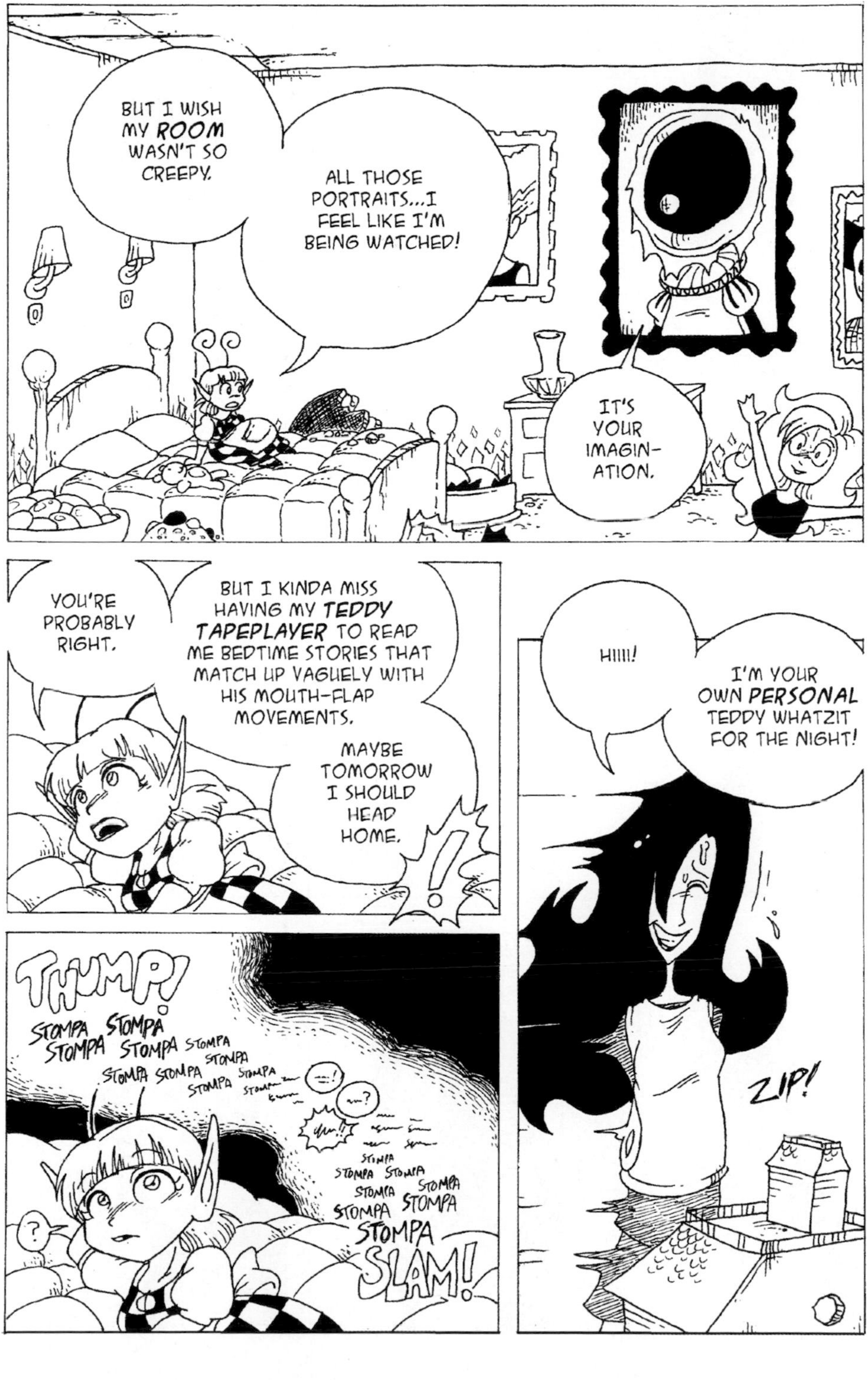
BUT I WISH MY ROOM WASN'T SO CREEPY.
ALL THOSE PORTRAITS...I FEEL LIKE I'M BEING WATCHED!
IT'S YOUR IMAGIN-ATION.
YOU'RE PROBABLY RIGHT.
BUT I KINDA MISS HAVING MY TEDDY TAPEPLAYER TO READ ME BEDTIME STORIES THAT MATCH UP VAGUELY WITH HIS MOUTH-FLAP MOVEMENTS.
MAYBE TOMORROW I SHOULD HEAD HOME.
!
HIIII!
I'M YOUR OWN PERSONAL TEDDY WHATZIT FOR THE NIGHT!
ZIP!
THUMP!
STOMPA STOMPA STOMPA STOMPA STOMPA STOMPA STOMPA STOMPA STOMPA STOMPA
?
STOMPA STOMPA STOMPA STOMPA STOMPA STOMPA STOMPA STOMPA
SLAM!

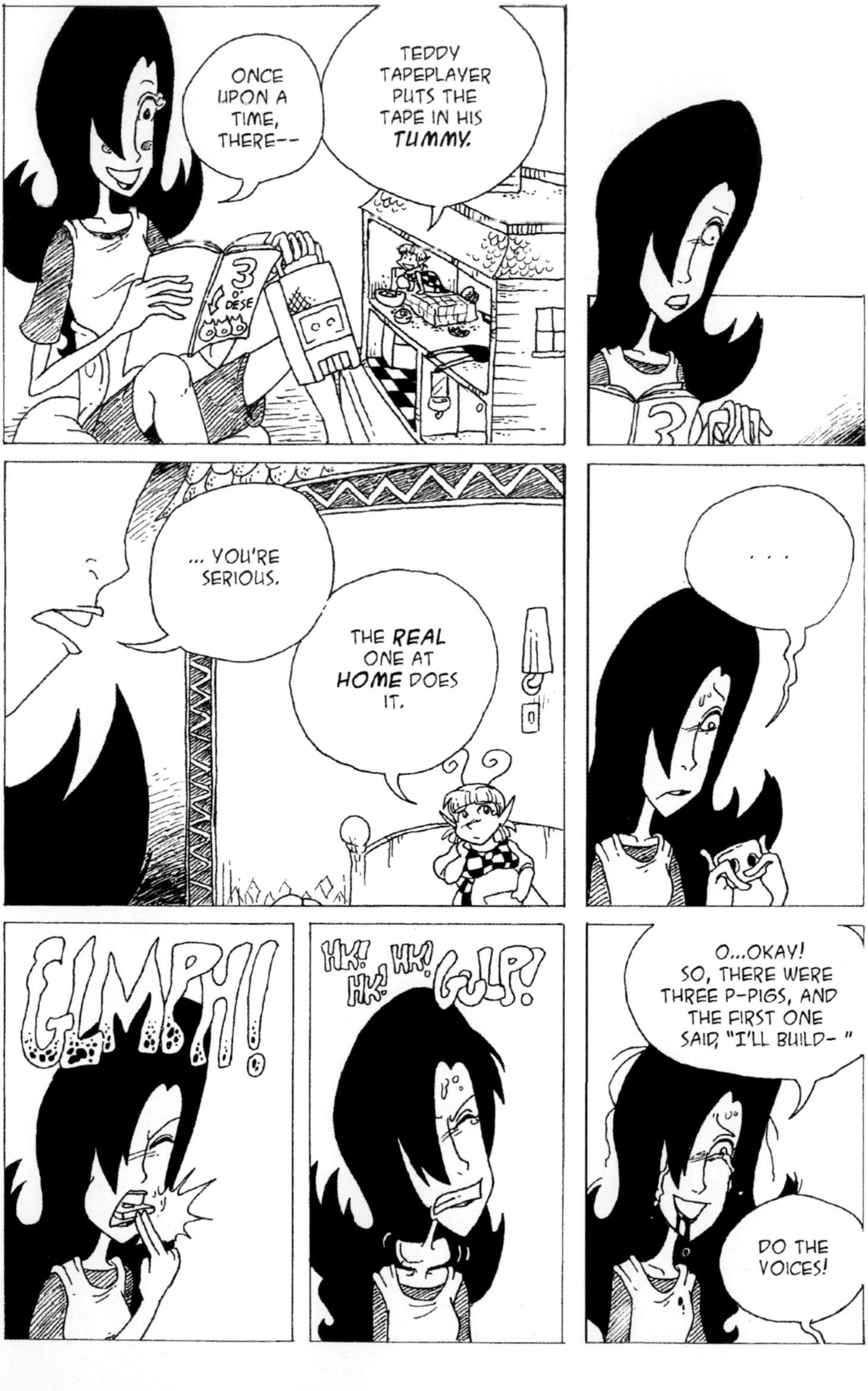
ONCE UPON A TIME, THERE--
TEDDY TAPEPLAYER PUTS THE TAPE IN HIS TUMMY.
3 O' DESE
... YOU'RE SERIOUS.
THE REAL ONE AT HOME DOES IT.
. . .
GLMPH!
HK! HK! HK! GULP!
O...OKAY! SO, THERE WERE THREE P-PIGS, AND THE FIRST ONE SAID, "I'LL BUILD- "
DO THE VOICES!

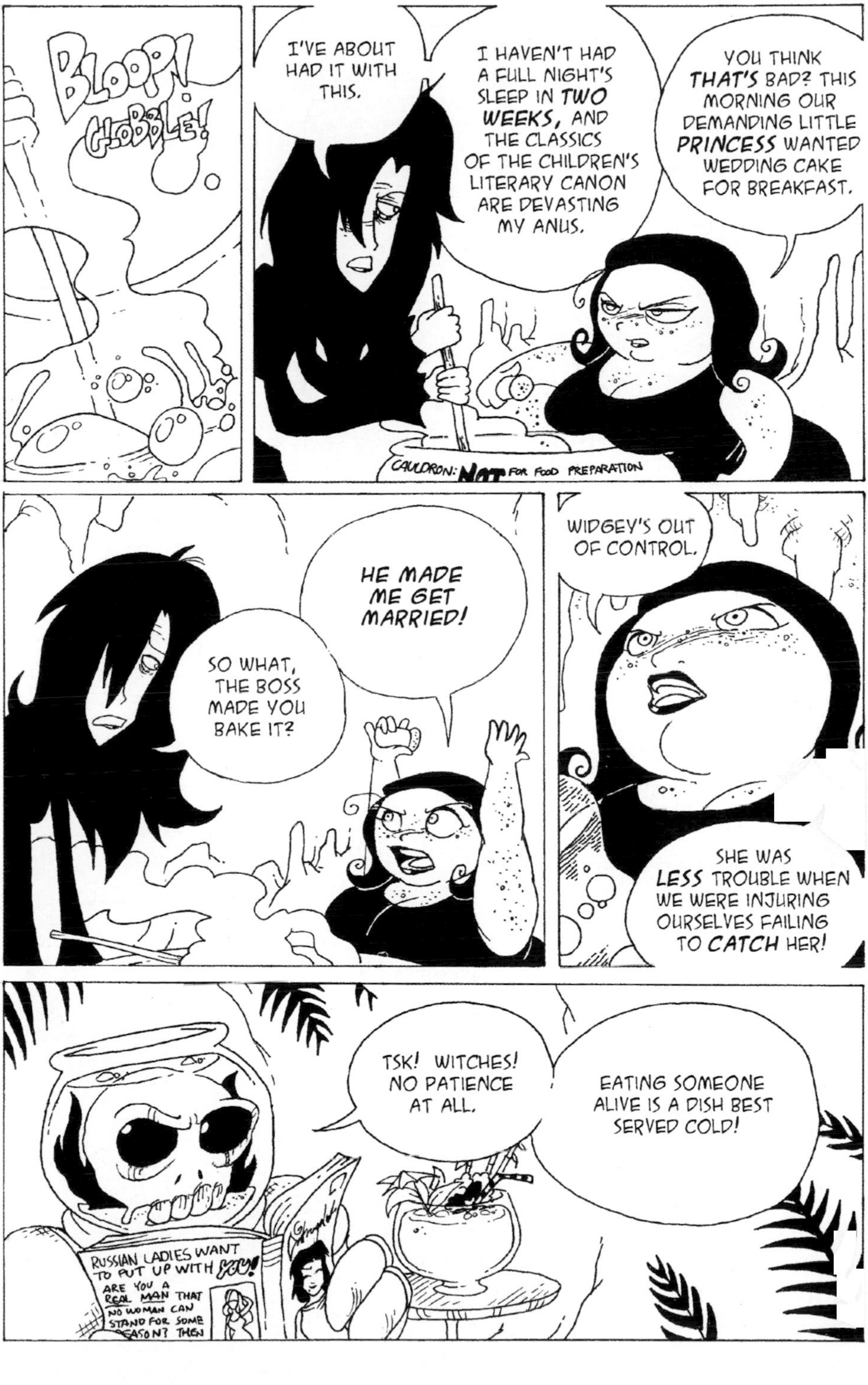
BLOOP! GLOBBLE!
I'VE ABOUT HAD IT WITH THIS.
I HAVEN'T HAD A FULL NIGHT'S SLEEP IN TWO WEEKS, AND THE CLASSICS OF THE CHILDREN'S LITERARY CANON ARE DEVASTING MY ANUS.
YOU THINK THAT'S BAD? THIS MORNING OUR DEMANDING LITTLE PRINCESS WANTED WEDDING CAKE FOR BREAKFAST.
CAULDRON: NOT FOR FOOD PREPARATION
SO WHAT, THE BOSS MADE YOU BAKE IT?
HE MADE ME GET MARRIED!
WIDGEY'S OUT OF CONTROL.
SHE WAS LESS TROUBLE WHEN WE WERE INJURING OURSELVES FAILING TO CATCH HER!
TSK! WITCHES! NO PATIENCE AT ALL.
EATING SOMEONE ALIVE IS A DISH BEST SERVED COLD!
RUSSIAN LADIES WANT TO PUT UP WITH YOU!
ARE YOU A REAL MAN THAT NO WOMAN CAN STAND FOR SOME REASON? THEN

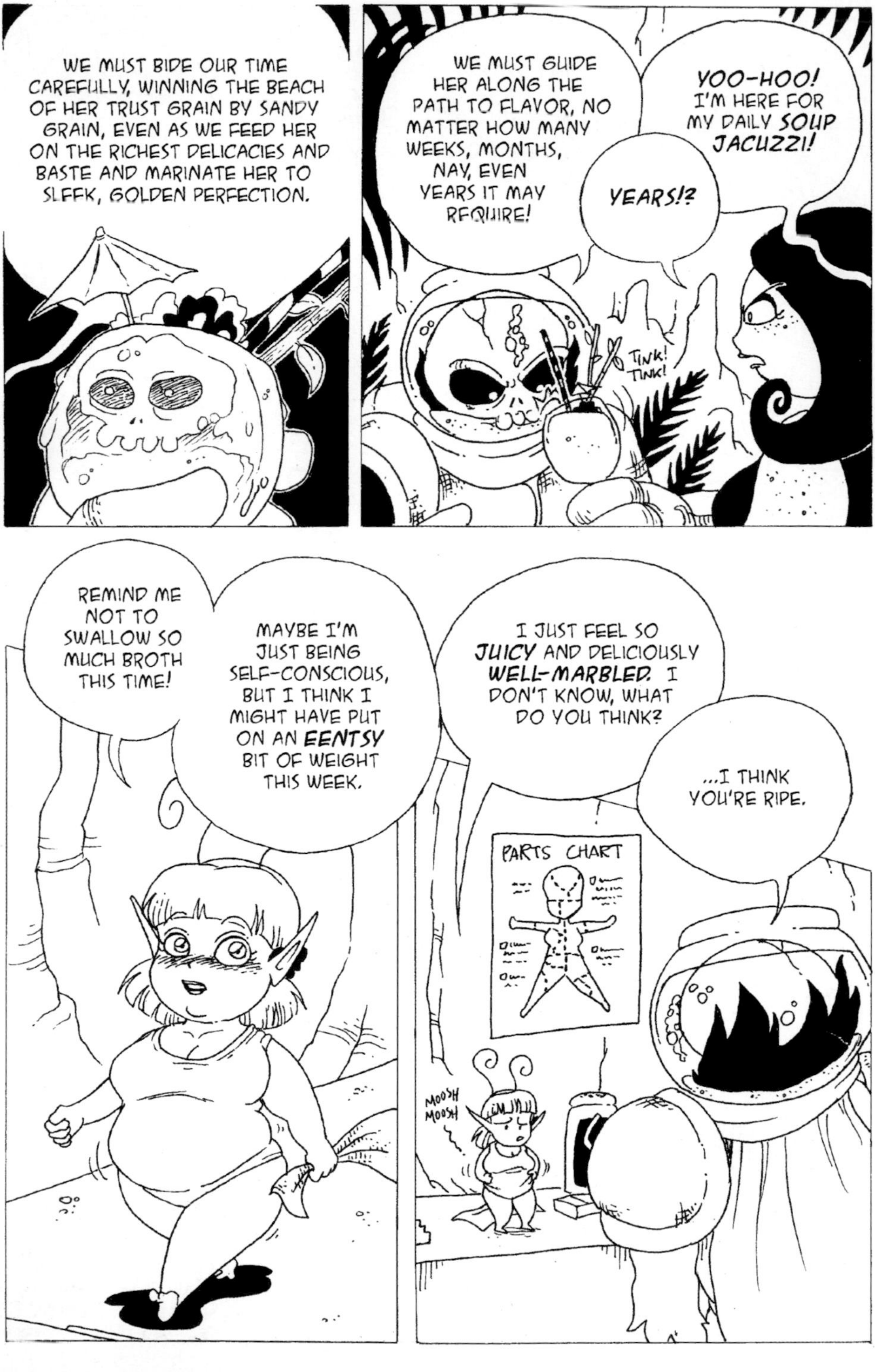
WE MUST BIDE OUR TIME CAREFULLY, WINNING THE BEACH OF HER TRUST GRAIN BY SANDY GRAIN, EVEN AS WE FEED HER ON THE RICHEST DELICACIES AND BASTE AND MARINATE HER TO SLEEK, GOLDEN PERFECTION.
WE MUST GUIDE HER ALONG THE PATH TO FLAVOR, NO MATTER HOW MANY WEEKS, MONTHS, NAY, EVEN YEARS IT MAY REQUIRE!
YEARS!?
YOO-HOO! I'M HERE FOR MY DAILY SOUP JACUZZI!
TINK! TINK!
REMIND ME NOT TO SWALLOW SO MUCH BROTH THIS TIME!
MAYBE I'M JUST BEING SELF-CONSCIOUS, BUT I THINK I MIGHT HAVE PUT ON AN EENTSY BIT OF WEIGHT THIS WEEK.
I JUST FEEL SO JUICY AND DELICIOUSLY WELL-MARBLED. I DON'T KNOW, WHAT DO YOU THINK?
...I THINK YOU'RE RIPE.
PARTS CHART
MOOSH MOOSH

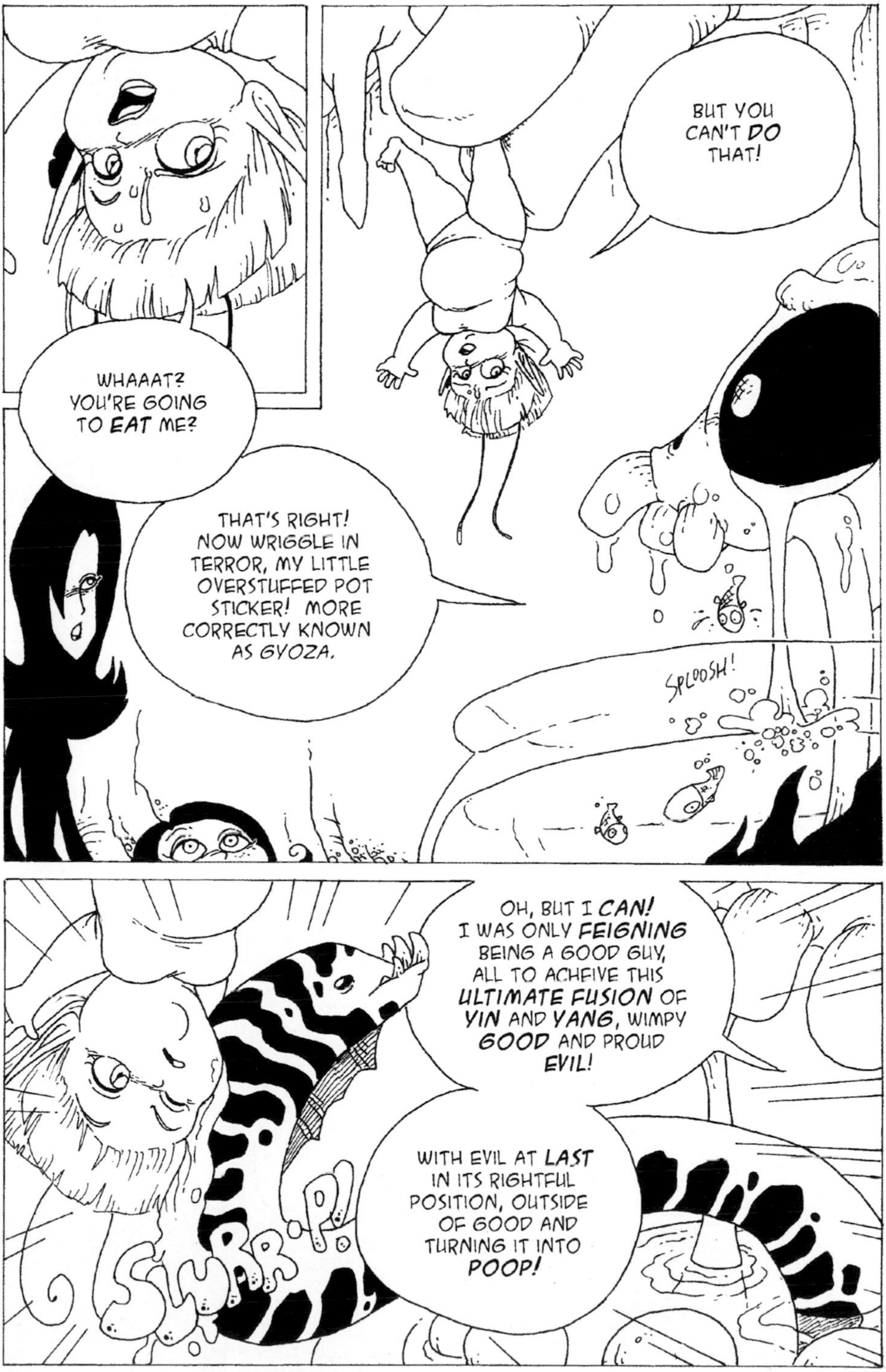
WHAAAT? YOU'RE GOING TO EAT ME?
THAT'S RIGHT! NOW WRIGGLE IN TERROR, MY LITTLE OVERSTUFFED POT STICKER! MORE CORRECTLY KNOWN AS GYOZA.
BUT YOU CAN'T DO THAT!
SPLOOSH!
OH, BUT I CAN! I WAS ONLY FEIGNING BEING A GOOD GUY, ALL TO ACHEIVE THIS ULTIMATE FUSION OF YIN AND YANG, WIMPY GOOD AND PROUD EVIL!
WITH EVIL AT LAST IN ITS RIGHTFUL POSITION, OUTSIDE OF GOOD AND TURNING IT INTO POOP!
SLURRP!

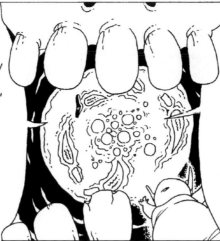

ALL THE GREAT RIVALRIES OF HISTORY EVENTUALLY BOIL DOWN TO ONE ANCIENT RULE, FORGED IN STONE BEFORE MAN KNEW IRON AND STAINED WITH THE BLOOD OF A THOUSAND VICTORY SUPPERS: EAT OR BE EATEN!

AS TOM ATE JERRY-- AS IAGO SUPPED UPON OTHELLO IN JELL-O-- AS THE SUGAR BREAKFAST CUPCAKES WEASEL EVENTUALLY ATE... EVENTUALLY... WELL, HE NEVER ACTUALLY GOT TO EAT THE CEREAL, BUT HE DID BLOW UP A POLICE STATION-- SO I WILL EAT YOU!

BUT ... YOU DON'T HAVE A STOMACH.

THAT'S NOT EATING ME, IT'S JUST KINDA MOVING ME THROUGH YOUR MOUTH.

HEY! I DO TOO HAVE A STOMACH.

IT DOESN'T LOOK LIKE IT CONNECTS UP.

IT'S DOWN... ROUNDABOUT DOWN HERE SOMEWHERE, I THINK.

I'LL SHOW YOU "CONNECTS UP"!

TOSS!

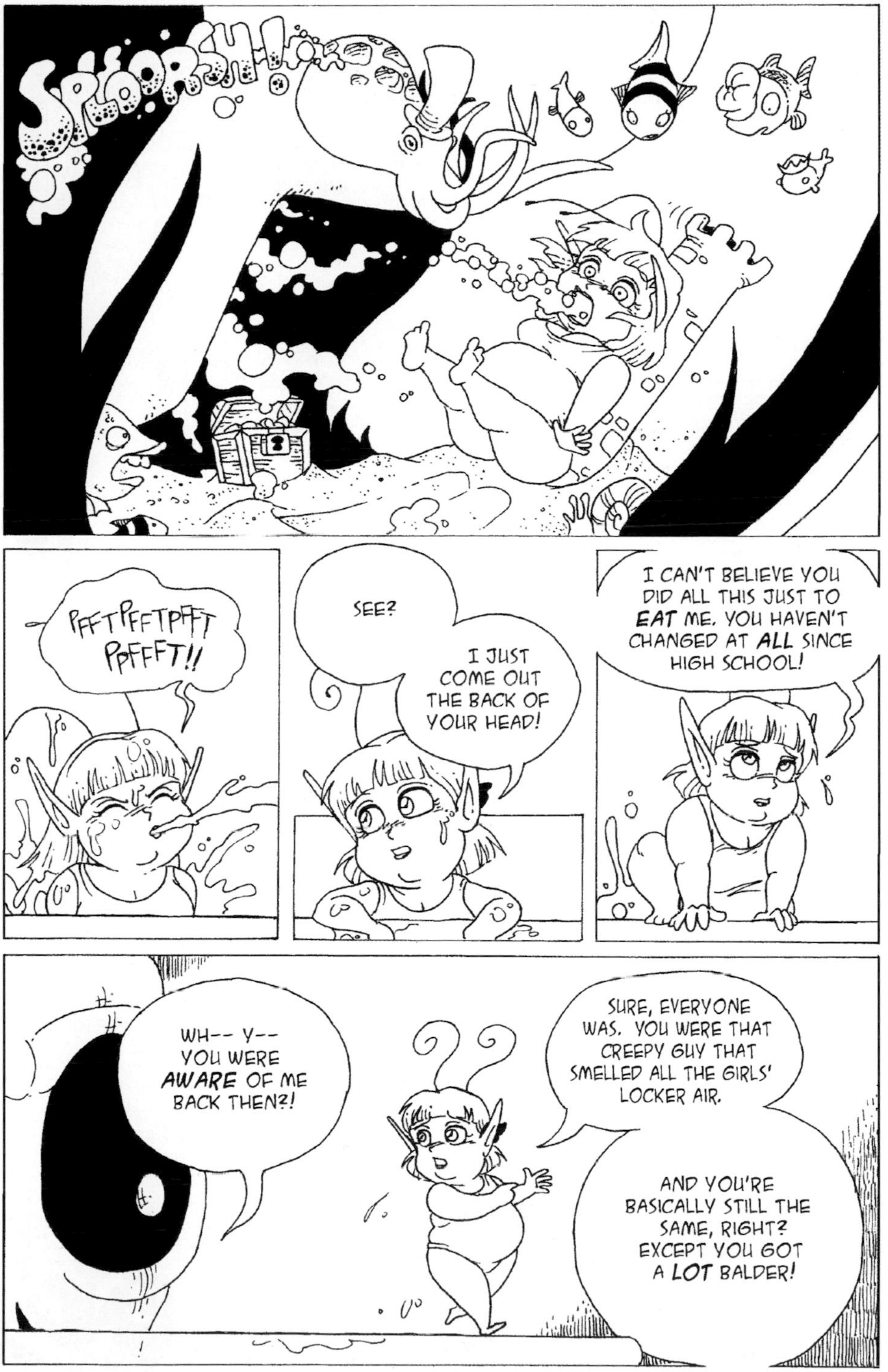
SPLOORSH!!
PFFTPFFTPFFT PPFFFT!!
SEE?
I JUST COME OUT THE BACK OF YOUR HEAD!
I CAN'T BELIEVE YOU DID ALL THIS JUST TO EAT ME. YOU HAVEN'T CHANGED AT ALL SINCE HIGH SCHOOL!
WH-- Y-- YOU WERE AWARE OF ME BACK THEN?!
SURE, EVERYONE WAS. YOU WERE THAT CREEPY GUY THAT SMELLED ALL THE GIRLS' LOCKER AIR.
AND YOU'RE BASICALLY STILL THE SAME, RIGHT? EXCEPT YOU GOT A LOT BALDER!

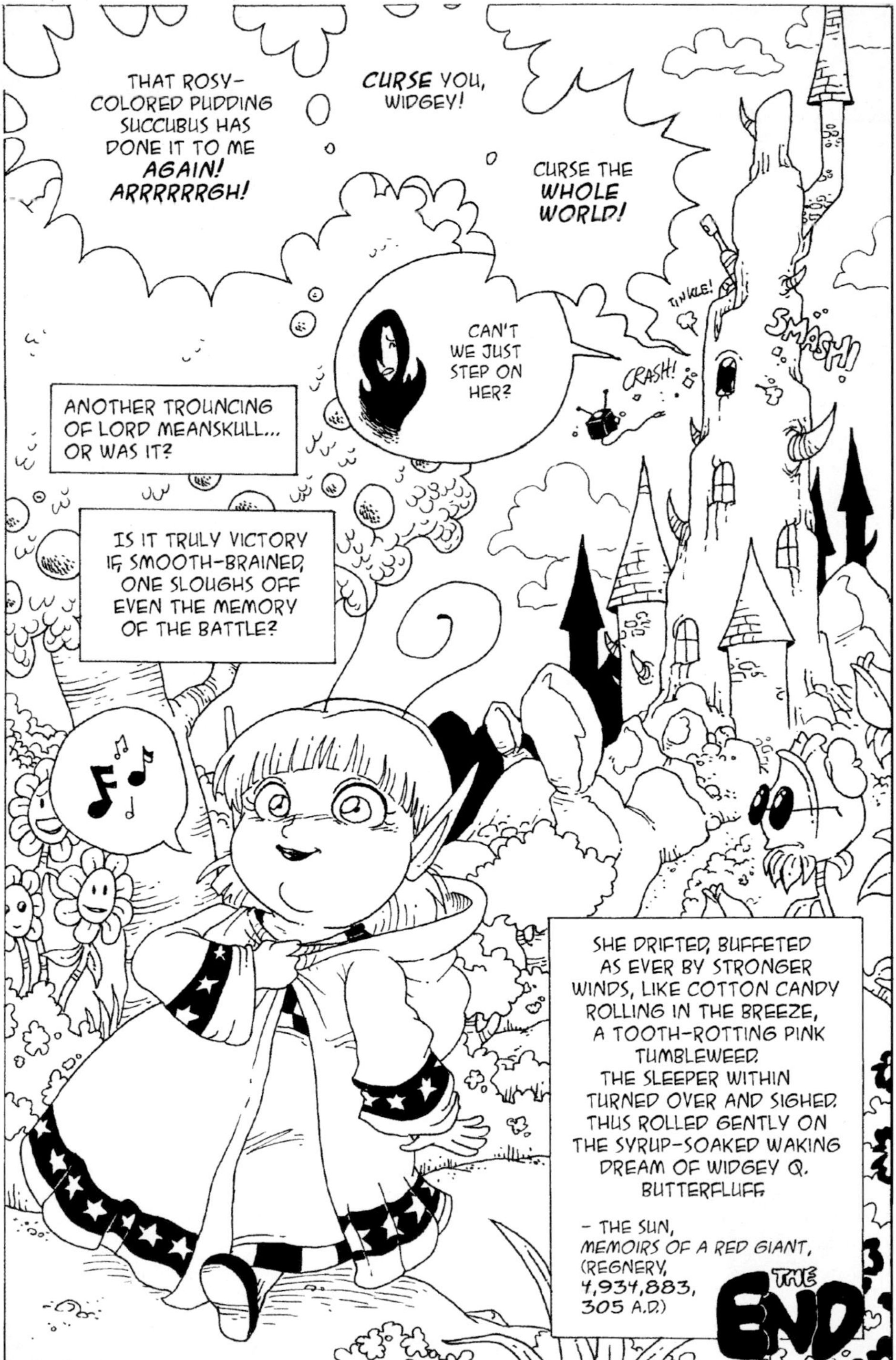
THAT ROSY-COLORED PUDDING SUCCUBUS HAS DONE IT TO ME AGAIN! ARRRRRRGH!
CURSE YOU, WIDGEY!
CURSE THE WHOLE WORLD!
CAN'T WE JUST STEP ON HER?
TINKLE!
SMASH!
CRASH!
ANOTHER TROUNCING OF LORD MEANSKULL... OR WAS IT?
IS IT TRULY VICTORY IF, SMOOTH-BRAINED, ONE SLOUGHS OFF EVEN THE MEMORY OF THE BATTLE?
SHE DRIFTED, BUFFETED AS EVER BY STRONGER WINDS, LIKE COTTON CANDY ROLLING IN THE BREEZE, A TOOTH-ROTTING PINK TUMBLEWEED. THE SLEEPER WITHIN TURNED OVER AND SIGHED. THUS ROLLED GENTLY ON THE SYRUP-SOAKED WAKING DREAM OF WIDGEY Q. BUTTERFLUFF.
– THE SUN, MEMOIRS OF A RED GIANT, (REGNERY, 4,934,883,305 A.D.)
THE END

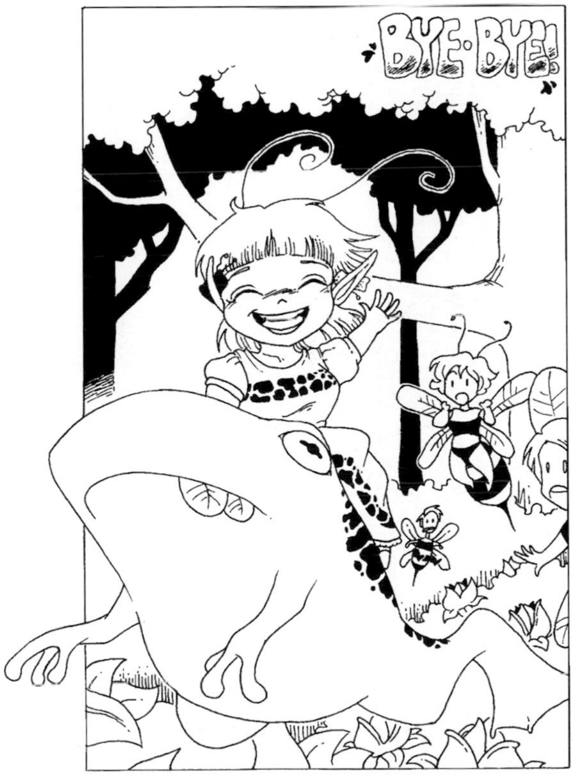
BYE-BYE!

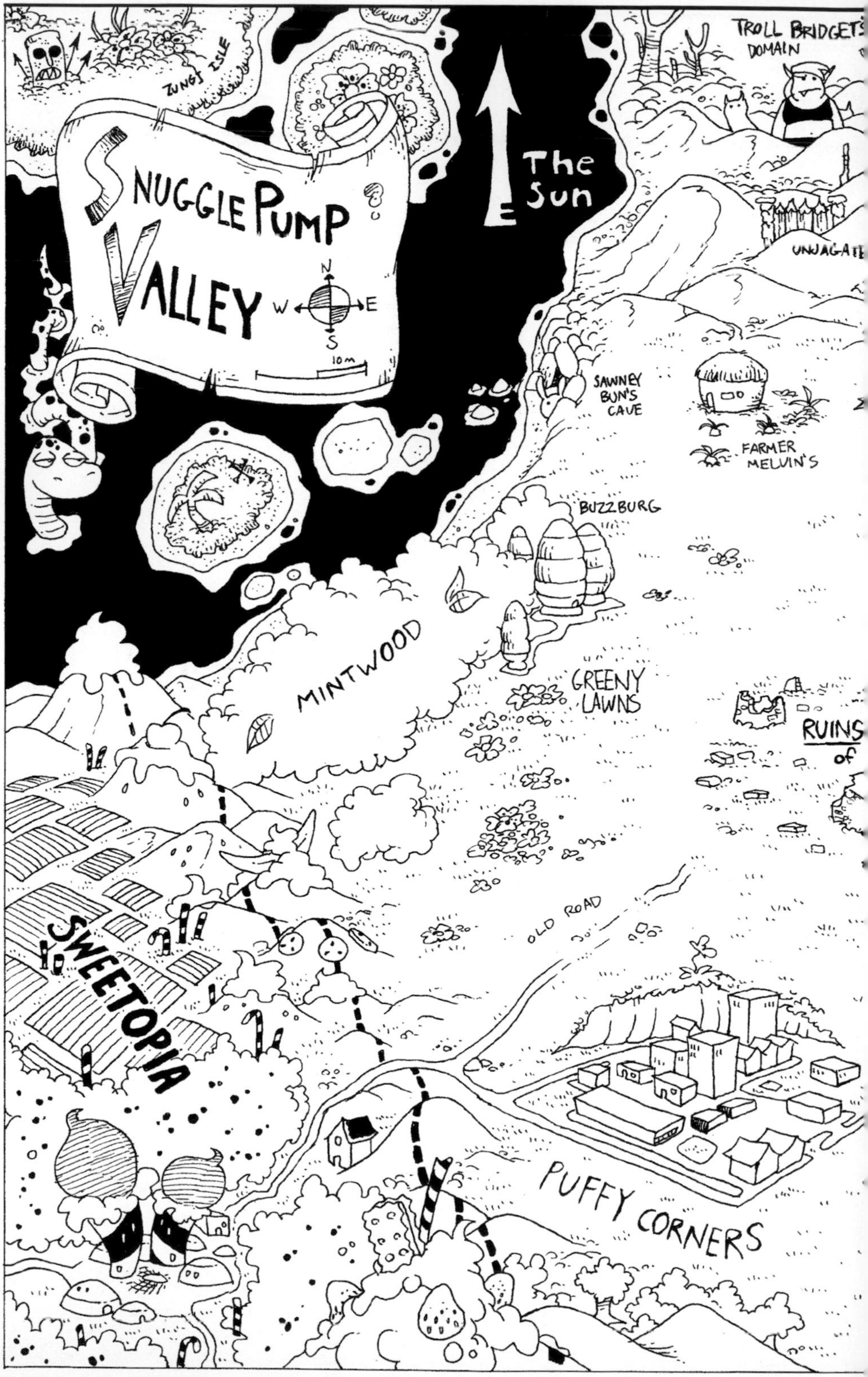
ZUNGI ISLE
TROLL BRIDGET'S DOMAIN
SNUGGLE PUMP VALLEY
N
W
E
S
10m
The Sun
SAWNEY BUN'S CAVE
FARMER MELVIN'S
BUZZBURG
MINTWOOD
GREENY LAWNS
RUINS of
OLD ROAD
SWEETOPIA
PUFFY CORNERS

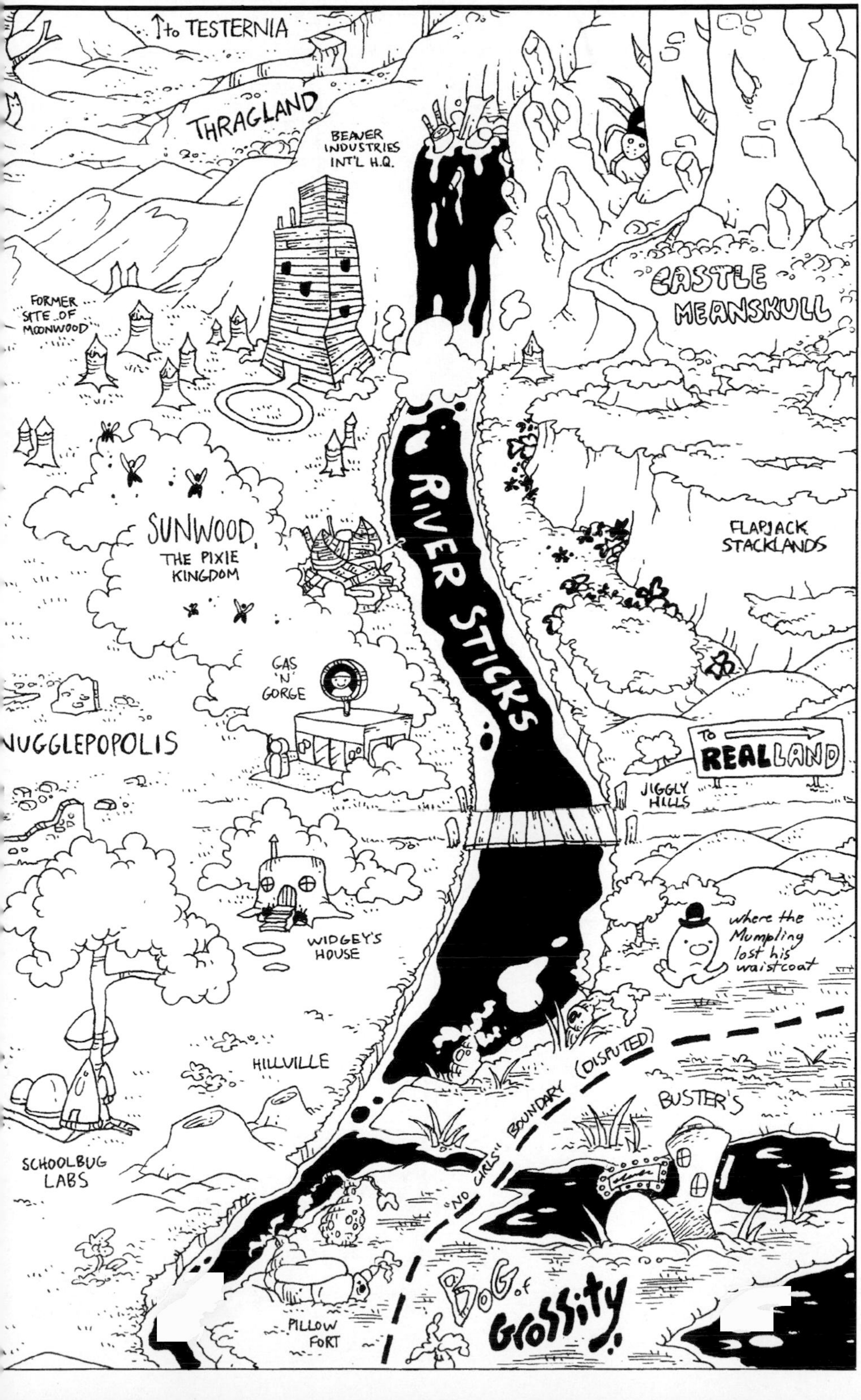
↑to TESTERNIA
THRAGLAND
BEAVER INDUSTRIES INT'L H.Q.
FORMER SITE OF MOONWOOD
CASTLE MEANSKULL
SUNWOOD, THE PIXIE KINGDOM
RIVER STICKS
FLAPJACK STACKLANDS
GAS 'N' GORGE
NUGGLEPOPOLIS
TO REALLAND
JIGGLY HILLS
WIDGEY'S HOUSE
where the Mumpling lost his waistcoat
HILLVILLE
"NO GIRLS" BOUNDARY (DISPUTED)
BUSTER'S
SCHOOLBUG LABS
PILLOW FORT
BoG of Grossity

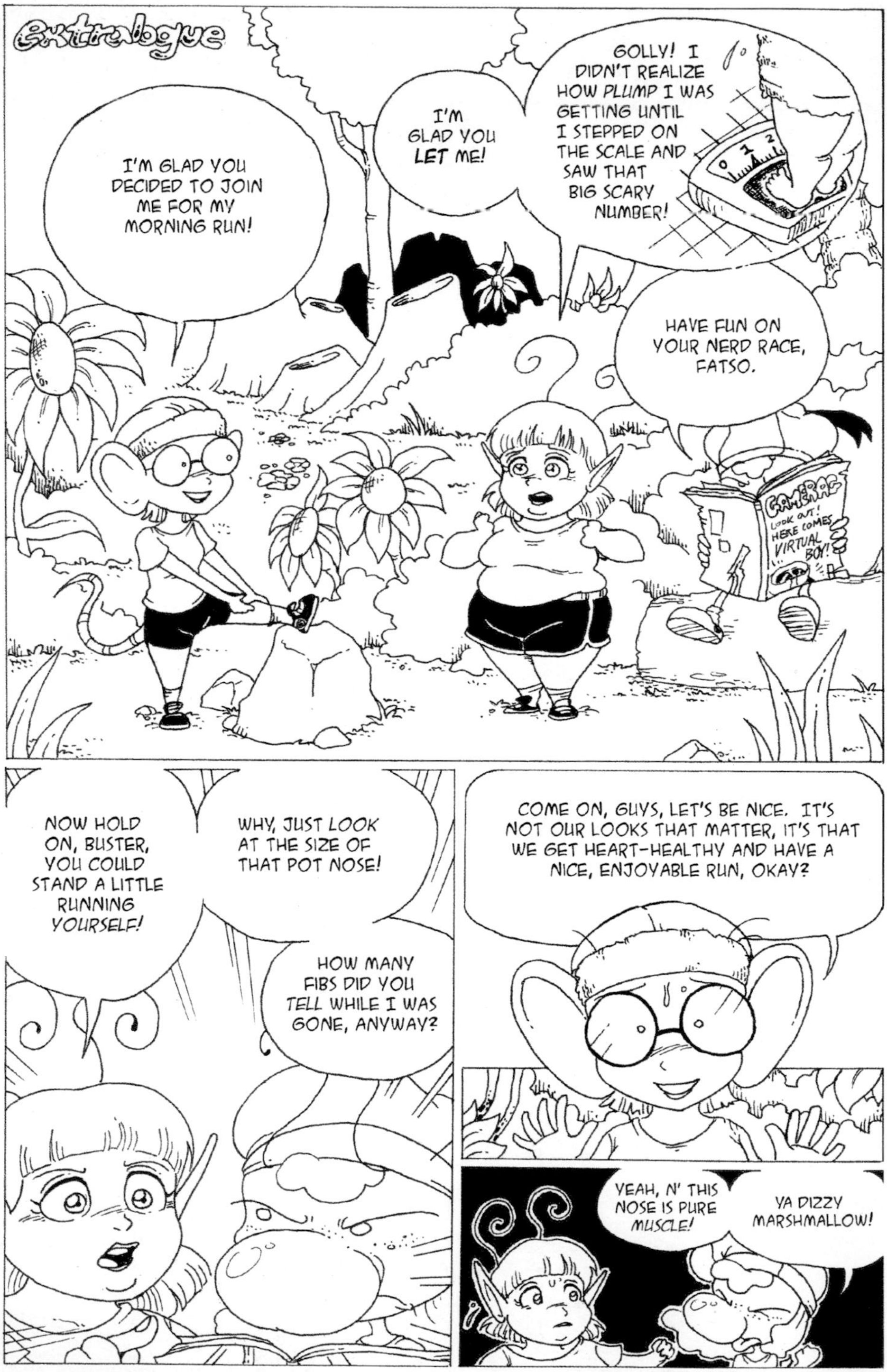
Extralogue
I'M GLAD YOU DECIDED TO JOIN ME FOR MY MORNING RUN!
I'M GLAD YOU LET ME!
GOLLY! I DIDN'T REALIZE HOW PLUMP I WAS GETTING UNTIL I STEPPED ON THE SCALE AND SAW THAT BIG SCARY NUMBER!
HAVE FUN ON YOUR NERD RACE, FATSO.
GAMERAG
LOOK OUT! HERE COMES VIRTUAL BOY!
NOW HOLD ON, BUSTER, YOU COULD STAND A LITTLE RUNNING YOURSELF!
WHY, JUST LOOK AT THE SIZE OF THAT POT NOSE!
HOW MANY FIBS DID YOU TELL WHILE I WAS GONE, ANYWAY?
COME ON, GUYS, LET'S BE NICE. IT'S NOT OUR LOOKS THAT MATTER, IT'S THAT WE GET HEART-HEALTHY AND HAVE A NICE, ENJOYABLE RUN, OKAY?
YEAH, N' THIS NOSE IS PURE MUSCLE!
YA DIZZY MARSHMALLOW!

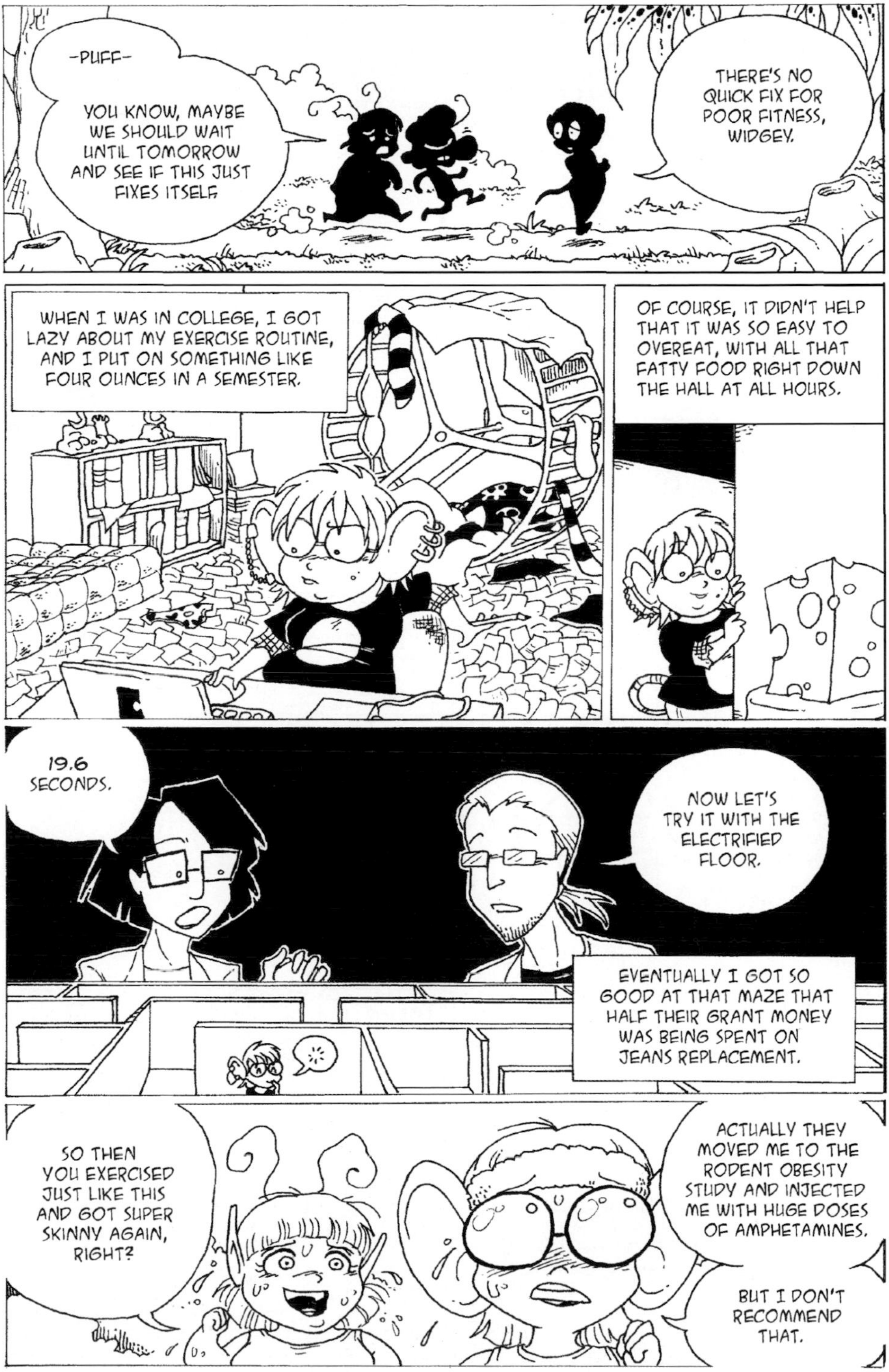
-PUFF-
YOU KNOW, MAYBE WE SHOULD WAIT UNTIL TOMORROW AND SEE IF THIS JUST FIXES ITSELF.
THERE'S NO QUICK FIX FOR POOR FITNESS, WIDGEY.
WHEN I WAS IN COLLEGE, I GOT LAZY ABOUT MY EXERCISE ROUTINE, AND I PUT ON SOMETHING LIKE FOUR OUNCES IN A SEMESTER.
OF COURSE, IT DIDN'T HELP THAT IT WAS SO EASY TO OVEREAT, WITH ALL THAT FATTY FOOD RIGHT DOWN THE HALL AT ALL HOURS.
19.6 SECONDS.
NOW LET'S TRY IT WITH THE ELECTRIFIED FLOOR.
EVENTUALLY I GOT SO GOOD AT THAT MAZE THAT HALF THEIR GRANT MONEY WAS BEING SPENT ON JEANS REPLACEMENT.
SO THEN YOU EXERCISED JUST LIKE THIS AND GOT SUPER SKINNY AGAIN, RIGHT?
ACTUALLY THEY MOVED ME TO THE RODENT OBESITY STUDY AND INJECTED ME WITH HUGE DOSES OF AMPHETAMINES.
BUT I DON'T RECOMMEND THAT.

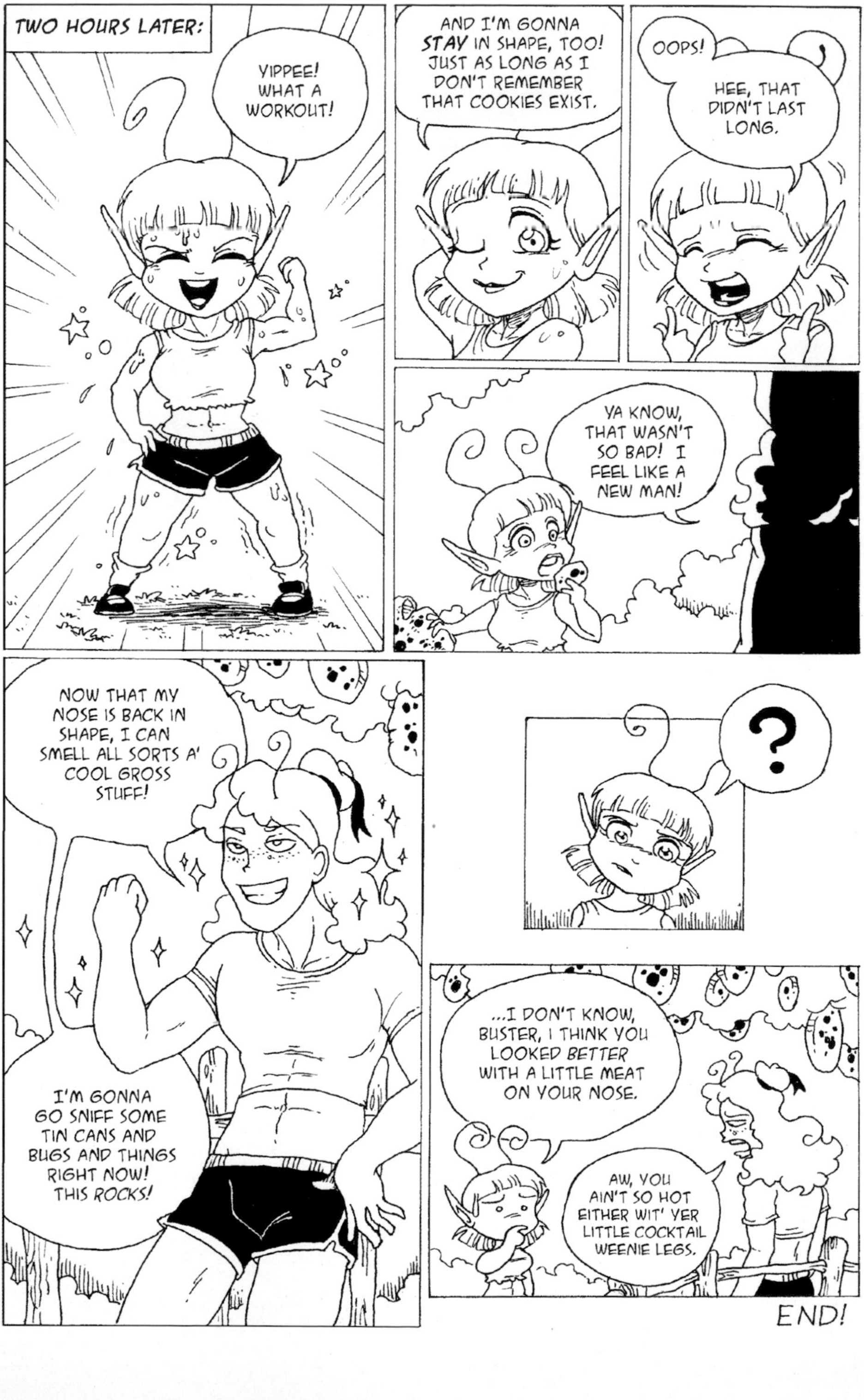
TWO HOURS LATER:
YIPPEE! WHAT A WORKOUT!
AND I'M GONNA STAY IN SHAPE, TOO! JUST AS LONG AS I DON'T REMEMBER THAT COOKIES EXIST.
OOPS!
HEE, THAT DIDN'T LAST LONG.
YA KNOW, THAT WASN'T SO BAD! I FEEL LIKE A NEW MAN!
NOW THAT MY NOSE IS BACK IN SHAPE, I CAN SMELL ALL SORTS A' COOL GROSS STUFF!
I'M GONNA GO SNIFF SOME TIN CANS AND BUGS AND THINGS RIGHT NOW! THIS ROCKS!
?
...I DON'T KNOW, BUSTER, I THINK YOU LOOKED BETTER WITH A LITTLE MEAT ON YOUR NOSE.
AW, YOU AIN'T SO HOT EITHER WIT' YER LITTLE COCKTAIL WEENIE LEGS.
END!

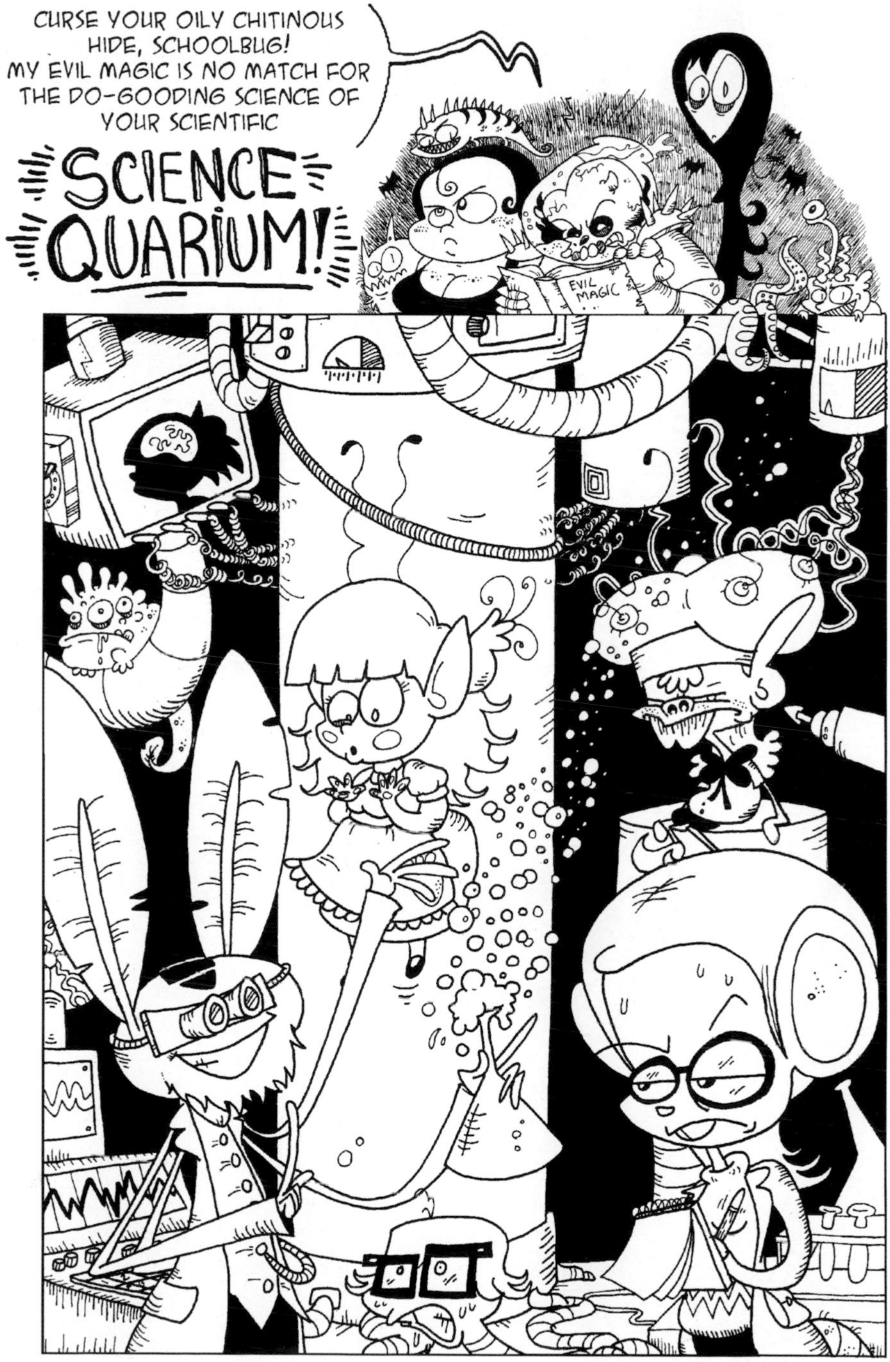
CURSE YOUR OILY CHITINOUS HIDE, SCHOOLBUG! MY EVIL MAGIC IS NO MATCH FOR THE DO-GOODING SCIENCE OF YOUR SCIENTIFIC
SCIENCE QUARIUM!
EVIL MAGIC

ILLUSTRATION BY AGOUTI-REX
WWW.GUTTERSNIPECOMIC.COM
HTTP://BUXOMPIRATEWENCH.COMICGENESIS.COM

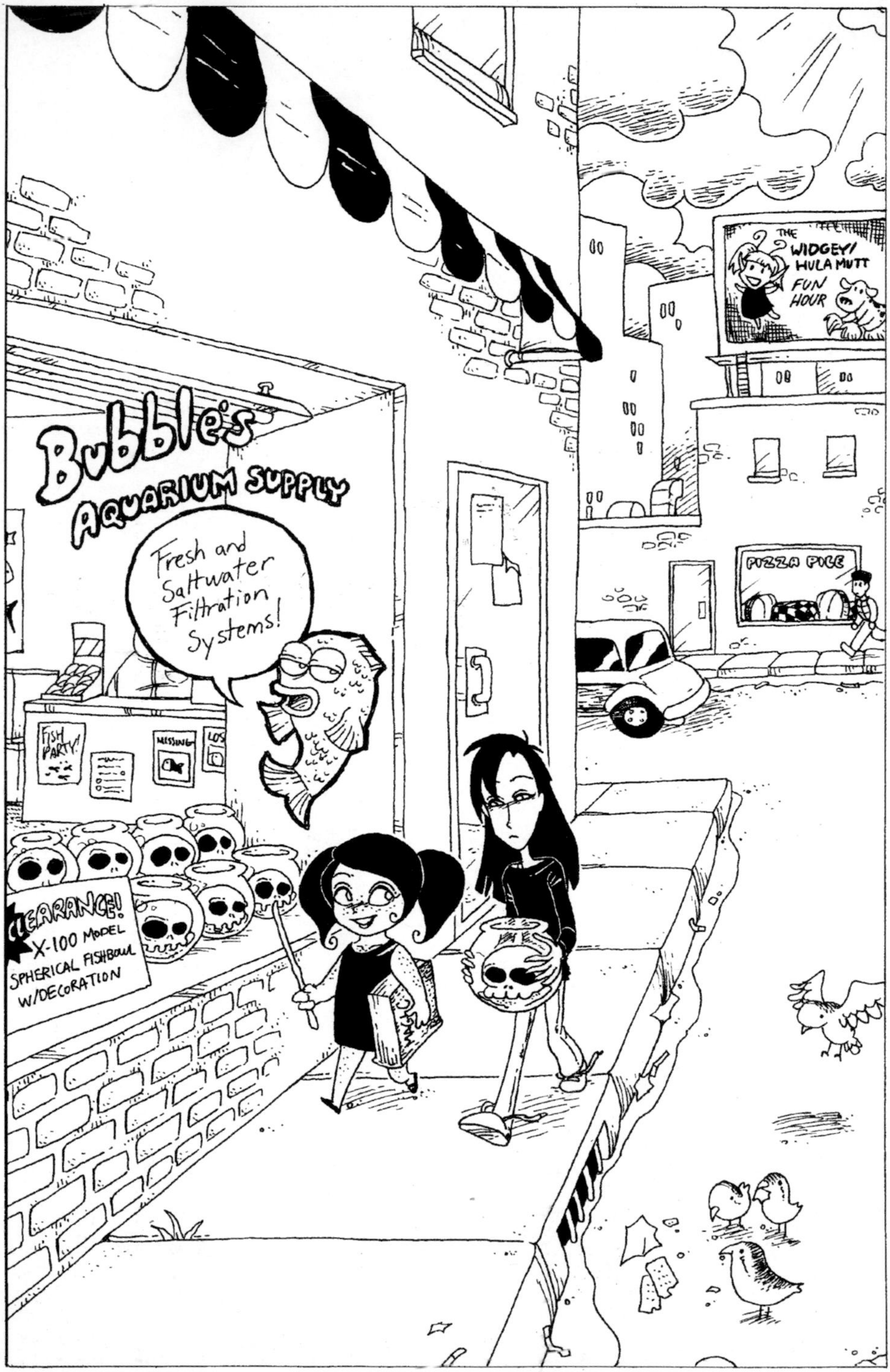
Bubble's
AQUARIUM SUPPLY
Fresh and Saltwater Filtration Systems!
FISH PARTY!
MISSING
CLEARANCE!
X-100 MODEL
SPHERICAL FISHBOWL
W/DECORATION
THE WIDGEY/HULA MUTT FUN HOUR
PIZZA PIE